MW00580661

AMALIA'S
MESOAMERICAN
TABLE

ANCIENT CULINARY TRADITIONS WITH GOURMET INFUSIONS

AMALIA MORENO-DAMGAARD

Author of **AMALIA'S GUATEMALAN KITCHEN: GOURMET CUISINE WITH A CULTURAL FLAIR,**
a bestseller and winner of nine international awards

WISE
INK

ISBN 13: 978-1-63489-451-7

Library of Congress Catalog Number
has been applied for.

Printed in the United States of America
First Printing: 2021

25 24 23 22 21   5 4 3 2 1

Book design by Evelin Kasikov
Photography by Todd Buchanan

Wise Ink Creative Publishing
807 Broadway St NE
Suite 46
Minneapolis, MN, 55413

To order, visit www.itascabooks.com
or call 1-800-901-3480.
Reseller discounts available.

DEDICATION

To Jesusito, my rock and the center of my universe.

*To my loving husband and son, Kenn and Jens.
Thank you from the bottom of my heart for your
love and support of my passion and work.
I love you both so much.*

*To my father, Doctor Marco Tulio Moreno Iriarte,
and my maternal grandmother, Mélida Guerra Jiménez,
for their wise teachings and unconditional love.
They illuminate me from heaven.*

*To my family in Guatemala, especially my sister, Gilda,
and the Santa Cruz family, for their love
and support of my work.*

*To my beloved country, Guatemala—you have
always been very near and dear to my heart.*

CONTENTS

PREFACE

ANCIENT TRADITIONS | MODERN INFUSIONS

Amalia's Mesoamerican Table is a Guatemala-centric sequel to *Amalia's Guatemalan Kitchen: Gourmet Cuisine with a Cultural Flair*, my first book, and aims to showcase the wide array of cuisines in the Central American region with close ties to Mexico, still relatively unknown to many. They come into close proximity with each other yet are unique, sharing not only key ingredients but a territory with synergies in culture and traditions.

Born and raised in Guatemala City, and now living in the United States and having traveled extensively in this area and on all seven continents, I feel privileged to make Guatemala once again the center stage of my second book. This is by design. As a professional chef and writer who respects and cares about other cultures, I have always believed that to confidently venture into other cuisines, it is important to first fully understand the cuisine you grew up with. This gives you a stronger base for creation, analysis, comparison, and appreciation.

Amalia's Guatemalan Kitchen informed me deeply about the cooking of my homeland and left me with the desire to learn and share more about how Mesoamerican cuisines are interrelated.

Writing a book is an arduous exercise for learning more about a subject, but the learning only begins there. For curious minds like mine, there's always another angle to a recipe or a new way to recreate an ancient dish. There is always a story behind every dish, cultural, historical, or anecdotal. Mesoamerican cuisines captivate me in part because I feel at home with them; they are a close encounter with who I am and allow me to reconnect deeply to the cuisines I cherish.

My goal with *Amalia's Mesoamerican Table* is to create awareness and continue fostering tradition and healthy eating. The wholesome foodways of Mesoamerica are ancient and still in practice today, but studies indicate they have been diminishing in the last seventy years. They are under constant threat of declining, in part due to the pervasive explosion of processed foods, sedentary lifestyles, and gradual disappearance of sustaining agricultural practices. We have been experiencing the results of this for several years through obesity and related diseases, such as type 2 diabetes, and more.

Living in Minnesota, I've been privileged to connect and work closely with farmers who practice and advocate for sustainable and regenerative farming. These practices are good for the land, the people, the environment, and the planet. We need more of this kind of work to help reverse unhealthy farming and land use practices. This needs to be a worldwide movement.

Amalia's Mesoamerican Table aims to highlight Mesoamerica as an important base and unifying factor in the cuisines and cultures of the Central American Isthmus and their close connection to their neighbor in the north, Mexico.

This book is for Mesoamerican adoptees and their parents, foodies, and anyone interested in gaining a broader understanding and appreciation of the culinary diversity and richness of the territory. It also is to provide Central American immigrants living in the United States who crave delicious home cooking with a base to reconnect to their cultures.

Time seems to go by at a faster pace elsewhere, especially in the United States, but in the Mesoamerican region, sometimes it seems to be at a standstill. This is more visible in the rural areas of each country, where ancient customs and traditions are still deeply ingrained.

I've had the fortune of spending extended time cooking in artisan and outdoor woodstove kitchens, grinding ingredients by hand with wise traditional cooks in Central America and central and southern Mexico. I am grateful to all the indigenous great-grandmothers, grandmothers, mothers, wives, mothers-in-law, daughters, and their close friends, from Mexico to Panama, for sharing their recipes and secrets with me unconditionally. These in-the-moment experiences have enlightened me and informed my cooking and writing in very special and unique ways.

Many ancient recipes we prepared together have been passed from generation to generation and have stood the test of time. Each family takes pride in their cooking ability and safeguarding traditions, and much respect is imparted in the kitchen upon the elders and matriarchs of each family. My memories of these community cooking gatherings will never be forgotten. They will live with me forever. I share them throughout this book, and they will continue to feed and inspire my insatiable craving for good and delicious artisan cooking.

I have traveled throughout my own country numerous times, and each time I have learned something new from a new place, cook, or practice. Every time I see the country with a new lens. This tells me that there's much more out there. I have learned that one must search for what lies beneath each country with an open mind, without ignoring historical and social injustice, political conflict, and economic strife. All countries have endured highs and lows at given points in time, and food often has been at center stage. It's part of the package.

Much has been written about Mesoamerica's anthropology, with an emphasis on archaeology, but little has been said about the cuisines and their importance from a cultural, agricultural, and strategic angle. What we know about the past is often being challenged by new research and findings, yet much still remains in the dark. This developing region continues to evolve and simultaneously plays catch-up with the rest of the developed world. It is a giant that is gradually waking up with the help of interconnectedness and digital technology.

Amalia's Mesoamerican Table contains 132 recipes plus recipe variations within many of them. It's important to highlight the variations because there is not one true or original recipe anywhere in all cuisines, but rather a recipe that represents basic common ingredients with variations in a particular dish. For example, moles are characterized by a set of culinary attributes, but there are many versions of mole by country and region. Taking this into account, I handpicked each recipe and focused on what recipes are representative of the cuisines and best fit this project based on my focused research and cooking experience in each country.

I have adapted all recipes to my cooking style, condensed them into fewer steps, and tested them to ensure they can be easily prepared with practical techniques in the comfort of your own home using the conveniences of the basic modern kitchen. I want to encourage home cooks to embark confidently into their kitchens with approachable recipes and easily accessible ingredients. Many recipes are naturally gluten free and vegan or vegetarian, or can be easily adapted to any diet with a few substitutions.

I am forever grateful to all the good cooks in Mesoamerica who shared their wisdom with me and welcomed me into their homes with open arms. These close encounters and enrichment journeys full of kitchen camaraderie informed me beyond what I could have learned in a classroom, cooking school, or book. I have expanded my culinary repertoire exponentially while making new and dear friends. These events have affected and enlightened my cooking and interpretation of these cuisines in profound ways.

I want to thank you for reading this preface and for your support. This work would be incomplete without you, the reader. I hope that you find in this book a sense of connection and comfort while you enjoy scrumptious dishes in the company of your family and loved ones.

¡Buen provecho! Happy eating!

Amalia

MESOAMERICA

A cultural and primary center of agriculture, origin, cultivation, diversification of edible plants, and interchange

Mexico

MESOAMERICA

AZTE

MAJOR CULTURAL TRAITS

PEOPLE: Major civilizations, the Olmec, Maya, and Aztec empires established strong agricultural and cultural patterns. Numerous indigenous tribes also flourished in Central America's cultural regions (see map), and contemporary indigenous peoples still inhabit the area, though they no longer go by their ancient ancestors' names.

FOOD: Domestication of maize (corn), beans, and squash (and other endemic plants), the fundamental base of nutrition, plus plants for religious or medicinal purposes (see sidebar: Native Edible Plants in Mesoamerica, page 15).

HOT SPOT: Microclimates in the Mesoamerican ecosystem act as mini labs, creating evolution and inducing biodiversity. Water is key in agriculture and fields (terracing, chinampas, or artificial islands).

EXCHANGE: Extensive trade networks of raw materials, foods, ideas, and concepts were held amongst the Gulf Coast of Mexico, the Mayan highlands and lowlands, and the Gulf of Honduras, as well as the ancient cultural regions of Central America (Ulúa River, Lempa River, Greater Nicoya, Central Caribbean, Greater Chiriquí, and Greater Coclé) from Guatemala to Panama, and extending to Colombia, Peru, and Ecuador.

Sources: National Museum of Anthropology–Mexico; Center of Regional Investigations of Mesoamerica (CIRMA)–Guatemala; "Cerámica de los Ancestros: Central America's Past Revealed," National Museum of the American Indian, Smithsonian Institution, Washington, DC, March 29, 2013–February 15, 2015; National Geographic.

Nomadic tribes from the north had been in the region of Mexico for thousands of years when hunter-gatherers turned to agriculture (about 7000–2000 BC).

Farming begins (1500 BC)

Olmec (1200–400 BC)

Maya (1000 BC–AD 1!

Plant domestication begins (7000 BC)

Preclassic Period (2000 BC–250 AD): The Olmec (1200–400 BC) development of foundational agricultural techniques, farming villages, pottery, trade, politics, religion; Preclassic Maya (1000 BC–250 AD): cultural boom, ceremonial temples emerge.

CENTRAL AMERICAN CONTEMPORARY INDIGENOUS PEOPLES

MAYA REGION: Large Maya groups (22) and languages in Guatemala are Kaqchikel (Cakchiquel), Ch'orti', Chuj, Ixil, Jacaltec, Kanjobal, Q'eqchi (Kekchi), Mam, Mopán, Pocomam, Pokomchi, Quiché, and Tz'utuhil (Zutigil). Q'eqchi, Mopán, and Yucatec Maya also live in Belize. Smaller, non-Maya, Garifuna (Afro-Caribbean) communities live on the Belize (and region) coast, and the Xinca, in southeastern Guatemala at El Salvador's border. || **LEMPA RIVER:** Area of the Lenca and Cacaopera (eastern), and the Pipil (Nawat), Q'eqchi, Pocomam, and Ch'orti' Maya (western). || **ULÚA RIVER:** Area of the Lenca and Xicaque (Jicaque or Tol). The Miskito, Sumo (Sumu), Garifuna, Pech (Paya), Pipil (Nawat), and Ch'orti' Maya inhabit other parts of Honduras. || **GREATER NICOYA:** Chorotega people live on the Matambú Reserve in Costa Rica's Guanacaste Province and in northern Nicaragua, and the Subtiaba (Ocanxiu) in León, Nicaragua's Pacific coast. Nicaragua's Nahoa people may descend from the Nicarao. The Cacaopera, Miskito, Sumo (Sumu), Rama, and Garifuna occupy northeastern Nicaragua and Caribbean coast. || **CENTRAL CARIBBEAN:** The Cabécar, Bribri, Brunka (Boruca), Teribe (Naso), and Huetar (Quitirrisi), earlier peoples' successors, live on numerous small reserves in Costa Rica's Limón, Cartago, San José, and Puntarenas's provinces. The Maléku occupy the Guatuso Reserve in northern Alajuela Province. Panama's Gaymí moved into southern Costa Rica. || **GREATER CHIRIQUÍ:** Guaymí, Ngöbe, and the Bokota (Buglé), earlier Panamanian peoples' descendants, occupy the Ngöbe–Buglé Comarca (indigenous territory extending to Greater Coclé) in Bocas del Toro, Chiriquí, and Veraguas provinces in Panama. The Teribe (Naso) lie in Bocas del Toro Province. || **GREATER COCLÉ:** Wounaan and Emberá peoples descend from Panama's earlier civilizations. Kuna, from Darién Province and northern Colombia, live in three comarcas in eastern Panama.

Gulf of Mexico

Yucatán Peninsula

MAYA

OLMEC

Belize

Gulf of Honduras

AZTEC

LEMPA RIVER

Guatemala

ULÚA RIVER

Honduras

El Salvador

Nicaragua

GREATER NICOYA

Pacific Ocean

Costa Rica

Costa Rica's Intermediate Area: Where cultures from the north overlapped with cultures from the south

CENTRAL CARIBBEAN

GREATER CHIRIQUÍ

GREATER COCLÉ

Panama

Colombia

N NE E SE S SW W NW

Mixtec (900–1521 AD)

Aztec (1200–1521 AD)

Huastec (1200–1521 AD)

otec (500 BC–1000 AD)

Toltec (950–1150 AD)

The Exchange (1492–1800 AD)

Colonization (1492–1504 AD)

Conquest (1517–1697 AD)

BC | AD

Classic Period (250–900 AD): Classic Maya (250–900 AD) urban state societies begin to emerge, mathematics, calendar, hieroglyphic writing.

Post Classic Period (900–1521 AD): Post Classic Maya (900–1521 AD); Aztec (1200–1521 AD) trade networks expand and intensify, Maya decline.

Slavery (1524–1829 AD)

Independence (1821 AD)

Garifuna (1797 AD)

WHAT IS MESOAMERICA?

Generally speaking, Mesoamerica, or Middle America, is the region that goes from south-central Mexico down to a precise part of Central America and up to Costa Rica's Gulf of Nicoya area. It's a land where ancient indigenous civilizations flourished and left major agricultural legacies based on sustainable practices that changed the lives of its people, from nomads to farmers. *Mesoamerica* is a term coined by German-Mexican anthropologist Paul Kirchhoff in 1943 to describe a specific area and historic hub that shared cultural, ethnic, and linguistic traits at the time of Spanish contact.

Central America is part of the North American continent. It is bordered by the Gulf of Mexico and Caribbean Sea on the northeast and the Pacific Ocean on the southwest and lies on the Ring of Fire, a seismic spot with deep ocean trenches, tectonic plates, and volcanoes. In consequence, the ecosystem is incredibly biodiverse and includes both dry forests and moist cloud forests and swamps, arid areas and deserts, high mountainous terrain and low coastal plains. It is home to about seventeen thousand species of vascular plants, with some three thousand of those endemic, in addition to over 3,300 fauna native species.

The geographic and microclimatic variety of the territory also produce diverse edible plants. Together, these factors function as mini labs, creating further evolution and inducing the growth of new plants. Of the currently identified 104 edible and cultivated native species in the region, about half are in Guatemala, near the center of Mesoamerica.

In terms of global importance, Mesoamerica is one of the three areas in the world where foundational primary crops originated and developed independently. Teosintes, wild grass ancestors of maize (corn), were first found in south-central Mexico around 7000 BC, and cultivation over thousands of years marked the beginning of agriculture in the region and beyond. Wheat and rice were the other major crops also originating independently, wheat in the Fertile Crescent (an area of the Middle East close to the Nile, Egypt, and Iraq) around 10,000 BC and rice in China around 5000 BC.

Mesoamerica's agriculture and foodways culture and history are complex, as they cover a long timeline over a large territory with incomplete information, and ongoing research and new findings continue to challenge some existing data. During archaic times in the area (7000 BC to 2000 BC), hunter-gatherers moved toward agriculture. The Olmec, a people known as the mother culture, flourished between 1200 BC and 400 BC in southeastern Mexico (Gulf Coast region). Notorious for their iconic large basalt head sculptures, the Olmec established two of the first major population centers, San Lorenzo and La Venta, and strong trade, agricultural, and cultural patterns that subsequent major civilizations—the Maya, Zapotec, Mixtec, Huastec, Toltec, and Aztec, to name the main ones in somewhat chronological order—followed and took to much higher levels in periods that continued until Spanish conquest in AD 1521.

These at times warring cultures interacted with coexistent cultures in the area and others in key Central American (and Caribbean) regions through bartering or trading objects and commodities, including jade, marble, obsidian, basalt, gold, copper, ceramics, cotton, salt, melipona honey, cocoa beans, and more (see pages 10–11). Jade (or jadeite) originating in the Motagua River Valley of Guatemala and salt were important economic drivers for the Maya. This social and trade interaction and possible north- and southward travels and migration may have contributed to the foodways and cultural synergies still present in the region.

That being the case, there's little difference between markets in remote parts of Mexico, Guatemala, and some neighboring countries. There are many commonalities in staple ingredients and cultural behaviors despite the fact that the countries have their own sets of indigenous cultures and native foods. Food, preparation techniques, cooking tools and vessels, and perhaps common languages (about sixty) or linguistics exchanged at the time (known as sprachbund, meaning a group of major indigenous languages with similar traits) may have made the exchange more feasible. Mesoamerican sprachbund was likely used to communicate through Aztec and Mayan times, the last empires before European conquest. There are dishes present from Mexico to Central America that carry Mayan and Aztec (Nahuatl-rooted) names, such as poc chuc, pul ik, kixnank', chilmol, and atole, tamale, pinole, pozole, respectively, among others.

The fertile Mesoamerican landscape combined with savvy agricultural prowess achieved solely with manual labor prior to Spanish contact contributed to developing one of the most important sustainable agroecosystems of all time still alive today, the Milpa, where corn, beans, and squash (and other edible native plants) grow in close proximity and perfect harmony with each other and provide complementary balanced nutrition. It's unknown how these early civilizations achieved these triumphs that became their major legacies for generations to come.

Other major achievements included how corn (maíz, maize, or *Zea mays*) evolved from simple grasses that resembled sprigs of wheat into the hybrid corn plants and cobs of today, which developed from very small teosinte sprigs with less than a handful of rows of kernels into multiple rows many times their size. Within the teosintes and hybrid corn plants, there are many varieties of corn that serve different purposes in cooking because they have different densities, sizes, and starch levels. They also have different colors, resulting in varying nutritional levels.

Very early indigenous cooking in Mesoamerica used rustic techniques and tools before clay cooking vessels appeared. Many of these techniques and tools (albeit more modern) are still around and include crushing, cracking, and grinding with the help of volcanic rock stones (metates and molcajetes), sun drying (applied to corn and coffee), toasting or cooking on hot stones, roasting in pits and over hot coals and ash, and baking in earth ovens with

rocks and large leaves (pibs). Drinking and fermenting vessels came from plants such as the morro or jícaro tree (*Crescentia alata*), which produce varying types of gourds that are soft on the inside and hard on the outside, allowing them to be easily hollowed out and adapted into bowls or water bottles.

Earthenware provided another means to take cooking and food to a new level. With ollas (clay pots), new techniques evolved, like cooking in water and steaming. Now corn (and other foods) could be boiled with ash (lye came later) to prepare masa from nixtamalized corn. This gave life to countless preparations with corn itself or masa (tortillas, atoles, tamales, and more). Clay griddles (comales) allowed for toasting corn and other ingredients prior to grinding, thus giving birth to many more dishes and beverages with toasted or toasted and cracked corn (pinoles and fermented foods). Ancient techniques combined with newer techniques revolutionized foodways.

Advancements in food preparation drove demand and further advancements in agriculture and crop variety, helping to nourish and support larger civilizations and their development. More crop variety of native plants plus wild land and water animals helped enlarge the culinary scene with guisos (stews), broths, and sauces, many of which revolve around the three major crops of Mesoamerica—corn, beans, and squash—as well as chiles, tomatoes, and tomatillos. Other important native crops are cocoa beans, avocados, vanilla, cactus, agave, chia, amaranth, and herbs, such as epazote and samat (*Eryngium foetidum*, also known as culantro). The food was strictly indigenous until the Columbian Exchange: the exchange of European (and other continents') and American cultures and native plants and animals.

The synergy and nonhomogeneous nature of ancient and present-day Mesoamerica is due to cultures of the region having deep influence and roots in advanced ancient civilizations and consequently sharing some cultural traits, practices, and culinary traits and ingredients while also having distinctive cuisines, ethnicities, languages, and, in some instances, customs and traditions.

Pre-Hispanic cooking evolved into the traditional cooking of today in Meso- and Latin America starting in the early sixteenth century, influenced by the colonial cooking of Spain and Portugal (in Brazil). During the Exchange and colonization (see page 11), new fauna, flora, spices, and cooking utensils and techniques were shared between Meso- and Latin America (the New World) and Spain (the Old World), affecting the culinary cultural landscapes of both regions (and the world) forever. See Mesoamerican Pre-Hispanic Foods and Spanish Contributions, page 92.

Modern Mesoamerican cuisines are rich in a large variety of native and nonnative fresh fruits and vegetables that grow in fertile landscapes and favorable weather. Dry and wet seasons and ancient agricultural practices combined with modern techniques continue to yield lusher and naturally imperfect delicious crops (heirlooms), which enjoy the privilege of ripening on the vine or tree, contributing to extraordinary fare.

The rural markets of Mesoamerica (especially in Guatemala and Mexico) are exotic, vivid, varied, and a feast for the senses. These are colorful indigenous centers of congregation for commerce, socializing, exotic eating, and pagan religious practice—very similar to ancestral times. One does not need to be a chef, cook, or foodie to experience their greatness. A heaven for a vegan, vegetarian, or celiac, here any dish or diet can be created, recreated, or adapted to anyone's needs. There is an abundance of all things green, orange, yellow, purple, bright pink, and everything in between. Here one can find many natural cures from plants for common ailments as locals do.

In the region, Mexico and Guatemala have the largest indigenous populations, and as such, the cuisines share some traits while staying unique. Because of this ethnic depth, the cuisines are also deep; even today there are remote ancient dishes that are only known in their areas of origin and nowhere else.

Mesoamerican cuisine is a group of cuisines sharing cultural and historical traits. As such, they deserve to be explored, discovered, and appreciated for their delicious uniqueness. Despite the passage of time, countries in close proximity in this area continue to share important cultural and agricultural commonalities as well as staples, causing dishes to sometimes resemble each other. Because of this, nuances by country make the region challenging to understand. From Mexico to Costa Rica, one can find foods that share a similar name but not looks or flavor. Foods that look like a dish from a neighboring country may taste completely different.

Mesoamerica does not include Panama, according to Kirchhoff, but culinary synergies suggest otherwise. Panama is an isthmus between the Caribbean Sea and the Pacific Ocean, and the land bridge linking North and South America, which shares many cultural and culinary characteristics (among other influences) with Costa Rica and Colombia, its closest neighbors. Because of this proximity, part of Costa Rica, sparsely populated by indigenous people, is called the "intermediate area," where Mesoamerican, Caribbean, and key Andean native cultures once overlapped and extended through part of the territory.

Mesoamerica is in essence an agricultural and cultural hub with very old, rich culinary traditions that are still alive today. But perhaps the strongest link amongst these ancient and contemporary cultures is an extensive pre-Columbian Central American pottery and artworks legacy spanning 2,000 years that helps tell part of their story through iconography on ceramics found in the cultural regions Maya, Ulúa River, Lempa River, Greater Nicoya, Central Caribbean, Greater Chiriquí, and Greater Coclé (see pages 10-11). Mesoamerica is on the short list of areas in the world where early advanced civilizations flourished and agriculture, sustainable agroecosystems, and writing arose and developed independently. Corn became a world staple. Beans, squash, cocoa beans, tomatoes, chiles, vanilla, and other important legacies (pyramids, the calendar, cosmovision) are gifts to humankind. Mesoamerica's cuisines are vibrant, colorful, nutritious, delicious, and full of history worth discovering.

NATIVE EDIBLE PLANTS IN MESOAMERICA

The following plants are native to Mesoamerica, as well as the region of Central America and Mexico.

- **Aguacate**
  Persea spp.
- **Aguacate de mico**
  Persea tolimanensis
- **Aguacate de Monte**
  Persea nubigena,
  Persea steyermarkii
- **Amaranth**
  Amaranthus
  hypochondriacus
- **Anona**
  Annona macroprophyllata,
  Annona purpurea,
  Annona squamosa
- **Arrowroot**
  Maranta arundinacea
- **Avocado**
  Persea americana
- **Ayote**
  Curcubita moschata
- **Badú**
  Xanthosoma violaceum
- **Bean, botil**
  Phaseolus dumosus
- **Bean, common**
  Phaseolus vulgaris
- **Bean, ixtapacal**
  Phaseolus lunatus
- **Bean, scarlet runner**
  Phaseolus coccineus
- **Bean, sword**
  Canavalia ensiformis
- **Bean, tepary**
  Phaseolus acutifolius
- **Bledo, leaf**
  Amaranthus cruentus
- **Caimito**
  Chrysophyllum caimito
- **Calabash tree**
  Crescentia cujete
- **Camote**
  Ipomoea batatas,
  Ipomoea tiliacea,
  Ipomoea trifida,
  Ipomoea triloba
- **Canistel**
  Pouteria campechiana
- **Capulín**
  Prunus serotina
- **Cassava**
  Manihot esculenta
- **Castilloa rubber**
  Castilla elastica

- **Century plant**
  Agave spp.
- **Cereza**
  Prunus capuli
- **Ceriman**
  Monstera deliciosa
- **Chan**
  Hyptis suaveolens
- **Chan**
  Salvia potus, Salvia
  polystachia
- **Chaya, leaf**
  Cnidoscolus aconitifolius
- **Chayote**
  Sechium edule
- **Chia**
  Hyptis suaveolens
- **Chia**
  Salvia spp.
- **Chicle**
  Manilkara zapota
- **Chilacayote**
  Curcubita ficifolia
- **Chipilín, leaf**
  Crotalaria longirostrata
- **Chucte, white avocado**
  Persea schiedana
- **Chufle, flower**
  Calathea allouia
- **Coco**
  Cocus nucifera
- **Cocoa bean**
  Theobroma cacao
- **Cotton, upland**
  Gossypium hirsutum
- **Coyol**
  Acrocomia aculeata
- **Cuajilote, fruit**
  Parmentiera aculeata
- **Cuje**
  Inga edulis
- **Custard apple**
  Annona squamosa
- **Grain amaranth**
  Amaranthus
  hypochondriacus
- **Guava, guayaba**
  Psidium guajava,
  Psidium friedrichsthalianum
- **Güicoy**
  Curcubita pepo
- **Güishnay, wixna 'i**
  Spathiphyllum phryniifolium

- **Güiscoyol**
  Bactris major
- **Güisquil**
  Sechium edule
- **Guayule**
  Parthenium argentatum
- **Henequen**
  Agave fourcroyes
- **Hierbamora, leaf**
  Solanum americanum
- **India-fig**
  Opuntia ficus-indica
- **Injerto**
  Pouteria viridis
- **Izote, flower**
  Yucca guatemalensis
- **Jaiba, fruit**
  Momordica charantia
- **Jícama**
  Pachyrhizus erosus
- **Jocote, fruit**
  Spondias purpurea,
  Spondias mombin
- **Kanaq'**
  Chiranthodendron
  pentadactylon
- **Kapok**
  Ceiba pentandra
- **Loroco, flower**
  Fernaldia pandurata
- **Madrecacao, flower**
  Gliricidia sepium
- **Maguey**
  Agave spp.,
  Agave atrovirens
- **Maize, maíz**
  Zea mays
- **Majcuy, leaf**
  Solanum nigrescens
- **Malanga**
  Colocasia esculenta
- **Mamey, fruit**
  Mammea americana
- **Manioc**
  Manihot esculenta
- **Manzanilla, hawthorn**
  Crataegus pubescens
- **Marigold**
  Tagetes patula
- **Matasano, fruit**
  Casimiroa edulis
- **Mezcal**
  Agave tequilana

- **Mezcal bean**
  Sophora secundiflora
- **Muta**
  Bromelia pinguin
- **Nance**
  Byrsonima crassifolia
- **Ñame**
  Dioscorea spp.
- **Pacaya, palm flower**
  Chamaedorea tepejilote
- **Pan de la Vida,**
  fruit
  Pouteria hypoglauca
- **Panic grass**
  Panicum sonorum
- **Papaya**
  Carica papaya
- **Pataxte, fruit**
  Theobroma bicolor
- **Pepper, aji**
  Capsicum frutescens
- **Pepper, bell**
  Capsicum annuum
- **Pepper, chile**
  Capsicum annuum
- **Pepper, tabasco**
  Capsicum frutescens
- **Pimienta gorda, allspice**
  Pimenta dioica
- **Piña, fruit**
  Ananas comosus
- **Pitaya, pitahaya, fruit**
  Hylocereus undatus
- **Pito, tz'ite, flower**
  Erythrina berteroana
- **Prickly pear**
  Opuntia spp.
- **Prickly poppy**
  Argemone mexicana
- **Pumpkin**
  Cucurbita pepo
- **Orejuela, flower**
  Cymbopetalum
  penduliflorum
- **Quilete, leaf**
  Sinclairia sublobata
- **Ramón**
  Brosimum alicastrum
- **Samat, zamat herb**
  Eryngium foetidum
- **Sapodilla**
  Manilkara zapota

- **Sapote, black**
  Diospyros ebenaster
- **Sapote, white**
  Casimiroa edulis
- **Saúco, sauco**
  Sambucus Mexicana
- **Sea-grape**
  Coccoloba uvifera
- **Sisal**
  Agave sisalana
- **Soursop**
  Annona muricata
- **Squash**
  Cucurbita spp.
- **Sweet potato**
  Ipomoea batatas
- **Sweet sop**
  Annona squamosa
- **Teosinte**
  Zea spp.
- **Ternera**
  Euterpe precatoria
- **Tepejilote**
  Carludovica palmata
- **Tomate**
  Physalis ixocarpa
- **Tomatillo,**
  miltomate
  Physalis philadelphica
- **Tomatillo**
  de culebra
  Solanum lycopersicum
- **Tuna**
  Opuntia megacanthos
- **Vanilla**
  Vanilla planifolia
- **Yam, Mexican**
  Dioscorea floribunda
- **Yam bean**
  Pachyrhizus erosus
- **Yampí**
  Dioscorea trifida,
  Dioscorea tripilla,
  Dioscorea triloba
- **Zapote, fruit**
  Pouteria sapota
- **Zapotillo, fruit**
  Pouteria durlandii,
  Pouteria amygdalina
- **Zunza, fruit**
  Licania platypus

AMALIA'S MESOAMERICAN PANTRY

The key to creating great authentic dishes is starting with the right ingredients. Your despensa (pantry) need not be large to create the recipes in this book. My list is long simply so I can highlight important ingredients and explain all the ingredients thoroughly.

You may have noticed that in the past few years, Latin culture has become more visible in the United States. Latinos are now the number one US minority, and the

Latin American population continues to grow. Grocery stores are stocking more Latin items, and the number of Latin grocery stores in major cities has increased. You'll find that many of the items on this list are available at your local grocery store in the Latin or ethnic section, at Latin stores in your area, or online. (See "Ingredient Sources" on page 378.) For less-common items that may be challenging to find, I have listed close substitutes where possible.

Achiote:

Also called achote or annatto, achiote is the seed of the achiote or annatto tree, which is native to the tropical Americas. It is available whole, ground, or in paste form. Achiote is used for coloring, not for aroma or flavor; its orange hue adds visual appeal to dishes. (In large quantities, it can taste earthy or bitter.) You must immerse whole achiote seeds in medium-hot oil to extract the color. You can use ground achiote as a rub or dissolve it in water and add it to soups, sauces, and rice dishes. You must dissolve achiote paste in liquid before adding it to food; a little goes a long way.

Alguaishte Iwaxte or Iguashte:

Toasted ground pumpkin seeds (shelled and unshelled pepitas) are widely used in the preparation of drinks, artisan sweets, moles, recados, salsas, and stews, and as a condiment on fresh vegetables and fruits. They impart a pleasant aroma and flavor to foods and, when combined with salt, chile powder, and lime, are a superb condiment for anything.

Cacao or Cocoa Beans:

A key ingredient in the cuisines of Mesoamerica, from beverages to savory dishes. They are easy to roast, peel, and incorporate into any preparation of choice. They are the most authentic and natural form of chocolate available.

Cal (Calcium Hydroxide):

Cal (a.k.a. slaked lime or pickling lime) has been used in Mesoamerica for millennia for processing corn into nixtamal. It also is used for making candied tubers and squash and for crystallizing certain fruits, such as figs, oranges, and chilacayote, a hard-shelled squash. It helps the fruit or vegetable retain its shape, become translucent, and acquire the desired crunchy yet soft texture. Buy it at your local Latin store or online.

Capers (Alcaparras):

Spanish capers are about the size of a raisin or larger and may be packed in salt, brine, or vinegar. Capers packed in salt are a bit bitter and have a stronger taste than capers packed in brine or vinegar. If Spanish capers are unavailable at your store, use nonpareil capers instead. Nonpareil capers packed in vinegar are top-quality, hand-harvested small capers from the Mediterranean.

Chile Peppers:

Chile peppers add not only heat but also much flavor and texture to stews, soups, and sauces. The following list describes several of the most widely used chiles in order of intensity from hottest to mildest. There are other chile varieties throughout Mesoamerica, and names can change by country and region.

Habanero: This chile is widely used in Mexican cooking, especially in Yucatán, although it is gaining popularity in Mesoamerica. A substitute can be Scotch bonnet.

Jalapeño: One of the most popular chiles in Mexican and Mesoamerican cooking. Although it can be quite spicy, some varieties are milder, especially larger chiles. It is called chipotle when smoked and dried.

Chipotle: A tasty smoked, dried chile that is called jalapeño when fresh. It's also available canned in adobo sauce. A little goes a long way.

Serrano: Another popular chile in Mexican and Mesoamerican cooking, oftentimes interchangeable with jalapeño in recipes.

Cobán (Cobanero): This chile is named after the town of Cobán in Guatemala's Alta Verapaz region. It is a small, hot pepper used both fresh and dried. The powder has a smoky flavor and is used widely in foods from fruit to soups. Substitutes are piquín or árbol.

Dog's Tooth (Diente de Perro): Dog's tooth is a small red pepper resembling a dog's canine tooth. Use it fresh or dried. Substitute with piquín or árbol.

Chocolate or Green (Chocolate or Verde): This chile is long and skinny (about 3 inches long). It's used for paches (spicy potato and pork tamales) when green, but it's also available dried. If chocolate chile is unavailable, substitute with serrano.

Chiltepe (Chiltepín): Chiltepe, also known as pequin or piquín, is the most widely used chile pepper in Guatemala. It is round, smaller than a pea, very spicy, and flavorful. Its color varies according to ripeness.

Guatemalans commonly use the chiltepe in its fresh form for sauces

and salsas. Although it is best fresh, it is also available dried and pickled at some Latin stores. If chiltepe is unavailable, substitute with fresh bird's eye chile (Thai chile).

Chamborote: Chamborote is a spicy pepper that resembles the habanero but is larger and less spicy. It's used fresh to garnish fiambre (marinated vegetables, meats, cold cuts, seafood, and cheeses), but it is also pickled and used in fresh sauces. Substitute with manzano.

Guaque: Guaque is a dried chile 3 to 5 inches long and about 3 inches wide. It gives great color and flavor and is one of the most popular chiles in Guatemalan cooking. A flavorful dark brown chile, guaque is often used along with pasa in recados (sauces) and stews. Substitute with Mexican guajillo.

Poblano: A larger flavorful chile used in Mexican cuisine in a variety of preparations. When dried, it is called ancho.

Pasa: The dried pasa is 4 to 5 inches long and 2 to 3 inches wide. It is one of the most popular chiles in Guatemalan cooking. It is a flavorful dark brown chile often used along

with guaque in recados (sauces) and stews. Substitute with Mexican ancho. Ancho is called poblano when fresh.

Zambo: This reddish-brown dried chile is about 2 inches long and 2 to 3 inches wide. It is used in sauces and stews in Guatemalan cooking. Substitute with mulato or new Mexico chile.

Morrón: This is a multicolored fresh sweet pepper that resembles a bell pepper. Even though they are from the same family, green bell pepper tastes uniquely different from the other sweet peppers, making morrón a favorite for sofrito, stews, soups, and other basic preparations in Mesoamerican and Latin cooking.

Chipilín (Chepil):

Chepil is a plant native to Guatemala. It produces small, delicate, aromatic, and flavorful leaves. Use the leaves in tamales, soups, rice, and beans. Chepil is available frozen.

Chocolate:

Guatemalan chocolate (regular and dark) has great depth of flavor. It's meant for drinking and cooking, not for eating right out of the package. Do not substitute with cocoa. Guatemalan chocolate comes in different shapes and sizes (thin rounds; long, thick tablets; and short, thick tablets), depending on the brand. The chocolate is very hard and must be broken for measuring. To break the chocolate, put it in a double layer of resealable plastic bags, wrap it twice in a kitchen towel, and pound it with the smooth side of a metal meat mallet until the chocolate is almost powdery. Then transfer it to a measuring cup and measure the desired amount. Substitute with Mexican chocolate.

Coffee (Café de Guatemala):

Guatemalan coffee is among the best in the world. The finest varieties come from the highlands. Substitute with other Mesoamerican coffees.

Corn and Corn Flour (Maíz and Masa Harina):

There are many colors and kinds of corn throughout Mesoamerica. Not all of them are turned into flour or masa.

Corn can be used fresh or dried, whole or broken, depending on the recipe.

Maíz: Dried corn (maize or field corn) of many varieties is used cooked in water and cal (slaked lime or calcium hydroxide) in fresh masa, or broken or coarse- and fine-ground and dry pan toasted in drinks, soups, stews, and other preparations in the Mesoamerican kitchen. Bob's Red Mill whole grain coarse-grind stone-ground cornmeal is a good substitute in Guatemalan pinoles (stews) and some Mesoamerican drinks.

Hominy: Corn without the hull (nixtamalized), available dried or canned. It is the base for pozoles in Mexican cooking.

Masa: Dough made from ground nixtamalized corn. It is used as a thickener and for tortillas, pupusas, tamales, and other dishes. Some Latin stores carry fresh masa made from scratch. Use fresh masa if you can find it in your area; there is a world of difference in taste and texture compared to the dried, powdered form.

Masa Harina (Instant Corn Masa Flour): This is masa that has been dried and further ground into a powder. It is available in white, blue, and yellow corn and is commonly used in multiple preparations, such as tortillas and tamales and more, in place of fresh masa because it's readily available and easy to prepare.

Harina de Salpor: Lighter than instant corn masa flour and made with a low-starch dried whole corn. It's used mostly for baking in Guatemala, but it also works great in pancakes and other recipes. Bob's Red Mill whole grain stone-ground corn flour is a good substitute.

Cornstarch (Maizena):

Cornstarch is used as a thickener for sauces, atol, or desserts.

Cream (Crema):

Crema is the Latin version of American sour cream. In Latin grocery stores and major grocery stores, there are two types of crema available, table cream and sour cream. The latter is known as agria (sour); it's tart, thick, and salted. Table cream is faintly sweet, thinner, and unsalted. Both types of cream are used in this book for savory and sweet dishes.

Culantro (*Eryngium foetidum*):

Not to be confused with cilantro, culantro (a.k.a. culantro de pata, culantro leaf recao, and samat) is an herb used in Caribbean and Mesoamerican cooking, especially in the Central American region.

In Guatemala, it's a key herb in the Mayan stew Kaqik. Culantro and cilantro (*Coriandrum sativum*), or Chinese parsley, have very distinct looks, flavors, and aromas.

Ducal or Kern's Juices (Jugos Ducal o Kern's):

Ducal and Kern's juices are juices from Guatemala made of common and exotic fruits, such as apple, mango, pineapple, pear, peach, and vegetables. They can be used to prepare cocktails or for cooking.

Flowers and Buds:

Native flowers and buds are commonly used in Guatemala and other Mesoamerican countries in a variety of preparations, such as beans, tamales, rice, soups, stews, drinks, and more.

Ayote: Squash blossoms that are stuffed, sautéed with crema, or added to soups. These are available online, or at farmers' markets when in season.

Izote: Izote is the flower of the spiky-leaved yuca plant. Guatemalans prepare izote steamed with lime, add it to stews, make it into fritters, and use it as a stuffing. Fresh izote is best; however, it also is available jarred in brine or frozen.

Pito: A slim, 1-inch-long edible flower bud that resembles a skinny whistle or tiny machete in its sheath. Pito is a plant native to Guatemala and Central America. The bud is bright red and encased in a bright-green stem. (Both are edible.) Pito buds taste similar to green beans but are more tender. They are used in bean dishes and others. Pito is available frozen.

Loroco: This is a delicate, flavorful, aromatic flower bud native to Guatemala and the surrounding region. It is used in tamales, stews, empanadas, and many other dishes. Loroco is available frozen or pickled. Fresh is always best, but for cooking, you can use frozen.

Hibiscus Flower (Rosa de Jamaica): Hibiscus flowers can be steeped in hot water to make an acidic infusion that looks like red wine. It's exquisite on its own and can be combined with other flavors, such as canela (Ceylon cinnamon), and more. Hibiscus tea is also available as a sweetened concentrate. The tea and concentrate can be used as a base for cocktails, sauces, dressings, braising meats, and more.

Manzanilla: Manzanilla is chamomile. Chamomile is used to make tea infusions, and the tea can be used to flavor desserts or to enhance other drinks. Manzanilla is available at Latin stores in bundles or in tea packages.

Herbs and Spices:

Guatemalan and Mexican spices have a deep flavor and aroma. You can find all of these spices at Latin stores. If you must, substitute with local spices.

Allspice (Pimienta Gorda): Allspice is used in recados (sauces), moles, desserts, and drinks.

Bay Leaves (Laurel): Bay leaves are used fresh or dried, usually whole.

Ceylon Cinnamon (Canela en Raja): Guatemalan cinnamon is also known as Ceylon cinnamon. It is softer, more aromatic, and more flavorful than the cinnamon found in most supermarkets (which is cassia cinnamon). Canela en raja has a barky texture, breaks easily, and quickly infuses deep flavor. If it's unavailable at your store, substitute with Mexican canela.

Cloves (Clavo): Cloves are used whole or ground.

Cumin (Comino): Cumin is used whole or ground.

Oregano (Orégano): Oregano is used whole, fresh or dried.

Pepper (Pimienta de Castilla): This refers to black peppercorns.

Spanish Paprika (Pimentón): Spanish paprika is sweet and smoky.

Thyme (Tomillo): Thyme is used whole, not ground. It may be fresh or dried.

Hierbabuena or Yerbabuena (Spearmint):

A strong mint-flavored leafy plant (*Mentha spicata*), widely used in the Mesoamerican region and key in preparations, such as marinades, recados, and sauces. It is essential for many Nicaraguan traditional dishes, such as nacatamales (Nicaraguan tamales), combined with achiote and sour orange, and more.

Leaves (Hojas):

Guatemalans and Mesoamericans use fresh and dried leaves for steaming a variety of foods such as tamales, baking meats, and wrapping cheeses and other foods; as vessels for serving food; and more. No close substitutes exist for any of these leaves. If you must, use parchment paper or aluminum foil as a substitute.

Banana Leaves (Hojas de Plátano): Fresh banana leaves are available at some Latin markets, and frozen fresh banana leaves are available at some major grocery stores and online.

Mashán Leaves (*Calathea lutea*): Leaves of a plant native to Guatemala used alone or in conjunction with banana leaves when making tamales.

Corn Husks (Hojas de Elote): These are fresh corn husks. Collect fresh corn husks in the summer when sweet corn is in season. When corn husks are dried, they are called tusas. Dried corn husks are available in plastic bags at most Latin stores and some major grocery stores.

Corn Leaves (Hojas de Milpa): These are the fresh leaves of a mature corn plant. They are used in rural Guatemala for wrapping small tamales and other foods.

Squash or Pumpkin Leaves (Hojas de Güisquil or Ayote): These leaves are used in Mayan cooking for wrapping tamales.

The entire tamale is edible when it is steamed in this leaf.

Legumes (Legumbres):

There are many varieties of beans and other legumes throughout Mesoamerica. These are some of the most popular.

Black Beans (Frijoles Negros): You can use them dried or canned.

White Beans (Frijoles Blancos): Substitute blancos with dried navy beans or great northern white beans.

Red Beans (Frijoles Colorados): Substitute colorados with dried or canned red kidney beans.

Piloyes: Large, round red beans native to Guatemala. They're used in piloyada Antigüeña, a bean salad from Antigua containing meats, cheese, and other fresh ingredients. Substitute piloyes with dried or canned red kidney beans.

Pinto Beans: Small, speckled pinkish beans popular in Mexican cooking.

Fava Beans (Habas): You can use fresh, dried, or canned fava beans for soups and atols.

Lentils (Lentejas): Use dried or canned lentils for soups and stews.

Garbanzos: Also known as chickpeas, use them dried or canned for soups and stews.

Other beans: Fresh beans are always best, but when you're short on time, use refried canned beans from Guatemala (Ducal brand). These are the next best thing. They're so tasty that you can eat them right out of the can. Kick up the flavor a notch by adding fried onions, or use canned refried Mexican beans.

Jocote:

Also known as red mombin and hog plum, jocote (*Spondias purpurea*) is a native fruit of Mesoamerica and tropical America with a thick, edible peel, sweet and tart flesh, and a large seed core. There are various kinds of jocote, and some can be eaten green, while others are best ripe.

Lizano Sauce:

A delicious sauce from Costa Rica and a key component in gallo pinto. The sauce is a staple in Costa Rican cuisine, and it resembles Heinz 57 Sauce in looks but not in flavor. The

sauce is widely distributed in the United States by Unilever.

Oils (Aceites) and Fat:

Aceite de maíz is corn oil. Aceite de cártamo is canola oil. Oliva is Spanish extra-virgin olive oil. Manteca is lard and is widely used in Mexican and Mesoamerican cooking even today. Mantequilla is butter; use butter sparingly in place of lard. Margarina is margarine and is used for spreading and baking.

Olives (Aceitunas):

These are Spanish olives stuffed with pimentos.

Pacaya Palm Flowers or Fronds:

These are the edible flowers of the pacaya palm tree (*Chamaedorea tepejilote*). The flower is bitter and a bit rubbery yet crunchy. It is best when fresh. It is also available pickled at Latin stores. If you can find frozen pacaya flowers, you can make them into salads or fritters with tomato sauce. Pacaya flowers are a key ingredient in fiambre. The flowers must be cooked in water to remove some of the bitter taste.

Panela or Piloncillo:

Unrefined whole cane sugar, panela (piloncillo in Mexico) is used for drinks, desserts, and sauces. It is also known as rapadura and other names in Mesoamerica. Panela's flavor depth is unique, but brown sugar is a close substitute. Panela is very hard and must be broken for measuring. To break it, put it in a double layer of resealable plastic bags, wrap it twice in a kitchen towel, and pound it with the smooth side of a metal meat mallet until the panela is almost powdery. Then measure the desired amount.

Raisins and Prunes (Pasas y Ciruelas):

Raisins and prunes are used in desserts, tamales, and hot drinks.

Rice (Arroz) and Rice Flour:

Use any long-grain white rice of high quality. Rice flour is used for tamales and for baking.

Rum (Ron):

Rum is used in cold and hot drinks and desserts. Ron Botrán and Zacapa Centenario are two different kinds of rum made by the same distillery in Guatemala City. Botrán is the name of the distillery's well-established line of rums. Zacapa Centenario is the distillery's newer line of rums. This award-winning newer line was introduced to commemorate the one hundredth anniversary of the foundation of the department of Zacapa in eastern Guatemala.

Both are great-quality rums. If necessary, you can substitute with Flor de Caña Nicaraguan rums.

Saffron (Azafrán):

Use Spanish saffron or any other good-quality saffron.

Salt (Sal):

Chefs prefer kosher salt (sal kosher) because it's flaky, dissolves easily, has a clean taste, and contains very few additives. Sea salt (sal de mar) is more healthful and flavorful than other salts because it's natural and contains traces of minerals. Some recipes in this book use coarse sea salt for flavor and tradition or as a garnish.

Sauces and Condiments (Salsas and Condimentos):

Chiltepe sauces are made with chiltepe chile (native to Guatemala) and are spicy and very flavorful. Guatemalan catsup is sweeter than American ketchup. Maggi sauce is a concentrated sauce resembling soy sauce in looks and salt content—but not in flavor (and it doesn't contain soy, though it does contain wheat

gluten). Picamás is a creamy and flavorful red or green chile sauce.

Seeds (Semillas):

Chia seeds (chan), pumpkin seeds (pepitas or pepitoria), and sesame seeds (ajonjolí) are available raw, toasted, and ground at most US grocery stores.

Sour Orange Juice (Jugo de Naranja Agria):

Native to southeast Asia, sour orange came to Latin America through Spain, and the juice is widely used in cooking in the Caribbean and Central America. It is also known as Seville or bitter orange. If unable to source it, use equal parts fresh orange and lemon juice to mimic its flavor.

Sugarcane Unrefined Alcohol (Aguardiente Venado or Indita):

Venado and Indita are two Guatemalan brands of a high-alcohol sugarcane brandy-like spirit. Use Bacardi white rum as a substitute.

Tamarind (Tamarindo):

Tamarind is available at most Latin markets in fresh (pod) form, in frozen pulp form, as paste, or in a sweetened concentrate (puree) form. It is used to make drinks and as a base for sauces.

Vanilla (Vainilla):

A key ingredient in chocolate, desserts, drinks, and other preparations. The best vanilla comes from the paste from the pod—easily recognizable by its flavor depth, aroma, and distinctive dark specks—or from its derivative, vanilla extract.

Vinegar (Vinagre):

Guatemalan Sharp brand vinegar is lightly flavored vinegar used in fiambre, salads, and escabeches. (Escabeche is a technique and sauce that consists of sautéing onions, garlic, fresh herbs, and spices in olive oil and finishing with good-quality vinegar. The term also refers to a quick, chunky sauce used to top fried fish or other seafood.) Substitute with champagne vinegar, white wine vinegar, or white vinegar. Red wine vinegar is also used in salads.

EASY, HEALTHY COOKING TECHNIQUES AND TIPS

Mesoamerican cuisine, like other cuisines, has its own distinct cooking techniques. When you use these techniques with certain key ingredients, you get the right results. Many Mesoamerican cooking techniques are rustic and have been practiced since ancient times. Savvy cooks are realizing that a modern approach can produce faster and healthier cuisine that's as delicious as ever. My professional background is in classic French cuisine, so I tend to blend that with Mesoamerican cuisine. The following pages describe some of the most common blended techniques and cooking tips that I use in my kitchen.

These first three terms are not techniques, but are important concepts to keep in mind before starting to cook.

Carryover Heat (Calor Adyacente)

Carryover heat is an important concept of the cooking process. It refers to the fact that food retains heat and continues to cook after you remove it from the heat source. The temperature will continue to rise by about 10°F while sitting on your kitchen counter, so it's best to slightly undercook vegetables, meats, and seafood by about 8 to 10°F. Planning for carryover heat can make the difference between properly cooked and overcooked food.

Mise en Place (Preparación y Organización)

Mise en place is a French culinary expression that means, roughly, to "put everything in place," to organize all ingredients for a recipe before you start cooking. Organization is essential in any kitchen. It makes the cooking process easier, smoother, and more fun. Reading and understanding the steps of a recipe before you begin is as important as having the right ingredients and equipment.

Seasoning and Tasting (Sazonar y Rectificar)

In Guatemalan and Mesoamerican cooking, *sazón* refers to the proper seasoning of foods. An outstanding recipe can produce poor results without proper seasoning. Basic seasonings like salt and freshly ground black pepper can make the difference between a bland dish and a delicious one. Tasting goes hand in hand with seasoning. You cannot possibly know how much seasoning you need without tasting.

Baking (Hornear)

Moderate baking (350 to 375°F) is useful for cooking vegetables and meats and for baking cakes. You can also use baking to finish meat that you've cooked partway on a grill or seared on the stovetop.

Baking Underground (Pib)

A pib is an earth oven and ancient dry cooking underground technique where foods wrapped in banana or other leaves are sandwiched between hot coals and stones, then buried with dried leaves and dirt. The prolonged cooking bakes, smokes, flavors, and tenderizes meat.

Braising (Cocer Lentamente en Agua o Fondo)

Braising meat is cooking it slowly in a covered dish, with enough liquid to cover the meat about three-quarters of the way. This can be done in the oven, on the stovetop, or in a slow cooker. Guatemalan cooks often dry-marinate meats and poultry prior to braising them in a clay Dutch oven. Braising is ideal for tough cuts of meat that need slow cooking to break down connective tissue and become tender. This technique works well with turkey too.

Broiling (Asar al Horno)

Broiling is grilling food from above. Cooks often use this technique for finishing foods after they are cooked.

Foods are quickly heated from above to melt cheeses or to quickly brown them.

Cooking in Natural Leaves (Cocer en Hojas Naturales)

Cooking food in corn, banana, mashán, or other leaves is an ancient technique. It's similar to the French method of cooking *en papillote* (inside a pouch usually made of parchment paper). Cooks enclose foods in the leaves and wrap them up like packages, then steam the food on the stovetop or bake it in a conventional oven or an outdoor oven over charcoal.

Crushing and Grinding with a Molcajete and Tejolote (Aplastar y Moler)

A molcajete is a concave grinding stone made from volcanic rock with an arm (tejolote) designed to grind or mash spices, seeds, and other ingredients for molcajete salsas and other preparations. It is used in traditional Mexican cooking. It is the equivalent of the mortar and pestle and is available in small, medium, and large sizes. This ancient pre-Hispanic tool is used in kitchens throughout Mesoamerica today.

Dry Pan Toasting or Roasting, Soaking, and Grinding (Tostar, Rostizar, Remojar y Moler)

Dry pan toasting or roasting consists of heating a dry skillet or griddle to pan toast or roast anything from tortillas to seeds to vegetables. The purpose of dry pan toasting or roasting is to char, toast, or brown a food, heightening flavors in the process, without adding any fat. Corn tortillas are cooked on a dry *comal*, or clay griddle. Peppers and tomatoes are charred to blacken them or to remove the skins. Pumpkin seeds and some spices are toasted to heighten their flavors. Soaking in a hot liquid is a technique used to reconstitute dry-roasted chiles or other dried ingredients for stuffing or pureeing. Grinding dried peppers or other foods in a spice mill is a technique used to pulverize ingredients for dry rubs and sauces.

Fire Roasting and Hot Oil Dipping (Asar a la Llama y Sumergir en Aceite Caliente)

These techniques char or blister vegetables for easy peeling or to enhance their flavor. Hot oil dipping consists of dipping a vegetable in very hot oil for a few seconds to loosen the skin. Fire roasting is charring the skins of vegetables, such as chiles or tomatoes, directly on the flames of a burner to enhance their flavor and make peeling easier. Sealing the charred vegetables in a plastic bag for a few minutes eases the peeling process. Use wet paper towels (not water) to remove bits of charred skin that are hard to peel, or just leave them on to enhance the look or flavor of a dish. Fire-roasted tomatoes and chiles make delicious sauces and stews.

Grills and Griddles (Parrillas y Planchas)

Grills are called parrillas in Guatemala and Mesoamerica, and griddles are called planchas. Large parrillas and planchas are more common in restaurants than in homes. *A la parrilla* means to cook in a parrilla, referring to grilled foods.

Grinding with Volcanic Rocks (Moliendo a Mano en Metate)

A metate is a long concave stone designed for making corn masa from fresh nixtamalized corn kernels or for pureeing cocoa beans or softened dried chiles or other ingredients. The mano is the arm used for grinding. These are ancient pre-Hispanic tools that are still used in kitchens throughout Mesoamerica today.

Marinating (Marinar)

Marinar is to marinate; it's also called adobar, depending on the preparation. Beef, chicken, or pork can be marinated in wet or dry rubs, or in a liquid preparation. Dry rubs can can contain a variety of spices and ground dried chiles. Wet marinades can include pastes combined with fresh fruit juices and oil, or can be liquid preparations involving spices and herbs, vinegar, and sometimes oil. Marinades are also called adobos and salmueras.

Marinating with the Escabeche Technique (Escabechar)

Escabechar is an ancient technique that came to Latin America from the Middle East through Spain. It consists of making a quick, chunky sauce (escabeche) in a skillet by sautéing onion, peppers, garlic, herbs, and spices in oil and finishing the sauce with vinegar. In Guatemala, escabeche is commonly used to marinate (marinar) chiles, carrots, and cauliflower. Escabeche varies from country to country in Latin America and can contain many other vegetables. This sauce can top pan-fried fish or other proteins, or it can stand on its own. It is the perfect complement to fried seafood, as it provides a nice break between fatty bites.

Nixtamalizing (Nixtamalizar)

Nixtamalizar is the process of removing the skin (pericarp) from corn kernels by cooking them in water and cal (calcium hydroxide) to make it digestible and increase its nutritional properties. In ancient times, ash was originally used. This process also softens the corn to produce masa (dough) for making a multitude of preparations in the Mesoamerican kitchen, such as tortillas, tamales, atoles, and more.

Oven Roasting (Asar o Rostizar al Horno)

Oven roasting is baking at a high temperature, usually 400°F or higher. Oven roasting gives the effect of frying without adding much—or any—fat. It is a delicious and healthy way to prepare potatoes, meats, and poultry. Oven roasting is a good alternative to pan roasting pumpkin seeds and sesame seeds—just keep a close eye on them so the seeds don't burn.

Pan Frying (Sofreir, Sofrito, and Refrito)

Sofreir is to make a quick sauce with a little oil, onions, garlic, and tomato. This is a basic sofrito or refrito, common in the cuisines of Mesoamerica and Latin America. The sauce can be added to soups and rice dishes or can be used to top meat or chicken. Depending on its purpose, the sauce can be built by adding more ingredients of choice, such as bell peppers, culantro, cilantro, yerbabuena (mint), and other herbs and spices.

Patting by Hand (Tortear)

This technique involves patting corn masa or dough into tortillas. After shaping it into golf-ball-size rounds, the dough can be flattened by hand to the desired thickness by patting and turning them at the same time. This is an art form and requires practice. The term *tortear* comes from the word *tortilla*. An alternative is to use a flattening device made of metal or wood lined with thick plastic. Tortillas can also be made by placing the dough on a flat surface on top of a round piece of thick plastic about the same size as the desired tortillas and flattening with your fingers while rotating the circle simultaneously.

Pickling (Curtir)

Curtir means "to pickle." This technique consists of either steaming or blanching vegetables al dente (until tender-crisp) and then pickling them in a spiced vinegar-based sauce. Guatemalans make curtidos or encurtidos (pickled vegetables) for various purposes: to preserve vegetables for later use, to make quick condiments and toppings, and to make salads. Curtidos must contain a balanced mixture of vinegar, water, spices, and seasonings.

Poaching (Sancochar)

Poaching is gently simmering food in a flavored liquid over low heat for a relatively short time. In Guatemalan cuisine, poaching is used mostly in making desserts such as dulces (sweets). These sweets are poached in spiced panela syrup. The poaching liquid often becomes the sauce of the dessert. Poaching with wine, herbs, and lemon is a great technique for cooking delicate fish or seafood.

Quick Blackening (Tostar Hasta Quemar)

Blackening is a technique used on tortillas, plantain peel, and other ingredients to add flavor and color. A quick way to blacken food is to toast it in a toaster oven on the darkest setting until the food looks medium brown (4 to 6 minutes), or to dry pan toast it on a nonstick griddle or skillet on the stovetop at medium heat.

Quick Pan Frying (Freír)

Stovetop pan frying is used to make foods that cook quickly, such as plantains and sofrito. Sofrito is a base for many Guatemalan dishes. Basic sofrito is a mixture of onions and tomatoes seasoned with salt. More elaborate sofritos can include other ingredients, such as garlic and bell peppers. Pan frying adds flavor and eye appeal. Guatemalan cooks often combine this technique with other techniques in making stews. Some stews are simmered or braised first and then finished by pan frying them quickly with onions and garlic to heighten their flavor.

Quick Soaking (Remojar Rápidamente)

A quick way to soak chiles or tortillas in stock or water is to heat them in a microwave oven for 1 to 2 minutes, then let them stand for about 10 minutes, instead of waiting 20 to 30 minutes to soak them in cold water.

Quick Steaming (Cocinar a Vapor Rápidamente)

Stovetop steaming is a fast, healthy way to cook vegetables and seafood. You can combine steaming with other cooking methods, such as broiling, to add eye appeal and flavor. Start with steaming: cook vegetables al dente and slightly undercook seafood. Then brush the food with olive oil, season it, and broil it quickly.

Resting (Descansar)

Resting is letting freshly grilled or roasted meats rest on your kitchen counter, slightly tented with foil, to finish cooking. This technique seals in the juices and allows the meat to reach the desired temperature. Grilled or roasted meats will be juicy and properly cooked if you allow them to rest for at least 10 minutes before slicing them.

Sautéing al Dente (Saltear al Dente)

Sautéing is cooking quickly over medium high heat. Sautéing vegetables al dente enhances their flavor, texture, and eye appeal. This technique is used to create vegetable side dishes like escabeche in minutes.

Searing and Oven Finishing (Sellar y Terminar en el Horno)

Searing is browning meat or vegetables in a little fat on the stovetop at high heat to heighten flavors, seal in juices, and add eye appeal. Oven finishing is transferring the seared food to the oven and cooking it to the desired temperature.

Simmering and Braising in Slow Cookers (Cocer en Agua o Fondo a Fuego Lento en Olla de Cocción Lenta)

Simmering and braising in a slow cooker is useful in many ways. You can brown foods on the stovetop first and then braise them in a slow cooker. You can cook dried legumes on the high setting without having to soak them first. This is stressless cooking; once all the ingredients are in the slow cooker, they cook by themselves with only minor supervision.

Simmering, Pureeing, and Pan Frying (Cocer Lentamente en Agua o Fondo, Hacer Puré y Freír)

This combined technique consists of simmering vegetables in some liquid first, then pureeing them, and lastly pan frying them to achieve the desired texture and flavor in stews, sauces, and soups. The vegetables are often dry roasted and soaked first.

Simple Grilling (Asar)

Guatemalans usually grill food on grates over natural charcoal. This grilling technique provides the best flavor and aroma. Before grilling, meat may be marinated with adobos or onions, oranges, herbs, and a little oil to prevent sticking. *Churrasco* is the Guatemalan term for "barbecue." Churrasco also refers to a grilled dish, such as grilled meats, or to a barbecue party. *Asado* refers to grilled meats.

Stewing (Guisar)

Guisar is to stew meat, usually searing or quickly browning it prior to adding sofrito and other ingredients in a recipe. Guisar is a slow cooking process that after searing them requires simmering foods, covered, to finish the cooking process or make tougher meats tender, blend flavors, and thicken broths or sauces (recados). A guisado is the end result, a stew.

Sweating (Sudar)

Sweating is a way to cook vegetables or fruits that naturally contain a great amount of water or juice, such as tomatoes, onions, cactus, pineapples, mangos, and more. Start with a dry skillet over medium heat. The skillet must be covered to allow for steady and consistent sweat to occur and cook the vegetables or fruits al dente, or as desired. Little stirring is needed. The food can then be added to other preparations or dressed with a sauce or made into a salad.

1

Bebidas y Cocteles
Drinks and Cocktails

ANCESTRAL AND TRADITIONAL DRINKS

All countries and regions have drinks unique to their cultures, and Mesoamerica has its fair share of them. Some have been around since ancient times. Others have a historical and ceremonial context and are seasonal. Made with fruits, vegetables, seeds, grains, legumes, flowers, or spices, these unique beverages are sweetened with natural syrups like agave, honey, panela (piloncillo), or sugar. The easy homestyle drinks provide a fresh and more nutritious alternative to empty-calorie carbonated drinks.

When sugarcane and other imports were introduced by the Spaniards to the Americas in the 1600s, a wide array of foods and drinks came into being, and existing creations were modified. Guarapo is freshly squeezed sugarcane juice enjoyed in Guatemala and other parts of Meso- and Latin America alone, on the rocks, or in a cocktail with other juices or liquors. Guarapo is the base of panela (unrefined whole cane sugar) and ultimately of aguardiente, a distilled spirit high in alcohol, and rum.

Fermented fruit-based drinks, often made with corn and panela, can contain low to high levels of alcohol depending on the type and are often connected to a special ritual or festivity. Súchiles (Fermented Spiced Fruit Brew, page 56), boj, cuxa or cusha, and chicha are all corn-based fermented drinks. These and caldo de frutas (aged aguardiente and fruit) are some of the better-known creations made in rural and urban Guatemala. Some are clandestine, prepared in homes by people who have a knack for making them or anybody who wants to sell them. Knowledge and recipes pass generationally, and sourcing them is often by word of mouth because some are illicit.

Tepache (Fermented Pineapple Brew, page 58) and tejuino (a fermented masa beverage) have been around Mexican culture since pre-Hispanic times and became a hybrid when piloncillo (sugar cane) was introduced.

Mesoamerican Wines

Wine production in Mesoamerica has been sporadic in a couple of countries due to varying factors: terroir, weather, skill, commitment, and political conflict.

Guatemalans have produced wine to conform to their own standards but ceased operations. They now successfully make good artisan wines with níspero and other tropical fruits.

Mexico has produced wine since the arrival of the Spaniards, though inconsistently due mainly to political strife, but lately production has been gaining momentum. There are now three key regions in Mexico producing good-quality wines, with Baja California producing about 90 percent of the wine. As a result, enotourism is booming.

Atol shuco is the Guatemalan cousin of tejuino, except the former is served warm with different toppings. There are versions of this atole in other Central American countries.

Mexico's tequila industry is well known today. Good tequila comes from the blue agave plant from the Jalisco designation of origin territory. The finer ones are meant for tasting and sipping, not to be taken in shots. Mezcal, called the nectar of the Aztec gods by Cortés, is higher in alcohol than tequila and also comes from the agave plant but not necessarily from blue agave. While visiting the land of mezcal—Oaxaca, Mexico—I discovered some exquisite brands. Pulque, harking back to Aztec times, is an unrefined cloudy-white fermented drink that comes from aguamiel, the sap of the maguey (agave) plant, and contains less alcohol than tequila and mezcal. To make it palatable, pulque is sometimes combined with other flavors, fruit pulp, or sugar.

Beer, another ancient brew originating in the early Middle East, is an import introduced to Latin America by waves of immigrants from Europe who brought the basic ingredients, barley and hops, and know-how. Each country in Mesoamerica has made beer recipes of its own, and today they are some of the best in Latin America. With good beer come other inventions and styles, including artisanal beer often mixed with local ingredients. Michelada con Boquita (Spicy Beer Cocktail with a Treat, page 40) is a tasty beer-based drink from Mexico mixed with a tomato juice cocktail and rimmed with spicy chile salt and sometimes paired with a botana or boquita (treat).

It's no secret that some of the best coffee comes from Mesoamerica, although it's not native. Coffee plants combined with volcanic terroir, favorable growing conditions, and expert growers have produced world-class coffee in the region for generations. Café con Canela y Agave (Aromatic Toasted Cinnamon and Blue Agave Coffee, page 35) is a classic cozy combination—agave is my personal preference instead of sugar.

Corn and cocoa beans did originate in this region and have been highly revered by ancient civilizations and their descendants. Corn and cocoa beans alone or together gave birth to a variety of delicious artisan beverages combined with spices. Tiste (Roasted Cocoa Bean, Corn, and Achiote Libation, page 55), Pinolillo (Toasted Corn and Cocoa Bean Shake, page 44), and Kixnank' (Artisan Chocolate with Vanilla Bean and Cinnamon, page 39) are some of the many liquid delights anyone can enjoy at home. Wholesome and full of flavor, these drinks are for the young and old, are easy to make, and are an opportunity to expand anyone's drink repertoire. Good drinks begin with the best raw materials, and Mesoamerica has them.

Whether you have an appetite for a virgin or a spicy cocktail, in this chapter, you will find a good sampling of some of the best artisanal drinks of the region. In the process, you'll discover something new and unique with a truly wholesome background.

Un Cafecito—A Social and Cultural Experience

A cafecito is a drink but also a cultural reference to a cozy rendezvous with a friend or relative at a home, cafeteria, restaurant, or coffee shop while enjoying some intimate conversation and a delicious cup of coffee.

It is a reference to an endearing time in good company sharing about family, friends, or relatives.

A cafecito is sometimes paired with pan de manteca or pan dulce (fresh sweet bread) or other treats.

CAFÉ CON CANELA Y AGAVE
Aromatic Toasted Cinnamon and Blue Agave Coffee

SERVES 1 to 2

3 tablespoons medium-roasted coffee beans (Mexican or Central American)

1 (½-inch) piece dry pan-toasted canela (Ceylon cinnamon) (see note)

1 ¾ cups water

⅔ cup steamed or hot milk (optional)

1 tablespoon blue agave nectar

A good coffee is simply one freshly made with good-quality beans and the right proportion of ingredients. It is no secret that Latin America produces some of the best coffee in the world. Café con canela is popular in Mexico and in some Central American countries, where brown sugar or panela (unrefined whole cane sugar) instead of agave is sometimes used. Agave nectar gives it a gourmet touch. Add some steamed or hot milk, room-temperature evaporated milk, or warm cream to elevate it to a new level. Combining cold milk with coffee is frowned upon by Latin Americans who appreciate a good cup of cafecito. A French press is ideal for small quantities of coffee, and I do believe that fresh coffee tastes even better when not filtered.

1. In a coffee grinder, combine the coffee beans and cinnamon and grind them to a fine powder.

2. Make the coffee in a traditional coffee maker, or boil the water and use a French press.

3. Combine the coffee with the milk (if using). Sweeten with the agave nectar and serve.

AMALIA'S NOTE

- The easiest way to toast canela is to first break it into small pieces, then put it on a preheated small skillet over medium low heat and dry pan toast it until barely aromatic, about 1 minute. Keep a close eye, as it can burn easily.

RECIPE VARIATIONS

Café con Leche (Coffee with Milk):
Make the coffee as above, but omit the cinnamon and use all the milk.

Café con Vainilla (Vanilla Coffee):
Make the coffee as Café con Canela y Agave, but omit the cinnamon. Add ⅛ teaspoon of vanilla pulp or extract per cup during step 2.

Café con Manzanilla (Chamomile Coffee):
Make the coffee as Café con Canela y Agave, but omit the cinnamon and water, and make the coffee using chamomile tea (1 teabag) as a base.

Café con Chocolate y Canela (Chocolate and Cinnamon Coffee):
Make the coffee as Café con Canela y Agave and add 2 tablespoons broken-up Guatemalan or Mexican chocolate pieces during step 3. Stir well. The coffee and milk must be very hot to dissolve the chocolate.

Café con Dulce de Leche (Caramel Milk Coffee):
Make the coffee as Café con Canela y Agave (omit the cinnamon or leave it in) and add 1 tablespoon dulce de leche per cup during step 3.

CHINCHIVIR

Spiced Limeade with Anise and Ginger

SERVES 1

Chinchivir is a traditional refreshing drink, usually lime based mixed with a combination of exotic spices from the region of Antigua, Guatemala. There are varying versions, including a fermented one made with cordoncillo, a native root. Make it your own by using other fresh fruit juices such as orange or pineapple as a base. Aguas frescas, or refreshing waters of varying flavors, are traditional in Mesoamerica and many Latin countries. Easy to prepare and delicious, they can be made with whole grains and cereals, roasted seeds, spices, fruits, vegetables, and more. This is my rendition of this special drink, which could be elevated to a cocktail with a good-quality rum.

1 cup cold water

1 teaspoon finely grated fresh ginger

1 (½-inch) piece canela (Ceylon cinnamon)

2 whole cloves

⅛ teaspoon anise seed

2 tablespoons brown sugar, panela (piloncillo), or granulated sugar

¼ cup freshly squeezed lime juice (from about 2 small limes)

Adorno (Garnish)

Lime slices and mint sprigs

1. Combine the water, ginger, cinnamon piece, cloves, anise seed, and brown sugar in a saucepan over high heat and bring to a quick boil. Reduce the heat to low and simmer, covered, until fully aromatic, about 3 minutes. Let cool.

2. Strain the spiced mixture into a glass or jar and combine it with the lime juice. Chill. Stir well and serve in a tall glass (with or without ice), garnished with lime slices and mint sprigs.

AMALIA'S NOTES

- Canela (Ceylon cinnamon stick) can easily be broken by hand or using a knife or scissors to measure the required amount.

- If using ice, increase the amount of sweetener used to compensate for dilution.

KIXNANK'

Artisan Chocolate with Vanilla Bean and Cinnamon

SERVES 1 to 2

¼ cup fresh cocoa beans

1 (½-inch) piece canela (Ceylon cinnamon), broken into small pieces

4 allspice berries

3 black peppercorns

2 tablespoons sugar

1 (¼-inch) vanilla bean pod piece, split, pulp removed with a paring knife (or ½ teaspoon vanilla extract)

2 cups water

"Elixir of the Gods" might be an appropriate term for this luxurious drink of Maya Q'eqchi' origin. When I tried this fresh cocoa bean drink for the first time, it elevated my taste buds for hot chocolate to a whole new level. I never forgot the experience. The velvety look and mouthfeel and flavor depth do not mirror the taste of any chocolate or hot cocoa you may have ever tried. Traditional of the region of Las Verapaces in north-central Guatemala and the surrounding region, the drink is God-worthy, and it's not surprising that the Maya revered chocolate as their supreme drink. It is simple, pure, and sublime.

1. Over low heat in a dry pan, toast the cocoa beans until they are fragrant and the shells turn medium dark brown, about 15 minutes. Keep a close eye on them and stir the cocoa beans frequently with a heat-resistant spatula for even browning. Let them cool in the skillet, then peel.

2. Dry pan toast the cinnamon, allspice berries, and peppercorns on a preheated small skillet over medium low heat, until aromatic, about 1 minute. Stir frequently. Keep a close eye on them, as they can burn easily.

3. Process the cocoa beans, spices, and sugar in a spice mill to a fine powder. Store the powder in a jar with a tight lid until ready to use.

4. To make kixnank', bring water to a boil over high heat, reduce the heat to low, and gradually add the chocolate powder mixture. Add the vanilla. Stir. Cook over low heat until slightly oily and velvety, about 5 minutes. The nature of this drink is to have bits of chocolate on the bottom. Strain with a fine-mesh sieve for a smoother consistency, if desired. Serve.

AMALIA'S NOTES

- To peel the cocoa beans, squeeze them gently between your fingers, and the peel should easily slide off. Discard the peel.

- Fresh cocoa beans are always best, but you can also use organic cacao nibs instead of whole cocoa beans. They are available at co-ops and online.

- Commercial Guatemalan and Mexican chocolate also comes in dried rounds or blocks of this mixture, which is later combined with hot water or milk. Commercially made chocolate (not cocoa) often has other flavorings, such as vanilla, in addition to cinnamon. Newer recipes also include chiles, molasses, and other flavorings. While dried chocolate starts in a similar fashion to the recipe above, the taste difference is night and day.

MICHELADA CON BOQUITA
Spicy Beer Cocktail with a Treat

SERVES 4

Micheladas originated in Mexico and are beer-based drinks mixed with other flavorings such as lime, tomato juice, chile, and mild and hot sauces. They provide a nice break in the traditional beer-drinking routine and can add party flair to any gathering. They are also a refreshing drink to go with ceviche at la playa (a Guatemalan or any other Central American beach). The recipe varies by maker and Latin country. My gourmet version of this festive drink uses spicy, smoky Cobán chile. The term *boquita* refers to a small bite or appetizer in Guatemala, where all alcoholic drinks ordered in a bar come with a delicious bite, or small treat.

1 Process the first 7 ingredients in a blender or food processor to make a puree. Chill until ready to use. Place four tall beer glasses or mugs in the freezer to chill.

2 Place the shrimp in a small bowl and drizzle it with the lime juice. Season with the Cobán chile powder, salt, and black pepper mixture. Coat the shrimp with the chopped cilantro and skewer them on four 5-inch skewers with 1 shrimp, 1 grape tomato, and a cilantro sprig per skewer. Set aside.

3 Rub the frozen glass rims with the lime wedge. Invert the glasses on a plate covered generously with salt and chile powder and coat the glass rims heavily.

4 Add the tomato puree to the four glasses, distributed evenly. Pour the beer into the glasses slowly, and stir gently. Garnish with the boquita skewers.

AMALIA'S NOTE

• Beer glasses and mugs come in different shapes and sizes. Likely not all the beer from a can or bottle will fit in the glass after adding half a cup of tomato puree. Just simply serve the rest of the beer on the side for your guests to add to their glass as they consume their drink.

PURÉ DE TOMATE (FRESH TOMATO PUREE) (MAKES 2 CUPS)

1 ½ Roma tomatoes, seeded and cut into large chunks
1 ½ tablespoons freshly squeezed lime juice
½ teaspoon Tabasco sauce
½ teaspoon Maggi sauce
½ teaspoon Cobán chile powder or Mexican Tajín
½ teaspoon kosher salt
Dash finely ground black pepper

BOQUITA (TREAT)

4 medium cooked whole shrimp, peeled (tail on) or unpeeled (whole)
1 tablespoon freshly squeezed lime juice
¼ teaspoon Cobán chile powder mixed with ¼ teaspoon kosher salt and freshly ground black pepper to taste
1 teaspoon finely chopped cilantro leaves
4 grape tomatoes
4 cilantro sprigs

A wedge of lime
Kosher salt, for coating the glass rims
Cobán chile powder
4 cervezas de barril (Guatemalan or Mexican raw or draft beer) or bottled or canned beer

SANGRITA Y TEQUILA
Fresh Spicy Tomato Juice Paired with Tequila

SERVES 4 to 6

SANGRITA
(SPICY TOMATO JUICE)
(MAKES 1 CUP)

2 vine-ripened tomatoes, seeded and cut into small pieces

2 tablespoons freshly squeezed orange juice

2 tablespoons freshly squeezed lime juice

2 tablespoons clam juice

1 teaspoon shredded onion

½–1 teaspoon minced pickled jalapeños

1 teaspoon pickled jalapeño juice

½ teaspoon Worcestershire sauce

½ teaspoon Tabasco sauce

½ teaspoon kosher salt

Freshly ground black pepper to taste

High-quality blue agave tequila

This sangrita is one of my favorite prepared juices to go with a fine tequila. The spicy juice is meant for sipping just like a fine tequila. Sip some tequila, follow it with a sip of sangrita, and so on. The flavor contrast is phenomenal and something unique. Make sangrita with fresh ingredients, and you have a fiesta in every sip. This can be your next gathering's welcome drink, or make it a starter for a formal sit-down dinner party. It works for casual and formal gatherings in any style you attach to this exquisite Mexican duo.

1. Process the first 11 ingredients in a blender until smooth. Chill or serve immediately after blending.

2. Serve the sangrita and tequila separately, in same-size small glasses.

AMALIA'S NOTES

- Clam juice is available in small bottles at major grocery chains.

- Shred the onion on a Microplane grater designed for shredding and zesting, or on a box grater. Shredding is important to allow the onion to blend well with the juice.

- Fresh sangrita is best the day it's made, but it can be stored in the refrigerator up to 2 days. After that time, it starts losing its quality.

- Sangrita can be medium thick or thinner. If you like it thinner, strain the juice. Note that yield will decrease.

PINOLILLO
Toasted Corn and Cocoa Bean Shake
SERVES 6

While in Nicaragua visiting friends and touring various key regions, I discovered this exceptional drink, which reminded me of tiste (find a recipe on page 55) from Quezaltepeque, Chiquimula, Guatemala (my grandmother's town). They share some ingredients, except tiste has achiote and omits allspice. While dining at La Cocina de Doña Haydée in Managua with a local chef friend, I tasted pinolillo and wonderful homestyle cuisine in a cozy environment. Pinolillo has a depth of flavor and unique mouthfeel, making this a snack drink that will leave you satisfied. It certainly is as nutritious as it is delicious. A key characteristic of pinolillo is the head or foam that forms when mixed vigorously with water. The drink should be served in jícaras, natural tall vessels from a native species of a tree in the gourd family.

1 cup whole grain coarse-grind stone-ground cornmeal (makes 1 ½ cups dried powder)
¼ cup fresh cocoa beans
1 tablespoon ground canela (Ceylon cinnamon)
10 allspice berries

Sugar

1. In separate skillets, dry pan toast the cornmeal and cocoa beans over low heat until medium dark brown, about 15 minutes. Keep a close eye on them. Stir the cornmeal and cocoa beans often with a heat-resistant spatula for even browning. Let them cool in the skillets. Peel the cocoa beans.

2. Combine the cornmeal and cocoa beans with the cinnamon and allspice berries and grind in batches to a fine powder in a spice mill. Store the powder in a jar with a tight lid until ready to use.

3. To make one serving of pinolillo, in a blender, mix 4 tablespoons of the powder and about 1 ½ tablespoons sugar (or to taste) with 1 ¼ cups cold water or milk. Blend on high for 2 minutes. The drink should be foamy.

4. Serve in glasses half filled with ice.

AMALIA'S NOTES

- Whole grain coarse-grind stone-ground cornmeal is available at major grocery stores and online.

- Dried corn can also be used in this recipe, but you will need a more powerful mill than the spice mill to grind the corn to the needed texture.

- Fresh cocoa beans are available at some Latin or Asian markets or online.

- To peel the cocoa beans, squeeze them gently between your fingers, and the peel should easily slide off. Discard the peel. Alternatively, leave the peel on, but you will need a more powerful mill to process the peel to a powder, or you will need to strain the drink with a fine-mesh sieve for a smoother consistency.

- Fresh cocoa beans are always best, but you can also use organic cacao nibs instead of whole cocoa beans. They are available at co-ops and online.

- I use a coffee mill to grind the cornmeal, cocoa beans, and spices. I use a high-powered Vitamix blender to make the drink, but a regular blender will work as well.

- The drink will have a small sediment after it sits.

- Drinks containing ice should be sweeter than room-temperature drinks to compensate for the dilution of melting ice.

MISTELA DE NANCE
Spiced Fresh Nance Fruit Spirit

SERVES 2

1 cup nance or chopped
  pineapple
¼ cup raisins
⅓ cup sugar
1 (2-inch) piece canela
  (Ceylon cinnamon)
4 whole cloves
1 cup cold water

1 cup aguardiente

ADORNO (GARNISH)

2 edible flowers, or

2 raspberries
2 blackberries
2 sprigs mint

All cultures have homestyle alcoholic beverages that have been invented out of wit or necessity. Mistela likely came to Meso- and Latin America through Spain. In Spain, mistela is a fortified sweet wine made with grape must and alcohol, yielding around 23 percent alcohol content. Homemade mistela is an exquisite drink adapted to local tastes, which can be as good as a commercially bottled brew or even better, as it is usually fresh and made in small batches. Mistela is one of many Honduran drinks made with pineapple, with cousins throughout Mesoamerica made with less-expensive liquor such as aguardiente (also referred to as guaro), a distilled brandy-like 30 to 40 percent liquor made from sugarcane. This drink can be a welcome chilled drink for a special gathering or a warm happy ending paired with a good cup of coffee. This is my special rendition using nance, a fruit traditional in Guatemala, native to the tropical Americas.

1 In a saucepan, combine the nance, raisins, sugar, cinnamon stick, cloves, and water. Bring to a quick boil over high heat, adjust the heat to medium low, and simmer for 5 minutes for nance and 10 minutes for pineapple. Let cool.

2 Add the aguardiente to the cooled mixture. Mix well and chill in a jar until ready to use. Serve in martini glasses or smaller cocktail glasses as is or strain it. Garnish with edible flowers or raspberries, blackberries, and mint.

AMALIA'S NOTES

• Nance is available in the frozen section of major grocery stores or online.

• Depending on how it is being used, you may opt to strain the mixture before serving. Traditionally it is served strained with bits of the same fruit used to make the mixture, and sometimes with the spices. I serve it both ways depending whether I am using it as a welcome drink (strained) or as a dessert (unstrained). Unstrained it can be used to top fruit desserts or ice cream too.

• Nance will fall apart if overcooked, so it's important to cook it for the time indicated. You may also garnish with frozen nance or fresh pineapple right before serving.

• When chilled, this drink will taste less sweet than at room temperature. Add more sugar to taste, if desired.

FRESCO DE REMOLACHA Y MÁS BEBIDAS
Beet, Orange, and Lime Refresher and More Drinks

SERVES 1 to 2

Frescos, refrescos, jugos, and aguas frescas are popular drinks throughout the Mesoamerican region. They are simple, fresh, easy to make, and refreshing. Market stands sell jugos (freshly squeezed juices) and frescos (juices with added water and sugar) that are made at the moment you order them. In Guatemala and Mexico, at the mercado, they fill a bolsita (a small upright bag) with the drink and some ice, insert a straw in it, and tie at the top. Sold at a low price, this is an economical and practical way to carry it around. Frescos can be made with a wide variety of fruits and vegetables or a combination of both, and they are also part of the daily meal routine at many homes. In my sister's home in Guatemala City, she makes a variety of frescos with seeds, flowers, and seasonal fruits that she keeps in the freezer. Many traditional restaurants also make these special drinks upon request. There are countless possibilities for frescos (see recipe variations below for more ideas). In the United States, at major grocery chains, frozen exotic tropical fruit pulp comes in bags ready to mix with water or milk.

½ cup peeled, diced fresh beets
½ cup freshly squeezed orange juice
2 tablespoons freshly squeezed lime juice
1 cup water
¼ cup sugar

Ice, for serving

1 Combine the beets, orange juice, lime juice, water, and sugar in the blender and blend until completely smooth to make the fresco.

2 Serve in glasses filled with ice.

RECIPE VARIATIONS

Fresco de Zanahoria y Naranja (Carrot and Orange Refresher): Use ½ cup diced carrots, ½ cup orange juice, 1 cup water, and ¼ cup sugar. Follow the directions above.

Fresco de Marañón (Cashew Fruit Refresher): Use 1 cup diced cashew fruit, 1 cup water, and ⅓ cup sugar. Follow the directions above. Fresh cashew fruit is best, but a good substitute is frozen cashew fruit pulp (available at well-stocked Latin markets).

Fresco de Mango (Mango Refresher): Use 1 cup diced ripe mangos, 1 cup water, and ½ cup sugar. Follow the directions above.

Fresco de Mora (Blackberry Refresher): Use 1 cup rinsed blackberries, 1 cup water, and ¼ cup sugar. Follow the directions above.

Fresco de Melon con Piña (Cantaloupe and Pineapple Refresher): Use ½ cup diced cantaloupe, ½ cup diced pineapple, 1 cup water, and ½ cup sugar. Follow the directions above.

Limonada con Soda (Limeade with Soda): Use ½ cup lime juice, 1 cup sparkling water, and ¼ cup sugar. Follow the directions above. Garnish with mint sprigs and maraschino cherries.

Fresco de Papaya con Piña (Papaya and Pineapple Refresher): Use ½ cup diced ripe papaya, ½ cup diced pineapple, 1 cup water, and ¼ cup sugar. Follow the directions above.

Fresco de Sandía (Watermelon Refresher): Use 1 cup diced seedless watermelon, 1 cup water, and ¼ cup sugar. Follow the directions above.

Fresco de Fresa (Strawberry Refresher): Use 1 cup hulled, rinsed strawberries, 1 cup water, and ½ cup sugar. Follow the directions above.

AMALIA'S NOTES

• Vary the proportion of fruit to water according to taste.

• Drinks containing ice should be sweeter than room-temperature drinks to compensate for the dilution of melting ice.

FRESCO DE PEPITA DE AYOTE

Toasted Pumpkin Seed and Cinnamon Refresher

SERVES 4 to 6

½ cup unshelled
   pumpkin seeds
1 (1-inch) piece canela
   (Ceylon cinnamon)
¼ cup sugar
5 cups water, divided

Ice, for serving

This is a nostalgic drink for me, as it reminds me of my grandmother who lived in Quezaltepeque, Chiquimula, Guatemala. This refreshing and delicious drink is traditional from the region of Oriente, where Chiquimula is located. The key to this refresher is using unshelled pumpkin seeds and pan toasting them to a medium brown to develop a deep flavor and aroma not present in shelled pepitas. I recall my grandmother using the ayote (squash) flesh in desserts and other preparations and then washing the seeds to sun-dry them before storing them for later use. Seeds contain oils, so they should be used within a few weeks of purchase or they will become rancid. A way to extend their life is by freezing them. They thaw in minutes.

1. Dry pan toast the pumpkin seeds in a small skillet over medium low heat until medium brown, stirring constantly, about 10 minutes. The seeds will pop and jump out of the pan while toasting. Just return them to the pan. Break up the cinnamon stick into pieces and pan toast it in the same pan as the pumpkin seeds until aromatic, 1 to 2 minutes. Keep a close eye on them, as the pieces can burn easily. Let cool.

2. Combine the pumpkin seeds, cinnamon, and sugar with 2 cups water in a blender and process on high to a fine consistency. Strain the mixture through a fine-mesh sieve. Pour the remaining water gradually into the sieve to extract more flavor from the seed mixture, stirring and pushing gently with a soft spatula to force the water through. Taste and add more sugar, if desired. Strain again for a smoother consistency, if desired.

3. Serve in glasses filled with ice.

AMALIA'S NOTES

- Unshelled pumpkin seeds are available at Latin stores and online.

- Drinks containing ice should be sweeter than room-temperature drinks to compensate for the dilution of melting ice.

ENSALADA SALVADOREÑA
Tropical Fruit and Lettuce Punch

SERVES 2

The first time a friend offered me an ensalada Salvadoreña, I thought I was ordering a salad. To my surprise, instead I was served an unusual drink that was intriguing to look at, and it piqued my interest immediately. Think of it as a fruit salad with lettuce in bits floating around a delicious fresh fruit drink base. Traditionally from El Salvador, this attractive drink can be a starter or dessert, or you can build it into a delicious cocktail by adding rum or white wine. Make it your own by using different juice bases, grabbing colorful ideas from Fresco de Remolacha y Más Bebidas (Beet, Orange, and Lime Refresher and More Drinks, page 48).

¼ cup each type tropical fruit, diced into bits (use 3 to 5, or more: pineapple, starfruit, papaya, mango, kiwi, coconut, dragon fruit, plum, or cashew fruit)

1 cup fresh or frozen fruit pulp (pineapple, passion fruit, or other)

1 cup cold water

¼ cup sugar

5 drops food coloring (choose the color according to the fruit pulp used)

¼ cup finely shredded romaine lettuce

ADORNO (GARNISH)

Choose 1 or 2 of each: strawberries, sliced dragon fruit, or sliced starfruit

Mint leaves

1. Distribute the fruit bits evenly between two tall glasses, cover with plastic, and refrigerate.

2. Incorporate the fresh or frozen fruit pulp into the cold water in a bowl or large measuring cup. Add the sugar and stir well. Add the food coloring. Chill until ready to serve.

3. Divide the fruit drink equally between the two glasses. Float half the lettuce on top of each glass. Garnish with with your fruit of choice and mint leaves.

AMALIA'S NOTES

- Use the food coloring to intensify the color of the liquid base for greater contrast with the fruit bits and lettuce. Use yellow for pineapple and passion fruit or a combination of colors to match another fruit chosen. Alternatively, you can also use bright, colorful fruit essences available at some grocery chains or online.

- The ratio of liquid to fruit is a matter of personal preference. If serving as dessert, my drink is heavier on fruit, and I use about half fruit and half juice and serve it with a spoon. If I serve it as a welcome drink, I add less fruit, as my guests may be mingling and walking around with a tall glass or wine goblet without access to a spoon. Either way, this is a fun drink to enjoy with friends or family.

TISTE

Roasted Cocoa Bean, Corn, and Achiote Libation

SERVES 10

¾ cup whole grain coarse-grind
  stone-ground cornmeal
  (makes 2 ½ cups dried
  powder)
⅓ cup fresh cocoa beans
1 tablespoon sesame seeds
1 tablespoon ground canela
  (Ceylon cinnamon)
¾ cup sugar
1 tablespoon achiote powder

Ice, for serving

Tiste is another nostalgic recipe from my maternal grandmother's hometown, where excellent cooks abound creating scrumptious regional cuisine. During my childhood, one of the two main restaurants in the tiny town specialized in this magnificent drink made right on the spot. It was served on ice with a froth or head, which is achieved by stirring the tiste in a deep clay pitcher with a molinillo (a special wooden whisk). Tiste in varying forms is popular from Guatemala to Nicaragua.

1 In separate skillets, dry pan toast the cornmeal, cocoa beans, and sesame seeds over low heat until medium dark brown, about 15 minutes. Keep a close eye on them. Stir the cornmeal, cocoa beans, and sesame seeds with a heat-resistant spatula for even browning. Let them cool in the skillets. Peel the cocoa beans.

2 Combine the cornmeal, peeled cocoa beans, and sesame seeds with the cinnamon, sugar, and achiote, and grind in batches to a fine powder in a spice mill. Store in a jar with a tight lid until ready to use.

3 To make tiste, in a blender, mix 4 tablespoons of the powder with 1 ¼ cups cold water, or 3 tablespoons with 1 ¼ cups cold milk. Blend on high for 2 minutes. The drink should be lightly foamy. Taste for sweetness and add more sugar to taste.

4 Serve in glasses half filled with ice.

AMALIA'S NOTES

• Whole grain coarse-grind stone-ground cornmeal is available at major grocery stores and online.

• Dried corn can also be used in this recipe, but you will need a more powerful mill than the spice mill to grind the corn to the needed texture.

• Fresh cocoa beans are always best, but you can also use organic cacao nibs instead of whole cocoa beans. They are available at co-ops, Latin or Asian markets, and online.

• To peel the cocoa beans, squeeze them gently between your fingers, and the peel should easily slide off. Discard the peel.

• Achiote is available as a fresh paste, dried seeds, and ground at most Latin stores, some grocery chains, and online.

• I use a coffee mill to grind the cornmeal, cocoa beans, sesame seeds, and spices. I use a high-powered Vitamix blender to make the drink, but a regular blender will work as well.

• The drink will have a small sediment after it sits.

• Drinks containing ice should be sweeter than room-temperature drinks to compensate for the dilution of melting ice.

SÚCHILES

Fermented Spiced Fruit Brew

SERVES 8 to 10

Súchiles is a deeply flavored homemade fermented drink and a tradition during Holy Week, although it also can be found in Guatemala City at other times of the year. The recipe varies by maker. The key to this delightful, complex, low-alcohol sweet-and-sour drink is a well-balanced combination of fresh fruit, spices, fermenting time, and skill. Traditionally it is fermented in clay vessels covered with a lid, but ceramic or glass containers work too. Fermenting time can vary according to the ambient temperature, as the warmer it is, the shorter the fermentation time will be. The aroma, flavor, and alcohol become more intense the longer it ferments, yet it's important to know when the drink is at its sweet-sour peak before it starts turning into vinegar. Súchiles can be a scrumptious base for braising chicken or pork as well. Mexican tepache and Salvadoran chicha de piña are two other delicious drinks similar to this recipe that have fewer ingredients and less fermenting time (see recipe variations below).

2 cups dried yellow corn

1 cup unhulled or pearled barley

2 (5-inch) sticks canela (Ceylon cinnamon), broken into pieces

14 allspice berries

1 tablespoon anise seed

Peel of 1 ripe, well-scrubbed organic pineapple

¾ cup tamarind concentrate

10 frozen jocotes (from a 14-ounce bag)

1 tablespoon grated fresh ginger

2 ½ quarts cold water

2 ½ cups panela (piloncillo), broken into bits (see note)

1. Dry pan toast the corn in a skillet over low heat until medium brown, about 15 minutes. When the corn starts smoking a bit, begin to stir constantly to allow for even browning. Repeat this procedure with the barley using the same skillet. Let cool.

2. Dry pan toast the cinnamon sticks, allspice, and anise seed in the skillet over low heat until aromatic, about 2 minutes. Let cool.

3. In a 6-quart stockpot, combine the corn, barley, cinnamon, allspice, anise seed, pineapple peel, tamarind concentrate, jocotes, ginger, and water. Bring to a quick boil over high heat, adjust the heat to low, and simmer over medium low heat, covered, until the mixture is fully aromatic, about 30 to 45 minutes. Let it cool, covered, completely. This may take three hours or longer. The residual heat will continue to almost fully cook the corn and fully cook the barley. The corn does not need to be fully cooked for the recipe to work.

4. In a gallon-size glass or ceramic storage container with a lid, combine the cooled corn mixture with the panela. Stir well. Cover loosely to allow the fermentation gas to escape. Place the container in a quiet corner on your kitchen counter and allow it to ferment anywhere from 4 to 6 days, skimming any foam that comes to the surface from time to time. The timing will really depend on your kitchen temperature.

5. The mixture is working when some fizzing begins. Taste it at the beginning, in the middle, and the end of the fermentation time so you can tell when the flavor starts to change. The flavor should be pleasantly spiced and sweet with a sour twang a bit on the strong side. If it's too strong or vinegary, the fermentation has gone too long, and the mixture might be best for cooking rather than drinking.

6. When it's ready to drink, strain and serve in tall glasses half filled with ice. Store leftovers in the refrigerator and consume within 1 week, or freeze it and save it for cooking.

Continued on page 58

RECIPE VARIATIONS

Tepache (Mexican Fermented Pineapple Brew): Use the pineapple peel only, or the peel and the fruit cut into small chunks, 1 (5-inch) stick canela (Ceylon cinnamon), ½ teaspoon whole cloves, 1 ½ cups panela (piloncillo) broken into bits, and 8 cups cold water. Combine all ingredients in a gallon-size glass or ceramic storage container, cover it loosely, and allow it to ferment for 3 to 5 days. Strain and serve in tall glasses half filled with ice.

Chicha de Piña (Salvadoran Fermented Pineapple Brew): Use the pineapple peel and about ½ cup of the fruit cut into small chunks, 1 ½ cups panela (piloncillo) broken into bits, and 8 cups cold water. Combine all the ingredients in a gallon-size glass or ceramic storage container, cover it loosely, and allow it to ferment for 3 to 5 days. Strain and serve in tall glasses half filled with ice.

AMALIA'S NOTES

- Unhulled barley is a complete grain, and thus more nutritious, while pearled barley has had its husk and bran layer removed.

- Tamarind concentrate comes in 14-ounce jars and is available in the Asian section of major grocery stores.

- Jocote is available in the frozen Latin section of major grocery stores or online.

- Panela is very hard and must be broken for measuring or melting. To break it, put it in a double layer of resealable bags, wrap it twice in a kitchen towel, and pound it with the smooth side of a metal meat mallet until the panela is almost powdery.

- It is best not to ferment the ingredients in a metal container of any kind, as the acidity can oxidize it, spoil the drink, and potentially make it toxic.

- Instead of using just the peel, add 1 cup pineapple chunks or more to the Súchiles recipe.

- Drinks containing ice should be sweeter than room-temperature drinks to compensate for the dilution of melting ice. Add more panela (piloncillo) according to taste.

2

Antojitos y Entradas
Little Cravings and Starters

COMFORT FOODS

Fondas, cafeterias, tiendas, and comedores are some of the places where people eat for sheer pleasure. These eateries provide delicious ready-to-eat foods in markets, streets, and anywhere large crowds gather.

I could say that antojitos or antojos are the ultimate comfort foods, as these are the foods that Latinos usually crave. This is typically what attracts people to fairs and places that specialize in traditional snacks or quick meals that can be enjoyed in a short visit or between errands. When I hear the word *antojitos* (little cravings), many foods from my childhood come to mind as well as foods I have enjoyed in the company of dear friends and family. Parks, plazas, small mom-and-pop shops, and even makeshift weekend food shops open up in people's garages in Guatemala. Here people from all backgrounds gather with a common mission in mind: to satisfy a craving.

The little cravings in this chapter are some of my favorites. I went through an extensive list of casual foods that are enjoyed in Mesoamerica and chose the ones that truly provide me that sense of comfort. These are also foods that anyone can make at home, as they are easy, fun, and delicious.

Take note that these quick foods can constitute a meal if you eat enough of them in one sitting. Also, they can provide an opportunity to expand your cooking repertoire and venture into unknown ingredients. When I gather with colleagues and friends, I often resort to fun and casual foods that I enjoy sharing with them.

What is special about these foods is the creativity that has gone into each one. In the Mesoamerican region, you may notice that some snacks resemble the foods from neighboring countries in looks but differ in name, such as Catrachitas (Crispy Corn Tortillas with Refried Beans, Queso Fresco, and Chimol, page 81)

Comidas Típicas

These are the foods that are iconic to a country or region and are native and traditional.

Comidas típicas usually satisfy palates hungry for comfort foods. These can be street or home foods, snacks, or main dishes.

As a whole, they are comfort foods that represent cultural identity.

and Baleadas (Green Onion Flour Tortillas with Beans, Scrambled Eggs, Avocado, Spicy Onions, and Cheese, page 65), which could be interpreted as tostadas (the former) or the makings of a burrito (the latter). In other instances, a name may indicate the dish is similar to one in another country, but in essence it may be quite the contrary.

While traveling in Nicaragua, I encountered many dishes that were similar to other Central American ones yet differed in ingredients and presentation. Quesillo (Fresh Corn Tortillas with Melting Cheese, Crema, and Spicy Pickled Onions, page 77) is a snack I discovered in Guiligüishte, literally a shack on the road from Managua to Masaya.

It is a quick stop at an unpretentious cheese-making facility where people line up to buy these stuffed tortillas packed in a plastic bag for portability. You receive a napkin and enjoy a fantastic treat while standing or in your car.

Pacayas Envueltas (Palm Flower Fritters with Guajillo Tomato Sauce, page 73) are a delicacy street food in eastern Guatemala. Eager vendors board commercial buses that travel from Guatemala City to Esquipulas, El Salvador, and beyond with baskets filled with treats and put pacaya fritters on top of warm corn tortillas and garnish them with tomato sauce. It's an easy, nutritious food on the go at a convenient place and price.

Coming from a land where corn and beans reign, I truly enjoyed cooking in Oaxaca, where the culinary culture closely resembles Guatemala's. There I cooked with generations of women artisans who have spent their lives cooking cultural foods. Two of those many foods are Tetelas (Beans and Oaxaca Cheese Stuffed Corn Masa Pockets with Guajillo Sauce, page 78) and Memelitas (Herbed Achiote Corn Masa Cups Filled with Chopped Flank Steak and Vegetables, page 87). They have become some of my favorites, and they may just become two of your favorite antojitos too.

And, of course, tamales are the ultimate comfort food, small or large. Tamalitos de Cambray, Requesón y Rosicler (Sweet Aromatic Corn and Rice Tamales with Latin Ricotta, Pork, Almonds, and Raisins, page 88) are not well known outside Guatemala, but they are very special. If you decide to try them, you will agree.

About Flour Tortillas

Flour tortillas came about with the introduction of wheat to the Americas. They coexist with the well-established corn tortilla, an artisanal and ancestral food in Mesoamerica.

Flour tortillas originated in northern Mexico and are used in a good number of casual Mexican foods, such as tacos, burritos, and more.

In Mesoamerica, only Mexico and Honduras use flour tortillas for their traditional dishes. Hondurans mainly use them for one of their best-known foods, baleadas, which has a recipe in this chapter.

BALEADAS

Green Onion Flour Tortillas with Beans, Scrambled Eggs, Avocado, Spicy Onions, and Cheese

MAKES 10 appetizer-size baleadas

MASA (DOUGH)

2 cups all-purpose flour

½ teaspoon kosher salt

2 tablespoons thinly sliced green onions

½ tablespoon vegetable shortening

6 tablespoons warm water

RELLENO (FILLING)

1–1 ½ cups bean puree or refried beans (see bean recipe options on pages 100 and 102)

4 eggs, scrambled alone or mixed with ½ cup cooked chorizo

1–1 ½ cups cooked chicken, beef, or pork roast (optional)

Avocado slices

Queso fresco (fresh Latin cheese)

Unsalted crema or crema agria (Honduran, Guatemalan, Salvadoran, or Mexican table or sour cream)

1 recipe **Encurtido de Cebolla** (Spicy Pickled Onions and Carrots, page 293)

Baleadas are perhaps one of the most talked about and known traditional Honduran fast foods, and I have enjoyed them freshly made at some gas station snack shops in Honduras as well as in eateries and restaurants where they are sold at a steal. How the word *baleadas*, literally meaning gunned down or shot, relates to the dish is uncertain. Some say the name refers to the black beans (bullets) used in the filling, although the beans are usually ground into a paste. Traditionally baleadas are created with just-made large flour tortillas, but I have also experienced them with corn tortillas in Roatán, Honduras, a healthier alternative. The fillings vary and include sencilla (beans and cheese), egg and avocado, beef, pork, chicken, ground beef, chorizo, longaniza (sausage), and more. Make them spicy with salsa de chile cabro amarillo (a native yellow hot pepper resembling a habanero in size) or with Encurtido de Cebolla (Spicy Pickled Onions and Carrots, page 293). Depending on the number of toppings used, they can be a snack to share or a meal on their own, as they are quite large and substantial. Make baleadas your own using your toppings of preference and serve them for breakfast, lunch, or dinner. Elevate them to a gourmet level by cutting all the toppings evenly and spreading them artistically. This is my special rendition as small gourmet appetizers.

1. Combine the flour, salt, and green onions in the bowl of a stand mixer with the paddle attachment. Stir at the lowest speed for 30 seconds. Add the shortening divided into small pieces, distributing them through the flour. Mix at speed 2 until the flour appears mealy, about 2 minutes. Gradually add the water and stop the mixer when the dough has formed a ball in the center of the bowl.

2. Transfer the dough to a large cutting board or other clean surface and knead it for 2 minutes. Form a large ball with the dough and let rest for 10 to 15 minutes. With a pastry cutter, divide the dough into five equal-size portions, then divide each portion into halves. Form a small ball with each portion of dough. Flatten each to paper-thin thickness or 5 to 6 inches in diameter using a rolling pin or a tortilla press lined with plastic. Use flour for dusting, if needed.

3. Preheat a nonstick griddle and cook the tortillas until small bubbles begin to emerge and the dough appears cooked, about 30 to 45 seconds per side. Keep the cooked tortillas in a tortilla warmer until ready to use. (If using ready-to-eat flour tortillas, warm them on a griddle and wrap them in a tortilla warmer or several layers of cloth.)

4. To assemble the baleadas, top each tortilla with your desired toppings, starting with the refried beans, then eggs, meat (if using), avocado slices, queso fresco, crema, and spicy pickled onions.

AMALIA'S NOTES

- Fresh flour tortillas are best consumed the day they are made.

- Instead of making fresh tortillas, you can use a ten-count package of ready-to-eat taco-size flour tortillas.

- Fresh pureed or refried beans are always best, but if you're short on time, use canned beans instead of preparing them from scratch.

CHILOTES CON CREMA
Fresh Baby Corn with Latin Cream

SERVES 2

While visiting the home of dear friends in Managua one evening, we sat outside to enjoy drinks and appetizers before a fantastic dinner. We had many delicious starters, but one that stuck with me is this one. Oftentimes I am inclined to the simplest and freshest foods. Chilotes (fresh baby corn) are a delicacy in my eyes, as they are the ultimate appetizer for entertaining. They are light, and you can dress them in any style you wish. Chilotes are also known as xilotes, shilotes, or jilotes in Mesoamerica. For a nice experience, and to keep them warm, serve the baby corn with the husks on and let your guests peel them on the spot and dip them in the crema. You can also combine chilotes with other fresh vegetables as in Nicaraguan Guiso de Chilotes con Pipián (Baby Corn and Chayote Squash Stew, page 168). Either way you have chilotes, you'll love them.

4–6 chilotes (fresh baby corn), husks on

½ teaspoon kosher salt

½ cup unsalted crema or crema agria (Nicaraguan, Guatemalan, Salvadoran, Honduran, or Mexican table or sour cream)

Shredded queso fresco (fresh Latin cheese) (optional)

1. Bring 4 cups water to a boil over high heat in a large pot, and add the corn and salt. Adjust the heat to medium, cover, and cook for 4 to 5 minutes.

2. Remove the baby corn from the hot water, and drain off any excess water. Serve the corn with the husks on with crema and queso fresco, if using, on the side.

AMALIA'S NOTE

- Buy young fresh corn through produce growers online. Substituting with jarred young corn will not give you the full experience.

GALLO DE PICADILLO DE PLÁTANO Y CARNE

Fresh Corn Tortillas Topped with Green Plantain Beef Hash and Cabbage-Cilantro Slaw

SERVES 4 to 6

1 cup instant corn masa flour

1 cup cold water

1 recipe **Picadillo de Plátano y Carne** (Green Plantain Beef Hash, page 272)

1 recipe **Ensalada de Repollo Tica** (Costa Rican Cabbage-Cilantro Slaw, page 184) (see note)

Thinly sliced hot chiles (serrano, jalapeño, or habanero) (optional)

Ticos, or Costa Ricans, call gallos an eating style. Gallos encompass a variety of foods eaten in a casual way using corn tortillas as the vessel to fill with available treats at the table, from roast meats and chorizo to a wide variety of picadillos (hashes). They are similar to tacos or a Mexican taquiza where everyone makes their own taco according to taste. In Guatemala, at state fairs and celebrations, street vendors sell tortillas con carne, corn tortillas filled with meats and sauces and other toppings, quite similar to gallos and taquizas.

1. Combine the masa flour and water in a medium bowl to make a very moist dough. It should not stick to your hands. If the dough feels dry, add a little more water. If it's too wet, add more flour. Divide the dough into six equal parts and form them into balls. Line both sides of a tortilla press with plastic wrap to prevent sticking and mess. Flatten the balls to about ⅛ inch thick (about 5 to 6 inches in diameter).

2. Put each tortilla on a preheated nonstick griddle over medium heat and cook until the edges loosen (about 1 minute). Flip the tortilla with a wide, heat-resistant spatula and cook for another minute. Transfer to a tortilla warmer or cloth and keep covered.

3. To assemble, top each tortilla with a tablespoon of the beef hash and about a tablespoon of the slaw. Garnish with the sliced hot peppers (if using).

AMALIA'S NOTES

- Fresh corn tortillas are always best, but if pressed for time, buy ready-to-eat corn tortillas and heat them on a nonstick griddle or in a small toaster oven right before using them.

- Gallos can be made with a wide variety of picadillos, shredded stewed meats, roasted and grilled meats, chorizo, and more. Refer to the Picadillo de Plátano y Carne (Green Plantain Beef Hash, page 272) for additional ideas on picadillo variations.

- Find the recipe for Ensalada de Repollo Tica (Costa Rican Cabbage-Cilantro Slaw) in recipe variations under Ensalada de Repollo (Spicy Cabbage Slaw with Lime) on page 184.

RIGUAS CON QUESO

Grilled Fresh Corn Cakes in Banana Leaves with Fresh Latin Cheese

MAKES 8 riguas

Riguas are one of my favorite Salvadoran fresh corn treats because they are scrumptious and easy and look as if they took a long time to make. Traditionally they are half-moon shaped. They are perfect as an appetizer, snack, or side. For a wow look, garnish with traditional toppings such as crema, use black bean puree and spicy sauce, or use them as a base to build a bigger dish. Another version of this dish is to fry them directly on the griddle (see recipe variations below).

1. Combine the corn, shredded queso fresco, sugar, and salt in a food processor and pulse until the mixture is a bit runny and slightly coarse.

2. Lay the banana leaves matte side up on a flat surface, brush the matte side lightly with butter, and divide the corn mixture evenly among the eight banana leaves (about 2 tablespoons per leaf). With a spatula, spread the mixture carefully from the center outward to extend it to a shape similar to a small corn tortilla, about 3 ½ inches in diameter.

3. Carefully fold the banana leaf in half against the grain at the center of each circle so that one side falls on top of the other.

4. Preheat a dry nonstick griddle over low heat for 2 minutes. Cook the riguas on the griddle until the banana leaf turns dark brown, about 5 minutes per side. Allow the riguas to cool slightly, then peel the banana leaves off slowly and discard the leaves. Butter the griddle lightly, then brown the riguas lightly on both sides on medium heat, about 45 seconds per side. Alternatively, omit browning the riguas and eat them in the banana leaves.

5. Serve immediately and garnish with a dollop of crema and a teaspoon of crumbled queso fresco.

RECIPE VARIATIONS

Riguas Fritas (Fried Fresh Corn Cakes):
To the recipe above, add 2 large beaten eggs to the corn mixture in step 1. Omit the banana leaves. Heat a nonstick griddle over medium heat, divide the corn mixture evenly into eight portions, and distribute evenly with a spoon to a diameter of 3 ½ inches. Cook with 2 to 3 tablespoons melted butter on one side until firm and medium brown, about 3 minutes. Carefully fold in half with a heat-resistant spatula and continue cooking until thoroughly cooked, about 2 minutes more per side. Garnish with crema and queso fresco.

Tortas de Elote (Fresh Corn Cakes):
To the Riguas Fritas recipe above, add ½ teaspoon baking powder and use canola oil instead of melted butter. Follow the same cooking technique, except do not fold the cakes, as they should be round. Garnish with crema or queso.

Tashcales (Guatemalan Corn Cakes):
Follow the recipe for Riguas con Queso, except omit the cheese and add 1 teaspoon kosher salt. Use banana leaves or fresh corn husks and cook as directed. Garnish with crema.

2 cups frozen corn, thawed, or fresh corn kernels (from about 4 ears of corn)
½ cup shredded queso fresco (fresh Latin cheese)
2 tablespoons sugar
½ teaspoon kosher salt
8 banana leaves, cut into 8x4-inch pieces, rinsed and wiped with paper towels
Softened butter, for brushing the leaves and buttering the griddle

ADORNO (GARNISH)

Unsalted crema or crema agria (Salvadoran, Guatemalan, Honduran, or Mexican table or sour cream)
Queso fresco (fresh Latin cheese), crumbled

AMALIA'S NOTES

• Queso fresco comes in 10-ounce round packages (and larger). Leftovers freeze well.

• Cooked riguas freeze well. If freezing them, do so in the banana leaves. When ready to eat, thaw them at room temperature for 20 minutes and reheat them in the banana leaves right before serving, about 2 minutes per side, on a preheated griddle over medium low heat. Garnish as indicated above.

PACAYAS ENVUELTAS
Palm Flower Fritters with Guajillo Tomato Sauce

SERVES 4 to 6

2 large eggs, separated
1 teaspoon cornstarch or
    rice flour
½ teaspoon kosher salt

Canola or olive oil, for frying

1 (14- to 16-ounce) package
fresh or frozen pacaya,
cooked al dente, or
1 (15- to 16-ounce) jar
pacayas in brine, drained
and patted dry with
paper towels

1 recipe **Salsita de Chile
Guaque** (Guatemalan
Guajillo Tomato Sauce,
page 316) (see note)

Pacaya palm flowers are a favorite food in Guatemala and El Salvador. The pacaya palm tree is native to the Mesoamerican region and a little farther south. Its flowers are enclosed in a sheath that when peeled reveals a feather-duster-like bunch of pale yellow fronds. The flowers are bitter and a bit rubbery yet crunchy. They are best when fresh but are also available in brine in Latin stores. Pacaya flowers are a key ingredient in Guatemalan fiambre, a one-dish meal of marinated vegetables, meats, cold cuts, seafood, and cheeses, eaten traditionally on the Day of the Dead. Envueltos are a delicious tradition in Guatemala and surrounding areas. Envuelto comes from the verb *envolver* (to wrap), referring to the egg batter that coats the food. Envueltos can be made with any vegetable. Usually the batter is made with flour, but I often use cornstarch, rice, or corn flour instead to make it lighter or gluten free. Present them as a delicious appetizer, side, or sandwich with bread or corn tortillas as in this version.

1. Beat the egg whites until stiff peaks form. Continue beating, slowly adding the yolks one by one until well incorporated. Add the cornstarch and salt.

2. Line a plate with paper towels. Preheat 2 tablespoons oil in a medium nonstick skillet over medium heat. Dip the palm flowers in the egg batter and shake slightly to remove excess batter. Pan fry in batches of two until medium brown, about 1 minute per side. Place on the paper-towel-lined plate to absorb excess oil. Add more oil as necessary to the pan, and continue dipping and pan frying the remaining flowers in batches.

3. Serve with guajillo tomato sauce.

AMALIA'S NOTES

- Fresh or frozen pacaya or pacayas in brine are available at Latin markets or online. Depending on size, there may be six to eight pacayas per frozen package or jar. Scale the amount of egg batter according to the number of pieces available.

- Other raw or slightly cooked vegetables can be coated in egg batter and pan fried. Soft and leafy vegetables can be coated raw, such as eggplant slices, celery pieces, hearts of palm, spinach, kale, other greens, broccoli, and cauliflower florets. Harder vegetables should be cooked al dente prior to coating, such as chayote squash, ichintal (chayote squash root), malanga (tuber), nabo (turnip), salsify, cabbage, green beans, and more.

- Find the recipe for Salsita de Chile Guaque (Guatemalan Guajillo Tomato Sauce) in recipe variations under Salsa Criolla Fría (Quick Homestyle Sauce), page 316.

BOQUITAS DE TAJADAS DE PLÁTANO VERDE
Green Plantain Chips with Tomatillo-Avocado Salsa and Langostinos

MAKES 12 to 14 tajadas

Green plantains and bananas are used for soups, picadillo, chips, tamales, and many more preparations. Tajadas and tostones (or patacones) are a popular preparation in the Caribbean region of Central America and the Caribbean coast of South America. Although they are prepared with the same ingredient, they are unique. Tajadas are fried once, while tostones are fried twice. They are easy to make and can be an appetizer, snack, side, or base for a main dish. They pair well with spicy salsas, guacamole, and tart sauces made with vinegar or lime. In coastal cities, they are often served with seafood and ceviche. They are truly delicious! This appetizer turns heads when I pass it during cocktail receptions.

1 ½ cups canola oil

1 green plantain, peeled and sliced ¼ inch thick on the bias

Kosher salt

1 recipe **Salsa de Miltomate y Aguacate** (Tomatillo, Avocado, Serrano, and Cilantro Sauce, page 308)

24–28 langostino tails (use 2 per appetizer)

12–14 cherry tomatoes, halved

12–14 cilantro leaves

1 Line a plate with a thick layer of paper towels. Heat the oil over medium high heat in a deep skillet or saucepan until small bubbles begin to form. Test the oil with one plantain slice and make sure the bubbles increase considerably before adding more slices. Fry in batches of four to five pieces.

2 Fry the slices until they are golden brown, about 1 ½ minutes per side. Transfer them to the paper-towel-lined plate to absorb excess oil. While still hot, sprinkle the tajadas lightly with salt.

3 Serve immediately topped with 1 teaspoon sauce, two langostino tails, a halved cherry tomato, and a cilantro leaf.

RECIPE VARIATIONS

Tostones or Patacones (Twice-Fried Green Plantain Chips): Follow the recipe given, except slice the plantains 1 inch thick and do not salt them after the first fry. Fry the slices until medium brown (about 1 ½ minutes per side), remove them from the oil, and flatten them to ¼ inch thick while still hot with a flat utensil or the back of a small skillet covered with plastic. Fry them a second time to crisp them (this time about 1 minute total). Transfer them to a plate lined with paper towels and salt them just as they come out of the oil so the salt sticks.

Plátanos Fritos (Guatemalan Pan-Fried Sweet Plantains): Follow the recipe for Boquitas de Tajadas de Plátano Verde, except use peeled ripe plantains (see note) and slice them ½ inch thick on the bias. Pan fry them in ½ cup canola oil until medium brown on both sides, about 1 ½ to 2 minutes per side.

AMALIA'S NOTES

• To peel green plantains or bananas, slice off the two ends with a sharp paring knife. Score the peel carefully, making sure not to cut the plantain. Carefully lift a piece of the skin and slowly run your finger under it to remove it.

• Green bananas are slightly sweet. Green plantains are not sweet. They are harder and starchier than ripe plantains.

• Tajadas are best when just made. Once cold, they lose their crispness and can become tough. Refrigerated tajadas and tostones can be reheated in a toaster oven, but for best results, make them in small batches to enjoy crispy the day they are made.

• Ripe plantains are best when their peels look almost black. This is when their sugar level is at the highest, perfect for pan-fried sweet plantains.

QUESILLO

Fresh Corn Tortillas with Melting Cheese, Crema, and Spicy Pickled Onions

MAKES 6 quesillos

1 package of 10 quesillos (Nicaraguan melting cheese) (see note)

2 recipes fresh **Tlaxcalli** (Mesoamerican Corn Tortillas, page 97), made the same size as the cheese rounds (see note)

Crema agria (Nicaraguan, Guatemalan, Salvadoran, or Mexican sour cream)

1 recipe **Cebollas Encurtidas Simples** (Quick Nicaraguan Pickled Onions, page 293)

1 recipe **Chile Criollo** (Nicaraguan Spicy Tomato and Cucumber Salsa, page 316) (see note)

While traveling from Managua to León, I stopped by artisanal Quesillos Güiligüiste (willy-weestay), an unpretentious shop on the side of the road with a long line of customers, to have a simple and scrumptious snack. The shop is revered by locals as the place where they make a famous round and thin mild stringy melting cheese called quesillo (a cross between mozzarella and Oaxaca cheese). They put it on tortillas the same size as the quesillo, top with some salt and spicy pickled onions, and wrap them and stuff them into a long and skinny plastic bag that fits the roll just right. They add crema agria (sour cream) as a finishing touch. The bag is a good vessel to keep all the ingredients together and a great way to eat on the go without utensils. All you need is a napkin! This is my version using cebollas encurtidas and chile criollo to give it some kick and color.

1 Allow the cheese to sit at room temperature for 20 to 30 minutes to soften it a bit. Place a cheese round on top of a very warm corn tortilla so it softens even more and top with sour cream, pickled onions, and Chile Criollo. Roll up the tortilla and enjoy.

AMALIA'S NOTES

• Nicaraguan quesillo is available online. Panela and Oaxaca cheese or queso blanco can be a good substitute. Keep in mind that quesillo usually comes in large, thin rounds, while Oaxaca cheese and queso blanco come in different sizes. Adapt them to the recipe by cutting the rounds the long way and fitting them to the diameter of the tortilla.

• Follow the recipe for Tlaxcalli (Mesoamerican Corn Tortillas, page 97), except make the tortillas the same size of the quesillo rounds. Divide the dough into six equal parts and make balls as indicated, but flatten them by hand using a piece of sturdy plastic to flatten and pat the dough to the desired round size. Then cook as indicated in the recipe.

• Any leftover quesillo slices freeze well in resealable plastic bags.

• Find the recipe for Chile Criollo (Nicaraguan Spicy Tomato and Cucumber Salsa) in recipe variations under Salsa Criolla Fría (Quick Homestyle Sauce), page 316.

TETELAS

Beans and Oaxaca Cheese–Stuffed Corn Masa Pockets with Guajillo Sauce

MAKES 4 tetelas

I had the privilege to cook in Teotitlán del Valle and San Francisco Tutla in Oaxaca with some of the best cooks in town. What a special treat to share this experience with generations of great-grandmothers, grandmothers, mothers, daughters, sisters, aunts, and friends—all in the same kitchen. The collective wisdom was priceless. We made everything from scratch without fancy kitchen appliances or equipment. Our best instrument was our hands, and the desire to make moles, soups, and fresh corn-based treats like tetelas in outdoor settings using woodstoves, clay griddles, and large pots. Tetelas start with fresh masa patted into tortillas that are then filled with beans or cheese (or both) and folded as a triangle. Then they are griddled until fully cooked and light brown. As an appetizer, they are heavy and can constitute a meal if you have enough of them. I like to eat them with guajillo sauce to give them a delicious kick.

1. To make the guajillo sauce, combine the chiles, tomatillos, garlic, and salt in a medium saucepan. Cook, covered, over medium low heat until soft, about 5 minutes. Puree with an immersion blender or regular blender until smooth. Transfer the sauce to a serving dish and set aside.

2. Combine the masa flour and water in a medium bowl to make a very moist dough. It should not stick to your hands. If the dough feels dry, add a little more water. If it's too wet, add more flour. When you form the dough into a ball, it should hold its shape and should not crack when pressed. Keep it covered with a damp cloth, as it tends to dry out quickly.

3. Combine the refried beans and cheese in a small bowl to make a homogeneous paste.

4. Divide the dough into four equal parts and form them into balls. Line both sides of a tortilla press with plastic wrap (or use a gallon-size resealable plastic bag cut on both sides but still attached at one end) to prevent sticking and mess. Flatten the balls to about ⅛ inch thick (5 to 6 inches in diameter).

5. While still on the press, fill the center of each tortilla with 1 ½ tablespoons of the bean-and-cheese mixture. To make a triangle, fold two sides of the circle over and press gently to enclose the filling. Then fold the remaining side over on top of the two sides.

6. Put each tetela on a preheated nonstick griddle over medium heat and cook until it is medium brown, about 2 minutes. Flip the tetela with a wide, heat-resistant spatula and cook for another 2 minutes. Flip back and forth in intervals of 2 minutes per side to cook the inside dough, about 16 minutes total. The tetelas should be visibly cooked (lightly crispy on the outside and soft on the inside). Transfer them to a tortilla warmer or cloth and keep covered.

7. Serve the tetelas warm with guajillo sauce.

RECIPE VARIATIONS

Empanadas (Guatemalan Stuffed Masa Pockets): Follow the recipe above, except fold each tortilla in half instead of in a triangle. Cook as instructed above.

Memelas (Guatemalan Stuffed Masa Pockets): Follow the recipe for Empanadas, but shape as a plump and rounded tortilla, about ¾ inch thick and 3 to 3 ½ inches in diameter, carefully enclosing the beans inside. Cook as instructed above.

SALSA DE GUAJILLO (GUAJILLO SAUCE)

2–3 dried guajillo chiles, deveined and seeded (or use cascabel, pasilla, or japonés chiles)
8 small tomatillos, husked
2 tablespoons minced garlic
1 teaspoon kosher salt

1 cup instant corn masa flour
1 cup cold water

½ cup refried beans (see options on pages 100 and 102)
½ cup shredded Oaxaca cheese

AMALIA'S NOTES

• Fresh refried beans are always best, but if you're short on time, use canned beans instead of preparing them from scratch.

• Refer to Chapter 10, page 289, for more sauce choices.

CATRACHITAS

Crispy Corn Tortillas with Refried Beans, Queso Fresco, and Chimol

MAKES 16 appetizer-size catrachitas

4 store-bought corn tortillas
1 tablespoon canola oil
½ – ¾ cup refried beans
 (see note)
¼ cup queso fresco (fresh
 Latin cheese) or Cotija (dried
 Latin cheese), crumbled

CHIMOL (SALSA)

½ cup small-diced Roma
 tomatoes
¼ cup small-diced green
 bell pepper
¼ cup thinly julienned
 red onion
⅓ cup chopped cilantro leaves
1 tablespoon freshly squeezed
 lime juice
½ teaspoon kosher salt

Bottled hot sauce (optional)

Catrachitas comes from the word *Catracho*, a nickname for people from Honduras. In Guatemala, we call ourselves Chapines and refer to our land as Chapinlandia. This is a tradition of all Central American and many other Latin countries. It is a warm way to refer to our Latin heritage in a uniquely cultural way. In this recipe, catrachitas (-ito or -ita endings on words denote a small size or term of endearment) is the name of the fried tortilla to dress with a variety of toppings, similar to a tostada with Honduran flair. I am a fan of spicy foods and would add some minced chile to the chimol, but this is optional. Chimol (salsa) is present throughout Mesoamerica as chirmol, chilmol, and chilmole, with various recipes.

1. Preheat the oven to 350°F.

2. Brush each tortilla with the oil on both sides to coat lightly. Cut four circles out of each tortilla to make two bite-size rounds 2 ½ inches in diameter. Spread them on a baking sheet lined with parchment paper. Bake the tortillas for 15 to 20 minutes until crispy, rotating the pan at least once during baking time for even baking. Turn off the oven and let them sit until ready to use.

3. To make the salsa, combine the tomato, bell pepper, red onion, cilantro, lime juice, and salt in a small bowl and mix thoroughly.

4. Assemble the catrachitas in layers, beginning with about 1 ½ teaspoons of refried beans, followed by 1 teaspoon of cheese, and ending with 1 teaspoon of chimol. Top with hot sauce (if using).

AMALIA'S NOTES

- To cut small circles, use decorative cutters for pastry and cookies, either round or fluted round shapes.

- To make larger catrachas, do not cut the tortillas. This will make them snack size or can constitute a meal if you eat plenty of them.

- It is not necessary to use a large conventional oven for this recipe. If you own a countertop or smart oven, use it to bake the bite-size tortilla rounds.

- Fresh refried beans are always best, but if you're short on time, use canned beans instead of preparing them from scratch.

- Find the recipe for refried beans on pages 100 and 102.

ENCHILADAS NICAS

Pork Picadillo–Stuffed Corn Tortillas Topped with Cabbage-Tomato Slaw and Spicy Vegetable Pickles

MAKES 8 enchiladas

The concept of Nicaraguan enchiladas is similar to Guatemalan chilaquilas and Salvadoran chilaquiles, with varying ingredients and presentation styles. They are all delicious stuffed tortillas with layers of ingredients piled on top of one another. The nuances by country lie in the seasonings and variety of ingredients and layers. In Guatemala, the traditional enchilada is a multilayered colorful tostada and popular street food. In El Salvador, they are fried medium-size fresh masa tortillas with a few or several toppings. There's another version of Enchiladas Nicas resembling the Salvadoran ones, although the most popular enchiladas are stuffed. Most ingredients can be made ahead of time, making this dish perfect for a build-your-own enchilada party. In Mexico, the enchilada is a totally different dish; although sharing some ingredients, it consists of meat-, chicken-, or cheese-stuffed soft corn tortillas smothered in red or green sauce and garnished with crema and queso fresco.

1. To make the pork picadillo, in a medium wide, deep skillet over medium high heat, add the canola oil and sauté the onion, garlic, and bell pepper for 2 minutes. Add the tomatoes, vinegar, rice, pork, salt, and black pepper to taste. Continue cooking over medium low heat until the picadillo is no longer saucy, about 5 minutes.

2. To make the sauce, add the canola oil to a small skillet and cook the tomatoes, onion, sugar, vinegar, water, salt, and black pepper to taste, at low heat until chunky, about 5 minutes. Smash the cooked ingredients with a flat potato masher to give it a saucier consistency.

RELLENO DE CERDO (PORK PICADILLO)

1 tablespoon canola oil
½ cup finely diced yellow onion
1 teaspoon minced garlic
⅓ cup small-diced green bell pepper
6 tablespoons canned crushed tomatoes
2 teaspoons red or white vinegar
¼ cup cooked long-grain white rice
1 cup (about ½ pound) cooked chopped pork loin
½ teaspoon kosher salt
Freshly ground black pepper

8 ready-to-eat corn tortillas or fresh corn tortillas (see **Tlaxcalli**, page 97)
2 large eggs, separated
¼ teaspoon kosher salt
Canola oil, for frying

SALSA (SAUCE)

1 tablespoon canola oil
1 cup roughly chopped Roma tomatoes
¼ cup roughly chopped yellow onion
½ teaspoon sugar
1 teaspoon white or red wine vinegar
¼ cup water
1 teaspoon kosher salt
Freshly ground black pepper

ENSALADA DE REPOLLO CON TOMATE (CABBAGE-TOMATO SLAW) (SEE NOTE)

1 cup shredded green cabbage
¼ cup thinly shredded carrots (optional)
½ cup julienned red onion
½ cup diced vine-ripened tomatoes
2 teaspoons freshly squeezed lime juice
1 teaspoon champagne vinegar or white wine vinegar
¾ teaspoon kosher salt

CHILERO CRIOLLO (SPICY CHILE VEGETABLE AND ONION PICKLES)

½ cup finely chopped yellow or red onion
1 teaspoon minced garlic
½ cup finely diced carrots
½ cup finely diced unpeeled, seeded cucumbers
1 habanero chile, thinly sliced
1 serrano or jalapeño chile, thinly sliced
2 fresh or dried bay leaves
1 teaspoon kosher salt
½ cup white wine or apple cider vinegar
3 to 4 tablespoons cold water

ADORNO (GARNISH)

½ cup crumbled queso fresco (fresh Latin cheese)

Continued on page 84

3. To make the slaw, combine the cabbage, carrots (if using), onion, tomatoes, lime juice, and vinegar in a bowl and season with salt. Mix well and set aside.

4. To make the spicy pickles, combine the onion, garlic, carrots, cucumbers, habanero, serrano, bay leaves, salt, vinegar, and water in a medium jar that can be used for storing the pickles. Shake vigorously to combine and set aside.

5. Assemble the enchiladas. Warm the tortillas to make them pliable. To a tortilla, add about 2 tablespoons of pork picadillo, fold into half-moons, press gently to flatten, and repeat the procedure until all the tortillas and picadillo have been used. Distribute any leftover picadillo evenly amongst all enchiladas.

6. Beat the egg whites until stiff peaks form. Continue beating, slowly adding the yolks one by one until well incorporated. Add the salt and beat 30 seconds.

7. Preheat a medium nonstick skillet over medium high heat. Add 3 tablespoons of oil.

8. Quickly dip each enchilada in the egg batter to coat lightly and immediately place it in the skillet. Pan fry the enchiladas in batches of two, subsequently adding 3 tablespoons of oil per batch until they are light brown (about 1 minute per side.) Transfer them to a platter lined with paper towels to absorb excess oil. Cover them with a cloth to keep them warm. Repeat the procedure until all the enchiladas have been pan fried.

9. Top the enchiladas with salsa, slaw, spicy pickles, and crumbled queso fresco. Serve immediately.

AMALIA'S NOTES

• Use cooked chicken or beef for variety.

• You can make a simplified version of the Chilero Criollo with just onion, cucumbers, hot chile peppers, vinegar, and salt. Follow the same proportions and directions as in step 4, but increase the diced cucumber to 1 cup and adjust the vinegar and seasonings to taste.

• You can also make a simplified version of Ensalada de Repollo con Tomate with just cabbage, tomatoes, lime juice, vinegar, congo peppers or other hot peppers of choice, and salt (and freshly ground black pepper, if desired). Follow the same proportions and directions as in step 3.

• Leftover Chilero Criollo keeps in the refrigerator for up to 5 days. After that, it is still good, but some of the vegetables are not as crunchy.

MEMELITAS

Herbed Achiote Corn Masa Cups Filled with Chopped Flank Steak and Vegetables

MAKES 6 memelitas

1 cup instant corn masa flour

1 tablespoon achiote powder

¼ cup roughly chopped
   epazote

½ teaspoon kosher salt
   dissolved in 1 cup cold water

Canola oil

ADORNO (GARNISH)

1 recipe **Salsa de Miltomate
   y Aguacate** (Tomatillo,
   Avocado, Serrano, and
   Cilantro Sauce, page 308)

1 cup chopped lettuce

1 recipe **Carne Picada con
   Verduras** (Chopped Beef and
   Vegetable Hash, page 261)

½ cup crumbled queso fresco
   (fresh Latin cheese)

½ cup small-diced red or
   white onion

½ cup chopped cilantro leaves

While in Oaxaca, Mexico, I was seduced by these delicious treats. Memelitas are slightly thick corn masa cakes smaller than a typical corn tortilla, with a small ridge to keep fillings from oozing out of them. Sopes, another treat from the central and southern regions, are similar yet may be filled with other ingredients. In Mexico, as in all of Mesoamerica, some dishes may share traits and can be found in surrounding regions of the same country with varying sizes, ingredients, or toppings. Memelitas can be filled with just a few or many delicious sauces, spicy salsas, cilantro, and cheese, or they can be more elaborate. This is my creation for a casual or formal dinner party. Memelitas can be an appetizer, snack, or meal if you eat plenty of them.

1. In a medium bowl, combine the masa flour with the achiote and epazote, mix well, and add the salted water to make a very moist dough. It should not stick to your hands. If the dough feels dry, add a little more water. If it's too wet, add more masa flour. When you form the dough into a ball, it should hold its shape and should not crack when pressed. Keep it covered with a damp cloth, as it tends to dry quickly.

2. Divide the dough into six equal parts and form them into balls. Using two pieces of sturdy plastic, put one ball in between the plastic pieces and press carefully yet firmly with a large skillet to form a small and chubby tortilla 4 inches in diameter.

3. Put each tortilla on a preheated nonstick griddle over medium low heat and cook until the edges loosen, about 3 minutes. Flip the tortilla with a wide, heat-resistant spatula and cook for another 3 minutes. Let cool slightly. Quickly pinch the sides of each tortilla to form a ½-inch-tall ridge, pulling masa from the center outward.

4. Brush the memelitas with a light coating of oil. Return them to the griddle to finish cooking ridge-side up only, about 2 minutes. Transfer to a tortilla warmer or cloth and keep covered until ready to serve. Memelitas should be visibly cooked and slightly crispy outside and soft inside.

5. Assemble the memelitas, distributing the garnishes as desired starting with a layer of the salsa, a layer of lettuce, and a layer of the meat, followed by queso fresco, onion, and cilantro.

AMALIA'S NOTES

• Any leftover meat can be the main protein on a plate, or it can be used for another meal.

• Other filling alternatives are refried beans and roast pork or chicken, or you can make them totally vegan or vegetarian. See Chapter 8, Delicias Costeñas (Coastal Delights, page 223), and Chapter 10, Salsas, Recados y Aliños (Salsas, Sauces, and Dressings, page 289), for other ideas.

• Without any toppings or oil, memelitas keep in the refrigerator up to 1 week. They also freeze well and can be thawed at room temperature for 20 to 30 minutes, brushed with oil, and reheated right before using.

TAMALITOS DE CAMBRAY, REQUESÓN Y ROSICLER

Sweet Aromatic Corn and Rice Tamales with Latin Ricotta, Pork, Almonds, and Raisins

MAKES: 12 to 14 tamalitos

Tamalitos de Cambray in Guatemala are sweet tamales with varying ingredients depending on the maker. One differentiating feature of these tamales is their specks of pink imparted by the pink sugar used in the dough. Sometimes they are made without pork and only a few ingredients. There are other tamales de Cambray recipes in El Salvador, Honduras, and Nicaragua, and they share some of the sweetness but not the color. They have more or fewer ingredients by country. Some are wrapped in banana leaves instead of corn husks. These tamalitos are an excellent snack or starter for a family gathering. Here I elevate them to a new level with requesón (Latin ricotta cheese) and two flours and more garnishes to make them more delicate and scrumptious.

1 To make the dough, in the bowl of a stand mixer with the paddle attachment, add the masa flour, rice flour, sugar, and salt, and stir to combine, about 30 seconds. Add the milk and anise extract and continue to stir to make soft, very moist dough. Add the butter and cheese, and fluff the dough for 3 minutes at speed 4. (Alternatively, put the dough ingredients in a deep bowl and beat vigorously with a wooden spoon for 3 to 5 minutes.) Divide the dough equally into twelve to fourteen portions.

2 To make the pink sugar, in a small bowl, combine the sugar with the food coloring and mix it well with a fork, making sure any dark specks of pink are thoroughly integrated into the mixture. The sugar should be dry and bright pink.

3 For each tamalito, sprinkle 1 teaspoon pink sugar throughout the center of each corn husk. Add one portion of dough on top of the sugar to cover it. With a soft spatula, flatten the dough slightly and fill it with 1 tablespoon of the pork. Divide the raisins and almonds equally among the tamalitos. Sprinkle another ½ teaspoon pink sugar on top of the fillings and dough of each tamalito. Gently press the filling and sugar into the dough. Wrap the husk to overlap the edges so the dough and fillings are completely enclosed. Lay the tamalito flat. Beginning at the pointed side, press carefully with your fingers to force the masa toward the center of the husk, leaving enough space on both ends for tying. Tie at both ends to make round tamales.

4 Fill a deep pot with 8 cups water. Place all the tamalitos vertically in a steamer basket and put the basket in the pot. Bring the water to a boil over high heat, cover the pot, and reduce the heat to medium low. Steam the tamalitos until they're cooked (about 1 hour). When they're done, the dough should hold the shape of the package and should be shiny and slightly translucent, not opaque.

5 When done, allow the tamalitos to sit in the pot for at least 30 minutes before serving. Peel the tamalitos when ready to serve, or serve them semipeeled with the edges folded under the tamalito. Sprinkle a bit of the remaining pink sugar on top of each for garnish.

AMALIA'S NOTES

- Tamalitos freeze well. To reheat them, steam them for 20 to 30 minutes. Reheat refrigerated tamales in the microwave for 1 to 2 minutes.

- Tamalitos de Cambray are traditionally served on their own, but to add variety, serve them with crema and then garnish them with the pink sugar.

MASA (DOUGH)

1 ½ cups instant corn masa flour

1 cup rice flour

½ cup sugar

½ teaspoon kosher salt

3 cups skim milk scalded with 1 (5-inch) stick canela (Ceylon cinnamon), cooled to room temperature

1 teaspoon anise extract

1 cup (2 sticks) unsalted butter, at room temperature

1 cup requesón (Latin ricotta cheese)

ROSICLER (PINK SUGAR)

½ cup sugar

12 drops pink food coloring

RELLENO (FILLING)

1 ¼ cups chopped cooked pork shoulder, lightly seasoned with kosher salt and freshly ground black pepper

½ cup raisins

½ cup sliced almonds, toasted

12–14 dried corn husks, soaked in hot water for about 20 minutes

24–28 ties made from additional soaked corn husks, torn by hand into strips ½ inch wide

3

Cocina Indígena y Exótica
Indigenous and Exotic Cookery

MESOAMERICAN PRE-HISPANIC FOODS AND SPANISH CONTRIBUTIONS

The foods the natives of Mesoamerica were eating prior to the arrival of the Spaniards and up to colonization were simple, rustic, and at times exotic. They depended on what was available on their land. This included wild plants, turkeys and waterfowl, mute dogs, deer, reptiles, rodents, fish, insects, and others. The tools and techniques to make food happen outdoors were fire pits, hot stones, and baking underground in pibs.

Indigenous Fare

The ancient Mesoamerican diet included exotic native proteins still popular today.

Chapulines (grasshopers), alacranes (scorpions), gusanos (agave plant worms), escamoles (ant larvae), a.k.a. the "Mexican caviar," hormigas chicatanas (ants and their eggs), and other exotic life are prepared in Mexico simply by salting and roasting them. Worms are often ground to a powder and combined with dried chile and fancy salts and used to garnish drinks.

In Guatemala and Central America, armadillo, iguana and their eggs, and tepezcuintle (lowland alpaca) are also eaten. Despite their endangered status, huevos de parlama (sea turtle eggs), considered by some to be an aphrodisiac and a hangover cure, are a street food prepared as a cocktail with orange juice or mixed with lime juice, salt, pepper, spicy sauces, and Worcestershire sauce.

The food of Mesoamerica is in essence antique, as it started to develop gradually from the time agriculture began in the region; corn became domesticated in Mexico about nine thousand years ago. Corn is to this area what wheat is to the Middle East and Europe and rice is to Asia, a means of sustenance and one of the crops that contributed to and continues to revolutionize agriculture, diet, and humankind.

The Mesoamerican territory was one of the world's prehistoric hubs for cultivating and domesticating plants. The Milpa system was a genius invention where corn, beans, and squash (the Mesoamerican Triad) grow strategically together, complementing each other in the field and acting in ecologic support of one another. Also known as the Three Sisters, this trio (often intercropped with other vegetables and fruits) still constitutes the main diet staples here and in the American continent.

The wisdom and legacy the ancient cultures of Mesoamerica left behind have been a unifying force for subsequent generations. The communion with land, nature, and indigenous beliefs continues to enrich current field practices. Some of the world's most advanced civilizations once lived here, and their higher knowledge of how to work the land manually in their favor forever shaped the agriculture and culture of the zone, despite not having work animals initially to help them prepare the soil.

With deep-rooted customs and traditions, today's Mesoamerican peoples continue to thrive, cultivating many of the same and some of the best crops on the planet. This is evident in many of the traditional open-air markets in specific parts of Mexico (Oaxaca, Puebla, Mexico City) and Guatemala (Guatemala City, Chichicastenango, Cobán, and Antigua), where agricultural activity is high (see Chichicastenango market on pages 132–133).

This chapter, by design, contains some of my favorite traditional Mesoamerican foods, which I chose carefully to represent indigenous staples combined with non-native plants and animals. Moles of many types and colors are contained in the regional cuisines of Mexico and Guatemala, as are pepianes, pinoles, tamales, and other indigenous stews unique to each area. Versions of these dishes, whether with similar names or under other names but with similar characteristics, are also present throughout Central America.

Exotic foods are still widely popular in the Mesoamerica of today and include chapulines (grasshoppers), gusanos de maguey (agave worms), huevos de parlama (turtle eggs), hormigas y huevos (ants and eggs), tepezcuintle (rodent), armadillo, iguana, and many more animals native to the lands. Markets come alive with baskets full of roasted insects or freshly killed rabbits, goats, and other unique species in Oaxaca, Mexico, the Guatemalan Mayan highlands, and beyond.

A wide array of fruits and vegetables (and their subspecies by region) make these markets a feast for the senses. Chiles, tomatoes, avocados, and myriad native plants and edible greens are available in different colors, shapes, and sizes, all vine or tree ripened. The texture and flavor of these fresh foods is superior in quality to any fruit or vegetable one can buy in convenience markets. Many of them are not known outside Mesoamerica to this day.

Mesoamerican cultures also relied on plants as medicine for physical and spiritual ailments and for cultural ceremonies, practices that are still alive in varying forms from Mexico to Nicaragua. Limpias (cleansings) are mystical healing rituals that include curanderos (healers) and a variety of ritualistic components such as cigars, smoke, wax, eggs, and herbs.

With colonization, pre-Hispanic food—or the native food of the land—became hybridized, as new animals, plants, herbs, spices, techniques, utensils, and culture were introduced during the Columbian Exchange and passed from ancestors to new generations. This came to enrich the diets of Mesoamerica, Spain, and the world, but at a high price.

In essence, the cuisines of Mesoamerica are interrelated by culture, language, and staple ingredients. The marriage of native ingredients with nonnative ingredients of European origin and beyond brought about by the Exchange created a blended mix of hybrid cuisines called *cocina criolla* and *mestiza*, terms that also apply to the people.

The traditional cuisines of the region are thus a fusion of native pre-Hispanic cuisines with Spanish cuisine, that is, the native cuisines of multicultural indigenous groups of the Mesoamerican region and Spanish cuisine influenced by all the cultures that invaded the Iberian Peninsula throughout its history. As a result, traditional Mesoamerican cuisines contain elements of ancient, medieval, and modern times.

Asia, Africa, Europe, and the Middle East contributed to Mesoamerica and Latin America alone or through Spain, with primordial ingredients that fused seamlessly with the local diet. This gradual process and union created the foundation upon which traditional cuisine is built and further evolved with other subsequent foreign influences.

Wheat flour and bread came to rival, and in some instances replace, the corn tortilla. Rice, so common in today's traditional cooking, meshed naturally with our local guisos (stews), caldos (broths), and sopas (soups) and ignited creativity for rice-based dishes imitated from paella.

Recipes introduced by the Spanish into the New World took a new meaning as they blended with native products and cooking techniques. Some of them morphed into new dishes that resemble others in name but are unique creations. This mix created nuances by region and country.

Barley fostered beer making. Sugarcane revolutionized our cooking altogether as a sweetener, flavor enhancer, and preservative, and it helped jump-start rum manufacturing. Sugar created a whole new category within the culinary space—artisan candy making of Spanish tradition and some of Arab ancestry—and together with flour and other imported ingredients, it fostered confectionery.

Grapes sparked interest in wine, and where vineyards flourished, new wine industries were born. Citrus, namely oranges and limes, came to enliven our drinks and food. A ceviche without lime would be a totally different experience. Other fruits—apples, pears, peaches, nectarines, bananas, mangos, and coffee—came to enrich and balance our menus.

New herbs and spices took cooking to a whole new level. It is interesting to think what a mole, pepián, tamale, or recado sauce would be like without the ingredients we now consider key and are so accustomed to using, such as onion, garlic, cilantro, parsley, mint, bay leaf, oregano, thyme, cumin, cinnamon, clove, and other nonnative ingredients.

Olive oil and vinegars transformed cooking and introduced ideas for further development of similar products using other base ingredients. These two, combined with herbs and spices, produce cold sauces, alone or as vinaigrettes, that dress salads or make good marinades. They help preserve foods by pickling them or can be ingredients to boost the flavor of a dish.

Along with new ingredients came new recipes, cooking techniques, and tools, as well as Spanish nuns who traditionally were good cooks, bakers, and artisans of fruits poached in almíbar (spiced syrup) and other sweets. In colonial times, nuns prepared their delicacies in large convent kitchens, which often had subkitchens that also functioned as pantries and dining quarters for their cook helpers. Cooking happened in poyos (stone stoves) in clay or copper vessels fueled by firewood.

Flavor Profiles

From Mexico to Costa Rica, there are not only staple ingredients such as corn, beans, squash, tomatoes, and chiles that appear repeatedly in recipes but also key seasonings.

Naranja agria (sour orange) was introduced during the Exchange and became a favorite flavor enhancer. It is key in some dishes in Yucatán and Nicaragua and is a go-to seasoning for simple preparations in the rest of Mesoamerica such as carne asada, salsas, and spicy sauces.

But perhaps what really came to alter the cooking of Mesoamerica even more was the introduction of domesticated animals, including cattle, pigs, goats, sheep, and hens, and their derivatives, meat, milk, lard, and eggs. Their byproducts, namely cheese and butter, became kitchen essentials. Horses became essential in agriculture. Turkeys, mute dogs, and other wild land and water fauna had been the primary sources of protein, but with these additions, some native vegan and vegetarian dishes were modified and enriched, and the door opened for other creations such as charcuterie or cold meats. Mesoamerican native food was transformed in ways that enhanced our living, but at the same time, it created other challenges.

The controversial nature of the Spanish invasion of the Americas and the flora and fauna brought by the conquerors and settlers enriched local diets and enhanced textures and flavors of native dishes, but all at the expense of the indigenous and enslaved peoples. In addition to imposing their culture and religion and taking over their land, the colonizers also introduced new diseases that further compromised the lives of these populations. A diet higher in animal protein and their byproducts further created the opportunity for new diet-related diseases. Pre-Hispanic cuisine and later Spanish contributions are a combination of all these factors and provide a base for the current fare and characterize contemporary Mesoamerican cuisine, which is primarily mestiza, a blend of the two that continues to evolve through interconnectedness, migration, and foreign influences.

TLAXCALLI
Mesoamerican Corn Tortillas

MAKES 1 cup masa

1 cup instant corn masa flour
1 cup cold water
or
1 cup fresh **Masa de Maíz**
(Fresh Nixtamalized Masa,
page 98)

More than the bread of Mesoamerica, corn tortillas serve as the vessel, wrapper, and even utensil to eat many foods at indigenous tables. Tlaxcalli, tortilla in the Nahuatl language, is one of the most antique and desired foods today at every meal in the region made with nixtamalized yellow, white, or blue corn, all of which have varying antioxidant properties and densities when making masa. As a child, I often stood by my grandmother's side when she prepared masa from scratch (recipe on page 98). Like making beans, this was the normal thing to do. At tortillerías (tortilla shacks or makeshift kitchens) in urban and rural Guatemala, Mexico, and Central America, many women still use fresh masa dough to make tortillas by hand. Tortilla density, size, and color vary by country and region, and the intended purpose dictates the end product. Fresh corn masa dough is always best, and it is available at some Latin markets, but corn masa harina flour is used often for convenience. Although not native, flour tortillas came about with the introduction of wheat during the Exchange and are also popular in northern Mexico and Honduras (see Baleadas, Green Onion Flour Tortillas with Beans, Scrambled Eggs, Avocado, Spicy Onions, and Cheese, page 65).

1. Combine the flour with the water to make moist dough. When you form the dough into a ball, it should hold its shape and should not crack when pressed. Keep it covered with a damp cloth, as it tends to dry out quickly.

2. The technique for making tortillas varies by country. Tortillas are shaped by hand using a sturdy plastic circle set on a table and then flattened and shaped with one hand while the other hand rotates the circle. Use the *tortear* technique (flattening the dough balls to the desired thickness by hand by patting and turning them at the same time) or use a tortilla press (see page 99).

3. To make different sizes and densities of tortillas and other preparations, use the Tortilla Guide following the Masa de Maíz Mote Pelado recipe options.

Continued on page 98

MASA DE MAÍZ
(Fresh Nixtamalized Masa)

MAKES 1 ½ cups masa

1 cup maíz (dried corn for
   nixtamalization)
2 teaspoons cal (slaked lime
   or calcium hydroxide)
5 cups cold water

1. In a medium stainless steel pot, combine the corn, cal, and water and stir well. Bring to a quick boil over high heat, adjust the heat to medium low, cover, and simmer over medium low heat until the corn is tender, about 2 ½ hours. Let it cool covered for 4 to 6 hours. Drain.

2. Put the corn into a wide mesh colander. Put the colander inside a slightly larger bowl. Rinse the corn thoroughly under running cold water to remove all traces of cal. While fully immersed in the water, rub the corn kernels between your fingers to losen and remove the skin (pericarp). The skins will rise to the surface and the corn kernels should look creamy white, and matte and be tender but not mushy. Rinse well a few times to remove any residual traces of skin and until the water runs clear. This process may take 5 to 8 minutes. One cup dried corn yields 2 cups cooked corn.

3. Use the nixtamalized corn whole in a recipe or process in a food mill or food processor alternating with small amounts of water (about ½ cup total) to make soft masa. Use immediately, or freeze the masa flattened in plastic bags for later use. When ready to use, thaw at room temperature for about 30 to 45 minutes and then adjust the water for the intended purpose (tortillas, tamales, atoles, or other).

RECIPE VARIATION

Masa de Maíz Mote Pelado (Fresh Masa with Dried Nixtamalized Corn) (see note): In a medium stainless steel pot, combine 1 cup dried maíz mote pelado with 4 cups water. Bring to a quick boil over high heat, adjust the heat to medium low, cover, and simmer over medium low heat until the corn is tender, about 2 hours. Rinse thoroughly. One cup dried nixtamalized corn yields two cups cooked corn and 1 ½ cups masa. Use the corn whole in a recipe or process in a food mill or food processor alternating with small amounts of water (about ¼ cup plus 2 tablespoons total) to make soft masa. Follow the recipe for Masa for freezing directions.

AMALIA'S NOTES

- Slaked lime or calcium hydroxide and fresh masa dough are available at Latin markets and online.

- Maíz mote pelado is a large corn kernel from South America that comes in bags dried and nixtamalized. It is available at Latin markets and online.

- When working with corn masa dough, it is helpful to have a bowl of cold water right next to you to moisten your hands each time you handle the dough.

- Once cold, store leftover tortillas wrapped in a kitchen towel inside a resealable plastic bag in the refrigerator. As they are made from fresh dough, they will not last as long as commercially made tortillas. Reheat them in a toaster oven or on a nonstick griddle.

- Fresh tortillas freeze well in plastic bags. When ready to eat them, thaw them at room temperature for 10 to 15 minutes, then reheat them in a preheated toaster oven or nonstick skillet for 3 to 5 minutes.

- When making fresh corn masa, cooking time varies according to the corn color used. Begin testing the corn after 2 hours of cooking time (take a corn kernel out, rinse it well, and bite into it to determine tenderness).

TORTILLA GUIDE

Mexican Tortillas (Thin and Medium-Thin Corn Tortillas):
Divide the dough into six equal parts and form them into balls. Line both sides of a tortilla press with plastic wrap to prevent sticking and mess. Flatten the balls to about ⅛ inch thick (5 to 6 inches in diameter). For larger tortillas, divide the dough into three parts instead of six and flatten them to the desired thickness and diameter.

Cook the tortillas on a dry preheated nonstick griddle over medium heat and cook until the edges loosen (about 1 minute). Flip the tortilla with a wide, heat-resistant spatula and cook for another minute. Transfer to a tortilla warmer or cloth and keep covered. Tortillas should be visibly cooked and pliable. (If they are crispy, they are overcooked and can be used for tostadas).

Guatemalan, Salvadoran, Honduran, Nicaraguan, and Costa Rican Tortillas (Medium-Thin Corn Tortillas):
Follow the procedure for Mexican Tortillas, but flatten the balls to about ¼ inch thick (3 ½ to 4 ½ inches in diameter). Cook as instructed above, adding more time as needed in intervals of 1 minute, flipping them back and forth until the tortillas are fully cooked. Because they are a bit thicker, they are doughy and satisfying.

Guatemalan Pishtones and Memelas (Corn Masa Cakes):
Follow the procedure for Mexican Tortillas, but flatten the balls to about ½ inch thick (3 to 3 ½ inches in diameter). Cook as instructed above, adding more time as needed in intervals of 1 minute, flipping them back and forth until the tortillas are not fully cooked. These thicker tortillas are popular in some rural parts of Guatemala.

Guatemalan Totopostes (Dried Salted Crispy Thin Tortillas): Follow the procedure for Mexican Tortillas, except add ½ teaspoon kosher salt. Flatten the balls to ⅛ inch thick. Allow the tortillas to cook slowly in a preheated nonstick pan over low heat to dry out and crisp.

FRIJOLES

Favorite Bean Traditions

MAKES 4 cups

I call frijoles a VIP dish because they are not only delicious but also nutritious (rich in iron, fiber, and protein). When combined with corn or rice, they make a whole protein. They may just be the perfect meal combination for a vegan, vegetarian, or a gluten-free diet. Just like corn, beans are an ancient food and one of the three basic foods of Mesoamerica along with corn and squash. From basic to more elaborate dishes, beans of all colors, shapes, and sizes lend themselves to any style of preparation. But not all beans are treated equal. In Guatemala, black beans are king, although piloyes and blancos (red and white beans) and fresh beans are also popular. In other countries in the region, pinto, pink, red, and black beans are also popular. Besides beans, legumes of other types, such as lentils, garbanzos, and favas, are also consumed. These are some of my favorite preparations for beans that you can use to elevate them to any level you wish.

2 cups dried black, pinto, red, or white beans, free of debris and rinsed

5 cups water

1 whole medium yellow onion, peeled and t-scored (see note on page 102)

1 whole unpeeled garlic head

1. Add the beans, onion, garlic, and water to a 3-quart slow cooker and cook on high for 3 ½ hours. Beans are done when they have doubled in size, remain whole, and can be smashed easily between two fingers.

2. Alternatively, soak the beans in the water overnight. Place the beans and soaking water in a large saucepan with the onion and garlic and cook over medium low heat until done, about 1 ½ hours.

3. For either method, discard the onion and garlic when done, or chop them finely and add it to your final preparation, if you wish.

4. Use this method as a basic guide or base for the following recipes.

RECIPE VARIATIONS

Frijoles de Olla (Mexican Black, Pinto, or Pink Beans): Follow the recipe given, except chop the onion, omit the garlic, and add 2 tablespoons lard and 2 tablespoons chopped epazote. (Epazote is only used with black beans. If using the other beans, leave the epazote out.) Cook as directed. Season with kosher salt to taste.

Frijoles Charros (Mexican Pork and Beans): Follow the recipe for Frijoles, except chop the onion, mince the garlic, and add ½ pound pork loin cut into 1-inch cubes, ½ cup chopped Roma tomatoes, ½ cup chopped cooked bacon, 1 minced serrano, 2 tablespoons chopped cilantro, and 2 tablespoons lard. Cook as directed at left. Season with kosher salt to taste.

Frijoles Refritos (Mexican Refried Beans): Start with 4 cups cooked beans and the broth from the Frijoles recipe at left. Mash the beans to a paste or puree in a blender to a smooth consistency. Pan fry over medium low heat 1 cup small-diced yellow onion in ½ cup lard (or substitute canola oil) until medium dark.

Continued on page 102

Add the bean puree and season with kosher salt to taste. Fry the bean mixture over medium heat, stirring constantly, until it is very thick and pasty, no longer sticks to the skillet, and can be shaped in any form. This will take 20 to 30 minutes.

Frijoles Parados con Pitos, Chipilín, Chile Pimiento o Pepita de Ayote (Guatemalan Whole Beans with Sofrito and Pito Buds, Chipilín, Bell Peppers, or Toasted Ground Pumpkin Seeds): Pan fry over medium low heat 1¼ cups chopped yellow onion in 2 tablespoons canola oil until medium brown. Add 1 tablespoon minced garlic and sauté for 1 minute more. Add 1 cup fresh pureed Roma tomatoes and ¾ cup of any of the following: whole pito buds, chipilín leaves, diced bell peppers, or ground toasted shelled pumpkin seeds. Cook for 2 or 3 minutes. Add the cooked beans and the broth from the Frijoles recipe to this mixture and season with kosher salt to taste. Simmer uncovered to thicken the broth, about 15 to 20 minutes. Alternatively, puree ¾ cup of the beans and return them to the pan to thicken the sauce faster.

Frijoles Colados (Guatemalan Bean Puree with Sofrito): Pan fry over medium low heat 1 cup chopped yellow onion in 2 tablespoons canola oil until medium brown. Add 1 teaspoon minced garlic and pan fry for 1 minute more. In a blender, puree the cooked beans and the broth from the Frijoles recipe and add them to the onion mixture. Season with kosher salt. Cook, stirring from time to time to blend flavors, until the puree has thickened to a runny or thick paste.

Frijoles Volteados (Guatemalan Refried Beans): Follow the Frijoles Refritos recipe, using a blender to puree beans to a smooth consistency. Use canola oil for frying.

Frijoles con Chile (Salvadoran Beans with Bell Peppers): Pan fry over medium low heat 1¼ cups chopped yellow onion, ½ cup red bell pepper, and ½ cup green bell pepper in 2 tablespoons canola oil. Add ¾ cup fresh tomato puree and the cooked beans and the broth from the Frijoles recipe, season with kosher salt to taste, cover, and simmer for 10 minutes.

AMALIA'S NOTES

- Use any color of beans in the basic bean recipe and add other ingredients, such as chicharrones, cooked chorizo, or pork loin pieces.

- To t-score an onion, make a ½-inch-deep cross-shaped cut at the narrowest end of the onion. The onion remains whole.

- More dishes containing beans and other preparations are in other parts of this book (see index).

Mint and Sour Orange Beef and Vegetable Stew with Fried Plantains

SERVES 4 to 6

1 ½ pounds brisket or flank steak

1 small onion, peeled and t-scored (see note)

12 cups beef stock, divided, store-bought or homemade (see page 198)

SOFRITO (QUICK SAUCE)

3 tablespoons canola achiote oil (see note)

1 cup finely chopped onion

1 tablespoon minced garlic

1 ½ cups julienned or diced chiltomas (or equal parts green and red bell peppers)

1 cup diced Roma tomatoes

SAZÓN (SEASONINGS)

4 tablespoons chopped mint

¼ cup fresh sour orange juice (jugo de naranja agria) or equal parts fresh orange and lemon juice

1 ½ teaspoons kosher salt

Freshly ground black pepper

PARA ESPESAR (THICKENERS)

1 cup instant corn masa harina diluted in 2 cups cold beef stock

or

6–8 corn tortillas, torn and soaked in 2 cups hot beef stock for 10 minutes, then pureed

ADORNO Y ACOMPAÑANTES (GARNISH AND PAIRINGS)

½ cup crumbled queso fresco (optional)

Mint, sprigs or chopped

Boquitas de Tajadas de Plátano Verde (green plantain chips with tomatillo-avocado salsa and langostinos, page 74) , or use cooked whole ripe or green plantains (see note)

While in León, Nicaragua, I had the opportunity to make Indio Viejo with a woman who was known for being a good cook. We went to the central market, bought a few ingredients, and went to her home on the outskirts of town. Her kitchen was in her backyard, and we prepped all the ingredients for this dish in the company of her pet parrot, Paco, and a few dogs. While Paco talked to us, we used a stone to pound the cooked meat for the stew so we could shred it. We made the dish with just a few ingredients, but this recipe, like many others, varies per region and cook. Then we sat at a table under a shady tree with other Nicaraguan friends to enjoy our creation. It was delicious. What's crucial in this recipe is to achieve the right balance of mint and sour orange, two key seasoning characteristics in some Nicaraguan dishes. Fancy equipment is not essential to create delicious food, but kitchen common sense and flavor intuition truly is.

1. In a medium braising pan, place the brisket with the onion in 6 cups stock and bring it to a quick boil over high heat. Reduce the heat to low, cover, and braise until the meat fibers separate easily when pulled apart, about 1 ½ to 2 hours. Check the meat while it cooks and make sure there's at least 1 ½ cups liquid in the pot at all times (adding ½ cup of the remaining stock at a time as needed). When the meat is done, transfer it to a cutting board. Cut it in half against the grain and shred it using two forks. Reserve the stock in a container, then chop the onion and set it aside.

2. In the same braising pan, heat the achiote oil over medium low heat, then add the onion and reserved onion, minced garlic, chiltomas, and tomatoes. Sauté for 2 minutes. Add the mint, sour orange juice, salt, and black pepper to taste and cook 1 minute. Add the shredded meat. Stir well to mix the ingredients, and cook for 2 minutes to blend the flavors.

3. Gradually add your thickener of choice and reserved stock while stirring constantly. Stir very well, as the sauce thickens quickly. Cook for 2 to 4 minutes while continuing to stir until the sauce consistency is medium thick, about the consistency of spaghetti sauce. If the sauce appears too thick, add more stock. If too runny, cook a bit longer to reduce the liquid. Garnish and serve immediately.

AMALIA'S NOTES

- To t-score an onion, make a ½-inch-deep cross-shaped cut at the narrowest end of the onion. The onion remains whole.

- The sauce should have a yellowish color, which is achieved with the achiote oil. Achiote oil and achiote powder are suitable for this dish, as they contain no additives. Achiote oil is often more effective than the powder, but you may use both to add more color. To make achiote oil, heat ½ cup canola oil in a small skillet over medium low heat until small bubbles start to form. Turn the heat off and add 2 tablespoons achiote seeds. Allow the seeds to color the oil for 5 to 10 minutes (or longer), strain the oil, and discard the seeds. The oil should be deep orange, not brown. Keep leftover achiote oil in the refrigerator for up to a month.

- Achiote is available in fresh paste, dried seeds, and ground at most Latin stores, some grocery chains, and online.

- To cook a whole plantain, trim the ends and cut it into 2-inch slices. Place the slices in a saucepan with enough water to cover and ¼ teaspoon kosher salt. Simmer, covered, until cooked, about 3 to 5 minutes. Peel and serve with this recipe.

PEPIÁN ROJO DE CONEJO

Spicy Rabbit Stewed in Tomato, Tomatillo, and Guajillo Sauce with Yukon Gold Potatoes

SERVES 4 to 6

Pepián rojo takes its name from the red sauce. There are also black and yellow pepiánes with varying ingredients, such as turkey, chicken, beef, pork, and exotic meats, in Guatemala department, Quetzaltenango, Suchitepequez, and other regions. Pepián was declared intangible cultural patrimony (heritage) of Guatemala along with four other Mayan stews (Jocón, Kaqik, Mole, and Pinol). All pepián varieties have some ingredients in common, such as pan-roasted seeds, dried peppers, tomatoes, and tomatillos, but they may have different finishing touches. Serve it with Arroz con Arvejas y Chile Pimiento (Rice with Baby Peas and Red Bell Pepper, page 140), which provides a nice break between spicy bites.

1 In a medium pot, cook the rabbit pieces in the stock with the onion over low heat for 25 to 30 minutes. Remove and reserve the onion. Set aside the pot of rabbit and stock.

2 Heat a skillet for 2 minutes over medium heat and dry pan roast the tomatoes, tomatillos, onion, and garlic. Reduce the heat to medium low and continue to pan roast the vegetables until they're charred all over and mushy, about 8 minutes.

3 Separately, dry pan toast the chiles over medium low heat for 1 ½ minutes per side. Then dry pan toast the pumpkin and sesame seeds separately over medium low heat until medium brown, stirring from time to time with a soft spatula. Keep a close eye on the chiles and seeds, as they can burn easily. In a medium bowl, soak the roasted chiles in 1 cup very hot water for 10 minutes. Grind the seeds separately in a spice grinder.

4 To a blender, add the pan-roasted vegetables, the reserved onion, the soaked chiles, half the chile soaking water, and ¾ cup hot stock from the rabbit pot. Add the thickener of choice and puree to a smooth consistency. The puree should look smooth and velvety.

5 Heat the oil in a medium skillet. Add the puree, ground pumpkin and sesame seeds, achiote, cinnamon, salt, and black pepper to taste. Cook for about 3 minutes. Add the sauce to the pot with the rabbit and remaining stock. Add the potatoes and stir. Simmer, covered, for about 15 minutes to blend the flavors. The sauce should be medium thin, about the consistency of steak sauce. If the sauce is too thin, cook the stew a bit longer to thicken it. If the sauce is too thick, add more stock or water. Serve immediately in bowls.

AMALIA'S NOTES

- Use other exotic meats for this recipe, such as venison or bison. Fresh rabbit and these meats are available from your local farmer or Asian grocery store, or online.

- To t-score an onion, make a ½-inch-deep cross-shaped cut at the narrowest end of the onion. The onion remains whole.

1 fresh whole young rabbit (liver included), cut into 8 pieces

2 cups vegetable stock, store-bought or homemade (see page 198)

1 small whole onion, peeled and t-scored (see note)

2 cups quartered Roma tomatoes

½ cup husked, quartered tomatillos

1 medium yellow onion, cut into 1-inch-thick slices

2 large garlic cloves, peeled

2–3 guaque or guajillo chiles, seeded

2 tablespoons shelled pumpkin seeds

2 tablespoons sesame seeds

PARA ESPESAR (THICKENERS)

Choose one of the following:

3–4 corn tortillas soaked in ¾ cup hot water for 10 minutes

3 tablespoons instant corn masa flour combined with ½ cup cold water

3 tablespoons white rice soaked in cold water for 10 minutes

1 tablespoon canola oil

1 teaspoon fresh achiote paste dissolved in a little cold water or 1 teaspoon achiote powder

½ teaspoon ground canela (Ceylon cinnamon)

1 ½ teaspoons kosher salt

Freshly ground black pepper

2 cups 1-inch-sliced Yukon Gold unpeeled potatoes, cooked al dente

BOXBOLES

Corn Masa Dumplings in Chayote Leaves with Spicy Toasted Pumpkin Seed Sauce

MAKES 7 to 9 dumplings

MASA (DOUGH)

1 cup instant corn masa flour
½ teaspoon kosher salt
1 cup chicken stock, store-
  bought or homemade
  (see page 198)

2 ½ tablespoons vegetable
  shortening
3 tablespoons crumbled Cotija
  cheese

7–9 fresh chayote squash or
  pumpkin leaves, plus the
  vines if available (roughly
  chopped)

IGUAXTE (SAUCE)
(MAKES 1 CUP)

½ cup shelled pumpkin seeds
1 large Roma tomato
2 medium tomatillos, husked
1 small onion, cut into ½-inch
  slices
2 small garlic cloves
1 teaspoon Cobán chile powder
  or other spicy ground chile
¾ teaspoon kosher salt

While traveling in the Guatemalan Mayan highlands, I was invited to cook with indigenous families in Nebaj and Chichicastenango in Quiché. Boxboles, or boshboles or woxwoles, are of Maya Ixil origin, the area of the Cuchumatanes mountains in northern Quiché, although now they are also made in Huehuetenango, Alta, and Baja Verapaz. We used a piedra de moler (grinding stone and arm made of volcanic rock) to make the masa and the sauce for these treats. This is the families' normal everyday routine for preparing various meals. Right next to the prepared masa, we had a bowl of freshly cut chayote leaves and the spirally vines. We took one leaf at a time, put in some masa and then some of the tender vines, and rolled it up to form long, thin cigars. We steamed them for about a half hour and sat down to enjoy one of the best vegetarian snacks I've ever had. The spicy sauce adds a delicious touch. As we exchanged niceties at the table, we grabbed several of the small steaming boxboles with our hands, dipped them in the spicy sauce, and ate them and their wrappings in a couple of fiery bites. Serve them as an appetizer or make them a side for a stew from this book.

1. In the bowl of a stand mixer with the paddle attachment, combine the instant corn masa flour and the salt. While beating at speed 2, gradually add the stock to make very moist dough. Add the shortening and increase the speed to speed 4 and beat for 1 minute. Stop the mixer and scrape the sides and bottom of the bowl with a soft spatula. Add the cheese and the chopped vines (if available), beat at speed 2 for 1 minute, and then fluff the dough at speed 6 for 2 minutes. (Alternatively, mix the ingredients by hand in a bowl with a wooden spoon and beat vigorously at the end to fluff the dough.)

2. Form the boxboles starting by dividing the dough into seven to nine equal portions. Put a scoop of dough at the center of each leaf, matte side up. With your fingers, gently shape the dough into a 3-inch cigar. Fold the top and bottom sides of the leaf on top of the dough and press gently to secure in place. Lift the right side of the leaf over the dough and then roll it to enclose the dough inside and form 3x1 ½-inch cylinders. Repeat until all the dough and leaves are used. Set aside.

3. In a medium pot with 3 cups water and a steamer basket, stack the boxboles horizontally and evenly (end side down) throughout the basket. Make sure the water does not touch them. Bring the water to a quick boil over high heat, adjust the heat to medium low, and steam the boxboles until cooked, about 20 to 25 minutes. They are cooked when the leaves have turned darker green and the dough is slightly shiny, not opaque. Let them sit in the pot for 10 minutes, or until ready to serve, with the heat off to firm up a bit before serving.

Continued on page 110

4. Dry pan toast the pumpkin seeds in a small skillet over medium low heat until medium brown, about 3 to 5 minutes, and keep a close eye on them, as they can burn easily. Separately, on a nonstick griddle, dry pan roast over medium low heat the tomato, tomatillos, onion, and garlic until charred all over and mushy, about 8 minutes. This whole process can take 12 to 15 minutes. Puree the pumpkin seeds and tomato mixture with the chile powder and ¾ teaspoon salt in a blender to make a fine and smooth pasty puree. Transfer the sauce to a serving bowl.

5. Serve the boxboles with the spicy sauce on the side.

AMALIA'S NOTES

- Look for chayote squash or pumpkin leaves at farmers' markets or through Community-Supported Agriculture hubs (CSAs).

- The size of the leaves used will dictate the size and quantity of the tamales.

- Cobán chile powder is available at Latin stores and online.

- Boxboles are traditionally made with water instead of chicken stock and no cheese, but they taste much better after adding these two ingredients. The entire tamale is edible, including the leaves.

PINOL DE CONEJO

Toasted Dried Corn, Roasted Tomato, Cilantro, and Rabbit Stew

SERVES 4 to 6

CALDO (BROTH)

1 rabbit, cut into 8 to 10 pieces
2 Roma tomatoes, quartered
1 medium onion, peeled
  and t-scored (see note
  on page 113)
2 cloves garlic
½ cup whole cilantro leaves
  and stems
½ teaspoon kosher salt
6 cups chicken or vegetable
  stock, store-bought or
  homemade (see page 198)

PINOL (CORN-BASED SAUCE)

3 Roma tomatoes
3 tomatillos, husked
1 red bell pepper, seeded
  and quartered
1 medium onion, in
  ¼-inch-thick slices
2 cloves garlic
1 guaque or guajillo chile,
  seeded
1 cup whole grain coarse-grind
  stone-ground cornmeal
¼ cup white rice
½ teaspoon canela (Ceylon
  cinnamon), broken
  into pieces
1 tablespoon sesame seeds

SAZÓN (SEASONINGS)

½ cup finely chopped
  cilantro leaves
1 teaspoon kosher salt
Freshly ground black pepper

ADORNO (GARNISH)

Cilantro sprigs

Pinol is a delightful dish and a pre-Hispanic Mayan stew from San Juan Sacatepéquez, Guatemala Department. The dish was declared cultural patrimony (heritage) by the Guatemalan government along with four other stews (Jocón, Pepián, Kaqik, and Mole). They collectively are national culinary symbols for their ancestral origin and technique, originally incorporating only native ingredients in their preparation. The key ingredient in the stew is ground toasted dried corn, which is combined with meats, a few vegetables, and herbs. Pinol, from the Nahuatl word *pinolli*, meaning stone-ground corn, became a blend of flavors and cultures during colonization and varies in ingredients and texture by region and maker. Here's another recipe for Pinol de Marrano con Chatate (Toasted Dried Corn, Pork Rib, and Chaya Leaf Stew, page 206), inspired by my maternal great-grandmother. Pinol is also an atole drink in Guatemala and Mexico (pinole) and a refreshing drink in Nicaragua (Pinolillo, see page 44) and other parts of Mesoamerica. This is my special rendition of this glorious dish. Serve it with vegetable rice for a superb experience (see Chapter 5, page 135, for ideas).

1. Combine the rabbit, quartered tomatoes, t-scored onion, 2 garlic cloves, ½ cup whole cilantro leaves and stems, ½ teaspoon salt, and stock in a soup pot and bring to a quick boil over high heat. Adjust the heat to medium low and simmer, covered, for 20 minutes. Remove the rabbit, tomatoes, onion, and garlic, and reserve. Discard the cilantro.

2. Heat a large dry skillet for 2 minutes over medium heat, then add the 3 tomatoes, tomatillos, red bell pepper, thickly sliced onion, and 2 garlic cloves. Pan roast until charred all over and mushy, about 8 minutes.

3. Separately, dry pan toast the chile in a small skillet over medium high heat, turning it at least once, until aromatic, about 2 minutes. In a small bowl, soak the toasted chile in ½ cup hot stock for 10 minutes.

4. Separately, dry pan toast the cornmeal in a medium skillet over medium high heat until medium brown, about 5 minutes, flipping it or moving it around with a soft spatula constantly. Set aside. Repeat the procedure with the rice. Keep a close eye on them, as they can burn easily if left unattended. In a spice mill, grind the rice to a fine powder.

5. Separately, dry pan toast the cinnamon and sesame seeds over medium low heat until medium brown, about 3 to 5 minutes, stirring from time to time with a soft spatula. Keep a close eye on the cinnamon and seeds, as they can burn easily. Grind the cinnamon and seeds separately in a spice grinder.

6. In a blender, combine the reserved onion, tomatoes, and garlic with the pan-roasted vegetables, the soaked chile with the stock, and an additional 1 cup hot stock from the soup pot. Blend until smooth.

Continued on page 113

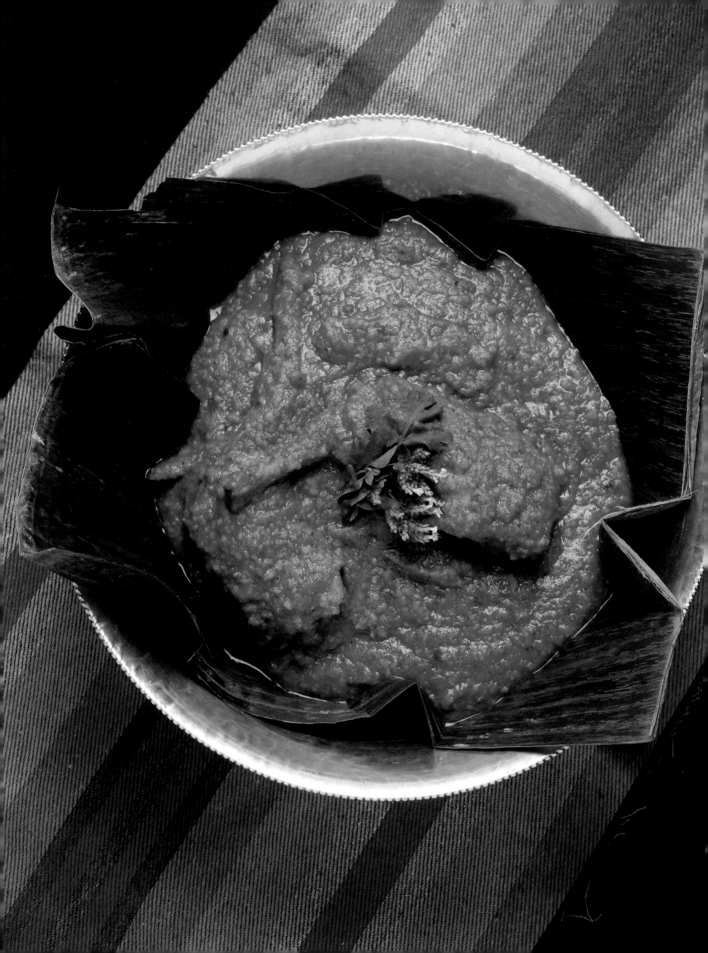

7. Add the blended ingredients to the soup pot and stir to combine with the remaining stock. While whisking continuously, gradually add the cornmeal and ground rice. Whisk to break up any lumps. Bring to a quick boil over high heat, adjust the heat to medium low, cover, and cook until the cornmeal is almost cooked, about 15 minutes. Add the ½ cup chopped cilantro, cinnamon, sesame seeds, 1 teaspoon salt, and black pepper to taste. Stir well, add the rabbit, and simmer gently, covered, to blend the flavors and to finish cooking the cornmeal, about 15 minutes. Serve garnished with cilantro sprigs.

AMALIA'S NOTES

- Fresh rabbits are available through local farmers, either whole or already cut up.

- To t-score an onion, make a ½-inch-deep cross-shaped cut at the narrowest end of the onion. The onion remains whole.

- Peel tomatillos under running water if you find the husks hard to remove.

- Whole grain coarse-grind stone-ground cornmeal is available at major grocery stores and online.

- Dried corn can also be used in this recipe, but you will need a more powerful mill than a spice or coffee mill to grind the corn to the needed texture.

- Increase the thickness of the stew by adding more cornmeal, or make it thinner by adding more stock.

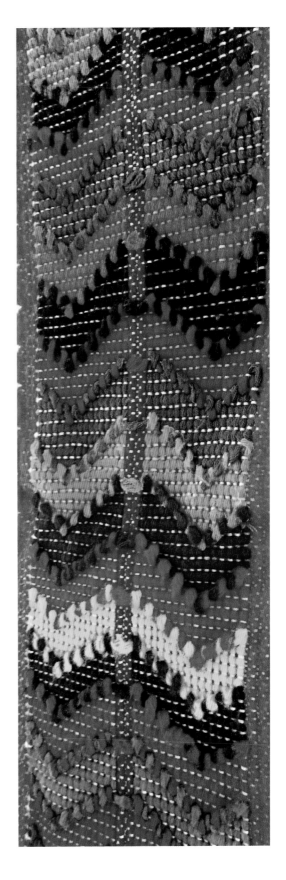

TOB IK

Chicken, Pork, and Beef in Cilantro-Cumin Stew

SERVES 4 to 6

This special soupy stew, also known as tobik or tabique, is from Totonicapán, Guatemala, located in the Mayan highlands at the southwest of the department of Quiché. The stew is simply as delicious as it is nutritious and easy to make. Traditionally made with beef and pork ribs, it lends itself well to other meats, so I have added chicken thighs. I like it spicy and added chiltepe, Guatemala's most popular and highly revered fresh chile pepper, also known as piquín in Mesoamerica. It's a complete meal in one dish that only needs warm corn tortillas and avocado chunks, if you'd like.

1 In a medium pot over medium low heat, simmer the chicken, pork loin, and top sirloin with the garlic in the stock, covered, for 20 minutes.

2 In a blender, puree the tomatoes, onion, ¾ cup cilantro leaves, chiltepe, and achiote. Add this puree to the pot with the chicken, pork, and beef. Season with 1 tablespoon chopped cilantro, cumin, and salt to taste. Stir well.

3 Add the cabbage, squash, carrot, and potatoes, stir, cover, and simmer gently over low heat for 15 minutes. Garnish with chopped cilantro or sprigs before serving.

2 boneless, skinless chicken thighs, cut into 3-inch strips
½ pound pork loin, cut into 3-inch strips
½ pound top sirloin, cut into 3-inch strips
1 head garlic
4 cups chicken stock, store-bought or homemade (see page 198)

RECADO (SAUCE)

2 cups roughly chopped Roma tomatoes
1 cup roughly chopped yellow onion
¾ cup whole cilantro leaves and stems
½–1 teaspoon minced chiltepe (fresh piquín chile) or bird's eye chile
2 teaspoons achiote powder

SAZÓN (SEASONINGS)

1 tablespoon finely chopped cilantro leaves
¾ teaspoon ground cumin
1 ½ teaspoons kosher salt

1 cup shredded green cabbage
1 güisquil or chayote squash, peeled and diced or in ¼-inch-thick strips
1 large carrot, peeled and diced, sliced, or in thick strips, cooked al dente
1–2 medium Yukon Gold potatoes, unpeeled, diced, sliced, or in thick strips, cooked al dente

ADORNO (GARNISH)

Cilantro, chopped or sprigs

BAHO

Sour Orange Beef, Yuca, and Plantains Steamed in Banana Leaves with Spicy Slaw

SERVES 4 to 6

1 pound brisket, sliced in half
 lengthwise and cut into
 2x4-inch pieces

½ pound cecina (dried salted
 meat), cut into 2x4-inch pieces

3 large Roma tomatoes,
 thinly sliced

2 large yellow onions, thinly
 sliced

3–4 chiltomas or 1 large green
 bell pepper, thinly sliced

2 tablespoons minced fresh garlic

2 cups fresh sour orange
 juice (jugo de naranja agria)
 or equal parts fresh orange
 and lemon juice

1 ½ teaspoons kosher salt

1 (16-ounce) package fresh or
 frozen banana leaves, rinsed
 and wiped on both sides
 with a damp cloth

1 pound fresh yuca, peeled,
 or frozen yuca kept whole
 or in large chunks

1 green plantain, peel on,
 washed, ends trimmed, cut
 into 2-inch-long pieces

1 ripe plantain, peel on, washed,
 ends trimmed, cut into
 2-inch-long pieces

ADORNO (GARNISH)

1 recipe **Ensalada de Repollo
 con Tomate** (Cabbage-Tomato
 Slaw, page 82)

1 recipe **Chilero Criollo**
 (Spicy Chile Vegetable and
 Onion Pickles, page 82)

SPECIAL EQUIPMENT

Disposable gloves
1 turkey-size oven bag

A dish unique to Nicaragua, baho (or vaho) is an indigenous delight representing a mix of local cultures with native and nonnative ingredients, traditionally topped with cabbage slaw and sometimes spicy salsa. Pecho, or brisket, is a tough piece of meat, and the long steaming time is needed to tenderize it. Some yuca species also take longer to cook than others. While on tour in Nicaragua, I experienced the dish very casually at the mercado and at a restaurant. They were similar yet different. When assembled and steamed in the banana leaves, the aroma of the meat, seasonings, and vegetables is delightful. Baho looks exotic and tastes amazing. One key ingredient here is the naranja agria (sour orange), a common seasoning in Nicaraguan and Central American cooking.

1. In a large bowl, combine the brisket, dried salted meat, tomatoes, onions, chiltomas, garlic, sour orange juice, and salt. Mix well with your hands (wearing gloves), cover, and marinate in the refrigerator overnight, or about 6 to 8 hours.

2. When you're ready to cook the dish, fill a deep pot with 8 cups water, cover it, and set it over low heat. Working on a countertop or table, line a steamer basket with the oven bag and then two layers of banana leaves, making sure the basket is entirely covered and the banana leaves also overhang on the sides enough to fold over the filling.

3. Layer all the ingredients in the basket, starting with the yuca, then the green plantains, the meat and marinade, and the ripe plantains last. Enclose the ingredients in the banana leaves, pulling the leaves from the sides on top of the

surface of the filling. Use additional leaves to ensure full coverage. Bring up the sides of the oven bag to enclose the filling, twisting the top loosely to allow the steam to escape. Do not tie it, or the bag could burst open at the bottom.

4. Place the steamer basket in the deep pot. Increase the heat to medium high, put the lid on top of the twisted bag, and steam the meat and vegetable mixture for 1 ½ hours. Reduce the heat to medium low and steam for 1 ½ hours longer. Keep a close eye on the pot, as steam builds up in the bag. Simply lift the lid for a few seconds to release the excess steam. After the 3 hours are up, check the brisket doneness. The meat fibers should separate easily; if not, continue cooking in 30-minute increments. Once the brisket is done, you can hold the pot on low heat, covered, until you're ready to serve.

Continued on page 118

5. When ready to serve, open the bag carefully and beware of the steam to prevent burns. Pull the bag down the sides of the pot. Using tongs, uncover the steamed ingredients. Move the meat slightly to the side, and using a large, deep spoon, scoop the yuca, plantains, and broth from the bottom of the pot.

6. Serve in plates lined with fresh banana leaves, starting with some yuca pieces, green and ripe plantain pieces (peels removed), the meat and pieces of the sliced vegetables, and some of the broth. Garnish with the Ensalada de Repollo con Tomate and Chilero Criollo.

AMALIA'S NOTES

- I use an 8-quart pasta pot with a deep steamer basket to make this recipe. The oven bag is needed to catch all the juices from all the ingredients; otherwise, they would be diluted and lost in the steaming water.

- Brisket is a tough cut, so slicing the meat in half lengthwise makes it thinner and speeds up the cooking process.

- Frozen banana leaves must be washed well, as they have residual ash from their baking on open fires. This is needed to make them pliable for packaging and cooking. Handle the leaves carefully to prevent tears.

- Fresh and frozen yuca are available at major grocery chains. Frozen yuca is peeled and ready to use. Fresh yuca must be peeled prior to using. To peel, use a peeler and make sure you remove the outer brown peel completely. The yuca should be completely white prior to using.

- Yuca has a stringy inner core that must be removed prior to eating. This becomes more visible when the yuca is cooked and split in half lengthwise.

NACATAMALES DE CERDO Y POLLO

Pork and Chicken Tamales with Sour Orange Sauce

MAKES 8 rectangular tamales

I am fond of all kinds of tamales, and nacatamales, nacatl-tamalli in Nahuatl, meaning "meat tamale," now have a special place in my kitchen. While visiting Granada, Nicaragua, I enjoyed them over and over at different places. All of them were slightly different but delicious. Most had few ingredients, but the ones I tried in Managua had many more. This is true for all tamales throughout Mesoamerica—they vary according to the maker and region. Nacatamales are one of the most important dishes in Nicaragua and perhaps the one that truly represents the blending of cultures. Pre-Hispanic ingredients combined with Spanish ingredients make for an interesting combination of flavors, much like in the rest of the region. Indigenous nacatamales were originally made with garrobo (native iguana), but today they are usually made with just pork, or pork and chicken. This is my rendition of the way I had them in Managua. They're worthy of celebration.

1. To make the sauce, combine the tomatoes, chiltomas or green bell pepper, yellow onion, garlic, mint, sour orange juice, ground achiote, and salt in a blender and puree to a smooth consistency. Pour 1 ½ cups of the sauce into a large bowl and add the chicken and pork pieces. Mix well so all the meat is coated. Cover and marinate in the refrigerator for 4 to 6 hours, or overnight. Wait until the chicken and pork are marinated before proceeding to the next steps, or make the dough and save it in the refrigerator after it has cooled, then proceed to assemble the tamales after the chicken and pork are marinated.

2. To make the dough, in the bowl of a stand mixer with the paddle attachment, combine the masa flour and salt with the chicken stock and sour orange juice and mix on low speed for 2 minutes. Add the rest of the sauce and vegetable shortening or lard and mix at low speed for 2 minutes. Fluff the dough for 2 minutes at speed 4. (Alternatively, put the ingredients in a deep bowl in the order listed and beat vigorously with a wooden spoon until well incorporated.)

RECADO (SAUCE)
(MAKES 3 ½ CUPS)

1 ½ cups diced Roma tomatoes
3–4 chiltomas, diced, or 1 cup diced green bell pepper
1 cup diced yellow onion
2 tablespoons minced garlic
1 ½ cups chopped mint, leaves and soft stems included
1 cup fresh sour orange juice (jugo de naranja agria) or equal parts fresh orange and lemon juice
1 ½–2 tablespoons ground achiote
3 teaspoons kosher salt

8 (3x2-inch) pieces chicken thighs, boneless, skinless
8 (3x2-inch) pieces country-style boneless pork ribs

MASA (DOUGH)

2 cups instant corn masa flour
1 ½ teaspoons kosher salt
2 cups chicken stock, store-bought or homemade (see page 198)
⅓ cup fresh sour orange juice (jugo de naranja agria) or equal parts fresh orange and lemon juice
¾ cup (about 6 ounces) vegetable shortening or lard

16 (14x11-inch) pieces banana leaves, wiped on both sides with a damp cloth
16 (60-inch-long) pieces cibaque (natural fiber), soaked, or kitchen twine, for tying

ADORNO (GARNISH)

9 tablespoons white rice soaked in cold water for 3 to 4 hours, drained
8 (2-inch) strips cooked bacon
8 (½-inch-thick) slices Roma tomato
16 (2-inch) pieces green bell pepper
16 thinly sliced onion rings
16 Congo chiles (chiltepe or piquín) or 8 bird's eye chiles
24 (½-inch cubed) pieces Yukon Gold potatoes, peeled
8 pitted prunes
24 raisins
24 Spanish capers
8 large Spanish olives stuffed with pimentos
8 large sprigs mint

Continued on page 120

3 Transfer the dough to a skillet and cook it on the stovetop over low heat, stirring constantly with a soft spatula to keep it from forming lumps and from sticking to the skillet until the dough is ready. It is ready when the spoon starts leaving tracks, the dough starts lifting from the edges, and the dough has thickened to a soft paste, about 10 to 15 minutes. Let the dough cool slightly, then divide into eight equal portions.

4 For each tamale, lay one piece of banana leaf (matte side up) on top of another piece of banana leaf so they're crisscross. Place one dough portion at the center of the banana leaves, make a small well with the spoon, and top with 1 tablespoon rice, 1 piece of chicken, and 1 piece of pork. Then distribute the remaining garnishes over the top of the tamale: 1 piece of bacon, 1 slice of tomato, 2 pieces of green bell pepper, 2 onion rings, 2 Congo or piquín chiles (or 1 bird's eye chile), 3 potato cubes, 1 prune, 3 raisins, 3 capers, 1 olive, and 1 sprig of mint. Top with some of the remaining sauce from the marinade (divide it equally among the eight tamales). Wrap the tamale and seal it tightly: Bring together the corners of the bottom leaf and make three small folds beginning at the top. Then press the leaves flat, from the outside in, to hold the ingredients in the center. Make one fold at each of the unsealed leaf edges so they overlap to form a rectangular tamale. Tie with cibaque or kitchen twine.

5 Fill a deep pot with 10 cups water. Place all the tamales vertically in a steamer basket and put the basket in the pot. Bring the water to a boil over high heat, cover the pot, and reduce the heat to medium low. Steam the tamales until they're cooked through, about 2 hours. When the tamales are done, the dough should hold the shape of the package and should be shiny and slightly translucent, not opaque. Let the tamales sit in the pot, covered, with the heat off for at least 1 hour before serving them. This resting time will bring their temperature down, and the tamales will firm up a bit.

AMALIA'S NOTES

- I use an 8-quart pasta pot with a deep steamer basket to make this recipe.

- These tamales are traditionally medium yellow. Add more or less achiote according to taste. Start with the lower amount listed under the sauce ingredients, then adjust the color while the dough is still in the mixing bowl. Never add achiote powder directly to the dough. Dilute it in a little cold water, then add it to the dough and fluff the dough for 1 minute. Achiote color intensifies during cooking, so another option is to add it while the dough is being cooked on the stovetop.

- Tamales freeze well. To reheat them, steam them for 30 to 40 minutes. Reheat refrigerated tamales by steaming them for 10 to 15 minutes.

CHILIMAL
Spicy Roast Muscovy Duck with Cobán Chile Stew
SERVES 4 to 6

1 (5 ½- to 6-pound) Muscovy
  duck, neck and giblets
  reserved (if provided)
1 tablespoon canola oil

RECADO (SAUCE)

4 Roma tomatoes
1 ½ large onions, cut into
  ¼-inch-thick slices
3 large cloves garlic, peeled
2 store-bought corn tortillas,
  torn into large pieces

2 ½ cups chicken stock,
  store-bought or homemade
  (see page 198)
1 ½ cups whole cilantro leaves
  and stems, plus more for
  garnish

SAZÓN (SEASONINGS)

2 teaspoons Cobán chile
  powder, plus more for garnish
1 teaspoons kosher salt
Freshly ground black pepper

1 cup ½-inch-sliced Yukon
  Gold potatoes, unpeeled,
  cooked al dente
1 cup ½-inch-sliced or diced
  güisquil or chayote squash,
  cooked al dente

A Mayan stew from the northern Quiché region of Guatemala, chilimal is one of the many varying types of indigenous stews throughout the country. While unique, the stew follows a cooking technique pattern inherent in other Mayan stews. Quite possibly this dish was originally made with exotic meats and native ingredients prior to colonization, but today it is made with pork combined with other nonnative ingredients. The recipe can be adapted as desired. A key flavor here comes from the spicy and smoky Cobán chile native to Alta Verapaz (Cobán is the capital). Like other traditional dishes in Guatemala and Mesoamerica, chilimal represents a blend of native and colonial flavors. Here I elevate the dish to a gourmet level using Muscovy duck, a leaner, meatier, tender, and flavorful duck native to Mexico and Central and South America, which has made part of the United States its home. This dish is perfect for entertaining.

1. Rinse and pat dry the duck. Remove the excess skin and fat from the duck and cut it into eight pieces. Season the pieces with salt and black pepper. In a braiser or wide nonstick deep skillet, pan roast the duck pieces skin side down in the oil at medium low heat until medium brown, about 12 to 15 minutes. Do not roast the other side. Roast the neck and giblets (if provided) on both sides for 5 minutes. Transfer the duck and other pieces to another dish, and keep warm. Discard the accumulated fat from the braiser but do not rinse it.

2. While the duck is roasting, prepare the sauce. In a separate skillet over medium high heat, dry pan roast the tomatoes, onion, and garlic until charred all over, about 8 minutes. Separately dry pan toast the tortillas until medium brown (keep a close eye on them, as they can burn easily if left unattended). This whole process will take about 12 to 15 minutes.

3. Simmer the stock with the cilantro over medium heat in a medium pan for 10 minutes. Soak the toasted tortillas in the hot chicken stock until soft, about 5 minutes.

4. In a blender, puree all the roasted and toasted ingredients, including the unpeeled tomatoes, onion, garlic, tortillas, cilantro, and stock. Add the Cobán chile powder, salt, and black pepper to taste and blend to combine.

5. Add the puree to the braiser. Bring it to a quick boil over high heat, reduce the heat to low, and nestle the duck pieces in the sauce skin side up. Braise over low heat uncovered for 20 to 25 minutes to finish cooking the duck and thicken the sauce. Do not turn the duck pieces at any time. Add the potatoes and squash, distributing them carefully where they fit within the stew, and braise for another 10 minutes.

6. Serve garnished with cilantro sprigs and additional chile powder, if desired.

AMALIA'S NOTES

- Cobán chile powder is available in select Latin markets and online.

- Free-range Muscovy duck, raised without antibiotics and hormones, is available through your local farmer or online. It is pricey but worth it. Pekin duck can be used instead of Muscovy duck if you are unable to source it and is less expensive. The flavor profile is different, and Pekin duck is less lean.

POZOLE BLANCO

Spicy Braised Pork Shoulder with Hominy, Oregano, and Cabbage

SERVES 4

Pozoles, or pozolli in Nahuatl, are traditional celebratory Mexican soups that can be white, red, or green, containing varying ingredients and garnishes depending on the color and cook. The basic component in all three is hominy (which means pozole). They also can be made with pig's feet and the head, honeycomb tripe, and other pork cuts. Found in several states in Mexico, pozoles are delicious, filling, and easy to make. Pozol also is a Costa Rican guiso (stew) with varying ingredients and similar traits. This version is one of my favorites because it's scrumptious and is made with ingredients that are conveniently available at grocery stores. A bowlful of this delight will leave you happily satisfied for hours. For a meal with friends, ladle the soup pork pieces, hominy, and broth in individual bowls and let your guests season and garnish their serving as they please. Accompany with warm corn tortillas and avocado chunks, if you like.

1 cup dried hominy, soaked in 3 cups hot water overnight
1 cup 2-inch-cubed pork shoulder
2–3 bone-in country-style pork ribs, or 1 pork foot cut into large chunks
1 cup roughly chopped yellow onion
1 teaspoon minced garlic
4 cups vegetable broth
Kosher salt
Freshly ground black pepper

SAZÓN (SEASONINGS)

¼ cup crumbled dried oregano
Piquín or other spicy dried chile powder, to taste

ADORNO (GARNISH)

2 cups finely shredded green cabbage
1 cup finely diced yellow onion
1 cup julienned or thinly sliced radishes
1 lime, cut into 8 wedges

1. Add the hominy and soaking water to a medium pot and bring it to a quick boil over high heat. Cover, reduce the heat to low, and cook until tender, stirring a few times, about 1 ½ to 2 hours. Keep the water level equal, making sure it covers the hominy at all times, adding more water during the cooking process to compensate for absorption and evaporation. The hominy will double in size.

2. Separately, in a braiser or large pot, braise over low heat the pork shoulder, pork ribs, onion, and garlic in the vegetable broth, covered, for 45 minutes. Add the cooked hominy, season to taste with salt and black pepper, and continue to braise, covered, for 30 additional minutes.

3. Remove the meat from the bones and discard the bones. Serve the soup in bowls and distribute its components evenly. Season each bowl with oregano and spicy chile powder, and garnish with some cabbage, onion, radishes, and a wedge of lime.

RECIPE VARIATION

Pozole de Maíz (Corn Pozole): Follow the recipe given, except prepare 1 cup cooked white rice for garnish, and use shredded lettuce instead of cabbage for garnish. To assemble the bowl, ladle in the pork, hominy, and soup, then add 2 tablespoons rice along with the rest of the seasonings and garnishes.

AMALIA'S NOTES

- Fresh hominy is best, but canned hominy may also be used. Since it is already cooked, combine it with the cooked meats and braise for 15 minutes to combine flavors.

- White hominy is the most popular, but there is yellow, purple, and white dried hominy.

MOLE AMARILLO
Cornish Hen and Costeño Chile Stew

SERVES 1 to 2

1 cornish hen, rinsed

3 cups chicken stock, store-bought or homemade (see page 198)

1 small yellow onion, peeled and t-scored (see note)

SALSA (SAUCE)

3 dried Costeño chiles or dried guajillo chiles, seeded, deveined, and dry pan toasted

1 cup diced Roma tomatoes

½ cup diced tomatillos

½ cup diced yellow onion

1 tablespoon minced garlic

¼ cup water

SAZÓN (SEASONINGS)

Dash ground cloves

Dash ground cumin

¼ teaspoon ground canela (Ceylon cinnamon)

½ teaspoon crumbled dried oregano

1 teaspoon kosher salt

Freshly ground black pepper

¼ cup instant corn masa flour combined with ¾ cup cold water

2 fresh or dried hoja santa (acuyo leaf)

1 cup peeled and ½-inch diced or thickly sliced chayote squash (about 1 chayote), cooked al dente

1 small bunch (8 to 10) whole green beans, trimmed, or sliced on the bias, cooked al dente

1 cup ¼-inch-sliced unpeeled Yukon Gold potatoes (about 4 to 5 potatoes), cooked al dente

CHILE DE AGUA EN RAJAS (SPICY CHILE SAUCE)

4 chiles de agua (or substitute jalapeño), cut into strips

¼ cup julienned white onion

¼ cup freshly squeezed lime juice

½ teaspoon crumbled dried oregano

Kosher salt

AMALIA'S NOTES

• To t-score an onion, make a ½-inch-deep cross-shaped cut at the narrowest end of the onion. The onion remains whole.

• Hoja santa is available in Latin markets in fresh and dried form.

• Costeño dried chiles are available in Latin markets or online.

While in Mexico City cooking with a few chefs, we made many versions of mole from throughout the country. This recipe stuck with me because it's simple, easy, and delicious, and the preparation technique is very close to Mayan stews from Guatemala. Moles, from the Nahuatl mōlli, meaning "sauce," can be savory or sweet, elaborate or simple, mild or spicy. This one has the right combination of meat and vegetables thickened with corn masa and flavored with hoja santa (sacred leaf, a.k.a. acuyo), native to Mesoamerica. Some moles include masa dumplings. The dish is inspired by the mole of the same name from Oaxaca, where I also had the fortune to cook with other great cooks. Moles can be light or heavier meals and can be paired with rice, corn masa tamales, or corn tortillas to make them into delightful experiences. Use pork, chicken, beef, or all three for another version of this exquisite stew. Mole amarillo takes its color and distinctive flavor from the Costeño chile native to Oaxaca, a medium-spicy and flavorful bright-yellow chile, as well as from the acuyo leaf. Here I use cornish hen, which is scrumptious in this aromatic velvety sauce. This is definitely a dish for entertaining.

1. In a medium saucepan, cook the cornish hen in the stock with the t-scored onion for 25 minutes. Then transfer the hen to another dish and keep warm. Remove and reserve the onion.

2. In a medium saucepan over low heat, cook the chiles, tomatoes, tomatillos, diced onion, and garlic in the water, covered, until soft, about 8 minutes.

3. In a blender, puree the cooked vegetables for the sauce. Add the puree to the stockpot. Bring to a quick boil over high heat, reduce the heat to low, and add the cloves, cumin, cinnamon, oregano, salt, and black pepper to taste. Stir well. While stirring constantly, gradually add the masa flour mixture. Stir well to prevent lumps. Add the hoja santa leaves and simmer, uncovered, for 5 minutes while stirring from time to time. The sauce should be medium thick and velvety. If it's too thin, cook it a bit longer. If it's too thick, add a bit more stock or water.

4. Add the hen and immerse the squash, green beans, and potatoes in the sauce and simmer, covered, for 10 minutes.

5. To make the spicy chile sauce, in a small bowl, combine the spicy chiles, onion, lime juice, oregano, and salt to taste.

6. Serve in a bowl topped with the spicy chile sauce.

4

Gastronomía Popular, Sacra y Social
Popular, Symbolic, and Social Fare

At the center stage of any celebration, food occupies one of the most important places at the modern Mesoamerican table. Deeply rooted rituals and customs are today a mix of native and colonial traditions. Popular, religious, or social, there are fare and protocols associated with all seasons or celebrations. These delicacies are highly revered in indigenous and communal gatherings because they reinforce cultural values. There are national iconic dishes and lesser-known regional plates. Here are some of the main festive events and foods, which at times can crisscross at some celebrations. This chapter, by design, contains no recipes but links important Mesoamerican celebrations with recipes found throughout this book.

Cofradías initially protected a patron saint and later grew into social gatherings that bring together indigenous and Catholic rituals (syncretism) under one celebration and give a voice and power to the indigenous people. Cofradías are headed primarily by elders who possess the wisdom to lead others. One symbolic and ceremonial food in Mexico is Mole Negro (Chile and Chocolate Sauce, page 298). In Guatemala, some of the dishes include Pinol de Marrano con Chatate (Toasted Dried Corn, Pork Rib, and Chaya Leaf Stew, page 206), Pinol de Conejo (Toasted Dried Corn, Roasted Tomato, Cilantro,

and Rabbit Stew, page 111), and Pulique de Pato con Tamalitos de Milpa (Duck and Vegetable Stew with Mini Tamales Steamed in Corn Leaves, page 278).

Día de los Muertos is a unique celebration of life-affirming qualities connected to death and is observed with great fervor, especially in Mexico and Guatemala. People take an active role in decorating graves, creating altars, and making popular traditional foods such as pan de muerto (festive sweet bread), moles, and tamales, including one of my favorites, Tamales Oaxaqueños (Oaxacan Mole Negro and Roast Pork Tamales, page 284) in Mexico, and Fiambre Rojo (Marinated Vegetables, Meats, Cold Cuts, Seafood, and Cheeses, page 188) in Guatemala.

Cuaresma and Semana Santa are the Lent and Holy Week celebrations especially big in Antigua, Guatemala. They are the most important religious celebration alongside Christmas in Latin and Mesoamerica. A regional Mexican favorite is Tortitas de Camarón (Shrimp Cakes with Ancho-Guajillo Sauce and Grilled Cactus, page 250). Other specialties include dried fish delights, Escabeche de Verduras (Marinated Vegetable Salad, page 171), and Súchiles (Fermented Spiced Fruit Brew, page 56) in Guatemala.

Noche Buena, or Christmas Eve, is more significant than Christmas Day because everyone awaits the birth of Jesus at midnight. **Las Posadas** (nightly processions that recreate the holy pilgrimage) precede these two important celebrations, and Mexican foods include aguinaldos (small colorful baskets with seasonal candies), dulces de colación (candy), tamales, and special drinks, like in Chapter 1, page 31. Family gathers for a special meal of ponche Navideño (aguardiente-spiked sugarcane fruit punch) in Mexico and Guatemala, Gallina Rellena (Roast Hen with Vegetable and Fruit Stuffing, page 281) in Nicaragua, and Tamales de Arroz y Pavo (Guatemalan Red Chile Sauce and Turkey Rice Tamales, page 265) in Guatemala, where children open presents following the special gathering.

Ferias are small or large fairs in honor of a patron saint. Large crowds gather to celebrate and eat local street foods.

These are some of the best places to appreciate food culture and traditions in a unique setting. In Mesoamerica, typical foods can include esquites in Mexico and Nicaragua, like Esquites Nicas (Nicaraguan Spicy Buttery Corn and Epazote Skillet, page 175), and many of the foods in Chapters 2, page 61, and 12, page 351.

Santo (saint), is the day of someone's birthday. This tradition developed when children used to be named after a Catholic saint's designated date on the calendar. While generally children may not be named after their saint today, the tradition of calling someone's birthday their Saint Day or santo is still alive. Children's santos are celebrated with elaborate piñatas (see opposite) and adults' santos with their favorite lunch or dinner, followed by a Pastel de Cumpleaños (Birthday Cake with Strawberry Compote and Vanilla Meringue, page 341).

Piñatas are important social gatherings associated with children's birthday celebrations (santos). In Guatemala, tradition dictates that children gather to play games and break a piñata or two filled with dulces (candies) or sometimes small toys before they sing "Feliz Cumpleaños" ("Happy Birthday"), blow out the candles, and eat cake or Pastel de Cumpleaños (Birthday Cake with Strawberry Compote and Vanilla Meringue, page 341), ice cream with barquillos (rolled wafers), small sandwiches, and other treats.

Bautizos are baptisms, which are big celebrations in Guatemala and some other parts of Mesoamerica. Family and friends gather at church for the christening and then for a big party that can involve a live band, an elaborate meal or buffet, a bar, and more at a country club, outdoor patio, finca (estate), or other special venues. This celebration also cements important responsibilities for the padrinos (godparents), who are carefully chosen for each child. Moles and grandma's stews are popular at these events in Mexico and Guatemala (see Chapter 3, page 91, and Chapter 9, page 253).

Quinceañeras are girls turning fifteen, and in Latin America, this is a very important day in the life of every girl, as it marks the rite of passage into womanhood. A Catholic mass initiates the celebration amongst godparents, family, and close friends, and it also involves a beautiful gown, a lavish meal that may include some of the quinceañera's favorite foods (sometimes following a formal protocol), live music, and other amenities. This festivity is quite elaborate in Mexico and Guatemala.

Mercados are some of the best places to observe culture and enjoy seasonal, native, and traditional foods. Eateries feature typical and popular street treats as well as antojitos típicos (traditional little cravings—see Chapter 2, page 61), guisos (stews) such as pozole (see Pozole Blanco, Spicy Braised Pork Shoulder with Hominy, Oregano, and Cabbage, page 124), and more in Mexico. Food stalls can be a feast for the eyes, as their displays are creatively presented to attract hungry customers.

Velorios are wakes, which can be very elaborate in Guatemala and other parts of Mesoamerica depending on a family's economic means. When wakes are held at home, visitors are served coffee, guaro (a liquor), and cigarettes while some play cards and others pray. Coffee and pozoles are popular in Oaxaca. At fancy funeral homes in Guatemala, wakes are held for several hours and overnight to allow for family who may live far away to say the last goodbye to a dead relative. During visiting hours, high-end funeral homes cater to the needs of the visitors and family members and pass appetizers, small soups and sandwiches, tamales, and hot tea and coffee throughout the entire stay at the home up to the time the body leaves for the cemetery.

Bendiciones are house christenings that usually involve blessing a brand-new home in Guatemala. These social gatherings bring family and close friends together to participate in a blessing tour of the house led by a priest. An elaborate meal often follows. Depending on location, celebratory foods can include Mayan stews (see Chapter 3, page 91, and Chapter 9, page 253) and pairings such as vegetable rice and tamalitos (small masa tamales) and desserts such as the special treats found in Chapter 11, page 319, and 12, page 351. In Oaxaca, tostadas are part of the menu. These foods can also be present in other celebrations throughout the year, including weddings, birthday parties, and even wakes and funerals.

Reuniones are casual weekend lunch or dinner gatherings to bring the family together. In my dad's large family, we often got together with his brothers and sisters and their families at someone's ranch or home. This gave us the opportunity to partake with our aunts and cousins regularly and enjoy a delicious Sunday lunch, which included carne asada, paella, or another special meal, such as the highly prized cocina de mamá o abuelita (mom's or grandma's cuisine). See Chapter 5, page 135, Chapter 7, page 193, Chapter 9, page 253, and Chapter 11, page 319, for other dishes.

Page 128: Repartición de Cofradías, Chichicastenango, El Quiché, Guatemala.
Page 130: Los Moros y la Danza del Torito, Feria San Pedro La Laguna, Sololá, Guatemala.
Pages 132–133: Mercado de Chichicastenango, El Quiché, Guatemala.

5

Arroces, Pastas y Papas
Rice, Pastas, and Potatoes

TONGUE PACIFIERS

I often refer to rice, pasta, and potatoes as tongue pacifiers because in Mesoamerican cooking, they provide a much-needed break in between spicy bites. Although not native to the Americas, rice and pasta are imports into our culture that came to pair well with our cuisine.

Rice is the perfect complement to our saucy guisos (stews), sopas y caldos (soups and broths), and a long list of legumes (beans, garbanzos, lentils, peas, and more). Rice gave birth to classic recipes in Mesoamerican and Latin culture such as beans and rice, arroz con pollo, and many of the rice and vegetable dishes found in this chapter, some of which were likely modeled after paella, which came to us via Spain.

From Rice, Beans, Legumes, Corn, Stock, and Herbs to Side Twists

Add cooked beans of any color or size, cooked garbanzos, lentils, or corn to any of the rice recipes in this chapter for complementary texture and nutrition.

Legumes and corn add fiber and protein, and when paired with rice, they make one whole protein.

Use vegetable stock instead of chicken stock to make these dishes vegan. They are naturally gluten free.

Increase the quantity of fresh herbs such as parsley, or add cilantro for a twist of flavor.

Pasta came to Mesoamerica through early Spanish settlers. An art form in itself, Mesoamericans have adapted pasta to their cooking styles, producing interestingly delicious hybrid versions of Latin, Italian, and Spanish classics. In Latin America, the Chinese have had some influence on the local cuisine as well; hybrid versions of chow mein, chop suey, and other popular Chinese dishes have been adapted to home cooking.

As in other cultures, pasta is also a comfort food in Mesoamerica, and we add it to soups as we would grains and legumes, although the result is not as nutritious. From the simple to the refined, we have managed to incorporate some of our classic sauces into a variety of recipes, such as Fideo con Pollo (Soupy Cumin, Tomato, and Chicken Vermicelli, page 148), Tallarines con Pitos y Crema (Spicy Tagliatelle with Pito Blossoms, White Beans, Jalapeño, and Latin Cream, page 151), Macarrones Verdes (Fire-Roasted Guaque Chile and Tomatillo Cream Sauce Macaroni, page 155), and more.

Potatoes (a large variety of them) are native to the Andean region and spread to the rest of the continent and the world from there. In Mesoamerica, a great variety of potatoes came to pair deliciously with indigenous soups and stews as well as with salads and other preparations, such as Papas a la Ranchera (Stewed Potatoes in Tomato and Guajillo Sauce, page 159), and many variations.

At some Guatemalan steak houses, Papas Asadas con Crema y Queso (Grilled Russet Potatoes with Chive Butter, Latin Cream, and Cotija Cheese, page 156) are a delightful side. In other instances, potatoes are used in Spanish preparations such as tortilla, an egg, onion, and potato skillet cake adapted to local tastes.

Undoubtedly, rice, pasta, and potatoes are today an inherent part of the Mesoamerican table, providing a much-needed break between spicy bites indeed.

Pasta Sides

In modern Mesoamerica, pasta is not usually the main meal but often a side dish. As such, pastas are very simple yet delicious.

Some contain onion, cream, and ham pieces, while others use quick homestyle tomato sauces.

In this chapter, I've created pastas that pair well with native flower blossoms, mild and spicy peppers, tomatillos, and crema.

ARROZ CON FLOR DE IZOTE

Izote Flower, Tomato, and Lime Rice

SERVES 4

1 cup long-grain white rice

1 tablespoon canola oil

3 ½ tablespoons finely chopped yellow onion

1 teaspoon minced garlic

½ cup julienned poblano pepper

¾ cup diced tomato

2 tablespoons fresh lime juice

2 cups frozen (or fresh, if available) whole izote flowers

¾ teaspoon kosher salt

Freshly ground black pepper

2 cups chicken or vegetable stock, store-bought or homemade (see page 198)

I grew up enjoying flor de izote straight from my grandmother's backyard. She poached it in water or vegetable broth along with tomatoes, onions, salt, and lime juice. Izote flowers, especially the bud or core, can be a bit bitter, but the petals are mild. Izote is native to Guatemala and the surrounding region and is quite popular in the cuisines of Guatemala and El Salvador (its national flower). Use them in a variety of preparations from rice dishes to stews to creamy sauces. They have a unique flavor and exotic look. I chose to mimic my grandmother's basic recipe and applied it to this rice dish along with poblano pepper for color contrast and complementary flavor. The end result is superb. It's a special dish to pair with anything spicy and saucy.

1. In a medium saucepan or skillet, sauté the rice in the oil for 1 minute over medium high heat. Add the onion and sauté for an additional 1 minute. Add the garlic and sauté for another 1 minute. Add the poblano pepper and sauté 1 minute more. Add the tomato, lime juice, izote flowers, salt, pepper to taste, and stock, and stir well. Bring to a quick boil over high heat, adjust the heat to medium low, and simmer, covered, until most of the liquid is absorbed, 15 to 20 minutes.

2. Fluff the rice and vegetables with a fork right before serving.

AMALIA'S NOTES

- Izote flowers are available frozen at Latin markets and online.

- I don't rinse packaged fortified rice because water washes away the added nutrients. Rinsing doesn't speed the process or do anything that cooking wouldn't do. This recipe makes delicious and fluffy rice in minutes. Rinse rice only if you are unsure of its source or its processing.

ARROZ CON CHIPILÍN

Chipilín Leaf and Red Bell Pepper Rice

SERVES 4

Chipilín is native to Mesoamerica and is very popular in the cuisines of Guatemala and El Salvador. The leaves of the plant are delicate, very flavorful, and aromatic. From tamales and soups to rice dishes, pupusas, and more, chipilín has been gaining popularity in the United States in the last few years. Add it to cream sauces containing mushrooms and serve it over pasta or pan-roasted chicken. Arroz con Chipilín pairs well with any of the stews, soups, and meat and chicken dishes in Chapters 3 (page 91), 7 (page 193), or 9 (page 253).

1 cup long-grain white rice
1 tablespoon canola oil
3 ½ tablespoons finely chopped yellow onion
1 teaspoon minced garlic
¾ cup julienned red bell pepper
1 ½ cups frozen (or fresh, if available) chipilín leaves, lightly chopped
¾ teaspoon kosher salt
Freshly ground black pepper
2 cups chicken or vegetable stock, store-bought or homemade (see page 198)

1. In a medium saucepan or skillet, sauté the rice in the oil for 1 minute over medium high heat. Add the onion and sauté for an additional 1 minute. Add the garlic and sauté for another 1 minute. Add the bell pepper and sauté 1 minute more, or sauté the bell pepper separately and use as a garnish (as in the picture). Finally add the chipilín, salt, pepper to taste, and stock, and stir well. Bring to a quick boil over high heat, adjust the heat to medium low, and simmer, covered, until most of the liquid is absorbed, 15 to 20 minutes.

2. Fluff the rice and vegetables with a fork right before serving.

RECIPE VARIATION

Arroz con Arvejas y Chile Pimiento (Rice with Baby Peas and Red Bell Pepper):
Follow the recipe given but substitute 1 cup frozen baby peas for the chipilín leaves. Add the peas near the end of the cooking time when the rice has absorbed most of the liquid so the peas don't shrivel. Then distribute them on top of the rice, turn off the heat, cover, and steam the peas with the residual heat for 5 minutes. Fluff the rice and vegetables with a fork right before serving.

AMALIA'S NOTE

• I don't rinse packaged fortified rice because water washes away the added nutrients. Rinsing doesn't speed the process or do anything that cooking wouldn't do. This recipe makes delicious and fluffy rice in minutes. Rinse rice only if you are unsure of its source or its processing.

ARROZ CON REMOLACHA
Beet and Vegetable Rice

SERVES 4

1 cup long-grain white rice
1 tablespoon canola oil
3 ½ tablespoons finely chopped
  yellow onion
1 teaspoon minced garlic
½ cup julienned red bell pepper
½ cup French-cut fresh
  green beans
1 ½ cups julienned fresh beets
¾ teaspoon kosher salt
Freshly ground black pepper
2 cups chicken or vegetable
  stock, store-bought or
  homemade (see page 198)

1 cup frozen baby peas

Beets and other vegetables alone or combined are a common addition to rice dishes in Guatemala. Vegetable rice is a traditional pairing with many dishes including soups, black beans, stews, chiles rellenos, and beyond. Carrots, tomatoes, black beans, red and green bell peppers, and peas are very common additions to rice. Beets add a unique flavor, aroma, and color to the dish. Serve this recipe warm or cold with saucy dishes, grilled meats, or roast chicken.

1 In a medium saucepan or skillet, sauté the rice in the oil for 1 minute over medium high heat. Add the onion and sauté for an additional 1 minute. Add the garlic and sauté for another 1 minute. Add the bell pepper and the green beans and sauté 1 minute more. Finally add the beets, salt, black pepper to taste, and stock, and stir well. Bring to a quick boil over high heat, adjust the heat to medium low, and simmer, covered, until most of the liquid is absorbed, 15 to 20 minutes.

2 Add the peas and distribute them on top of the rice, turn off the heat, cover, and steam the peas with the residual heat for 5 minutes. Fluff the rice and vegetables with a fork right before serving and serve immediately.

RECIPE VARIATIONS

Arroz con Verduras (Vegetable Rice): Follow the recipe given, except omit the beets and substitute with 1 cup julienned chayote squash, ½ cup julienned carrots, and ¼ cup diced tomato. Season with a pinch ground cloves plus salt and black pepper to taste.

Arroz con Tomate (Tomato Rice): Follow the recipe for Arroz con Remolacha, except omit the red bell pepper, green beans, and beets and add 2 cups chopped Roma tomatoes. Season with salt and black pepper to taste.

Arroz Verde (Green Rice): Follow the recipe for Arroz con Remolacha, except omit the red bell pepper and beets. Add 2 cups julienned green bell pepper and 1 cup chopped cilantro or parsley leaves. Season with salt and black pepper to taste.

AMALIA'S NOTE

- I don't rinse packaged fortified rice because water washes away the added nutrients. Rinsing doesn't speed the process or do anything that cooking wouldn't do. This recipe makes delicious and fluffy rice in minutes. Rinse rice only if you are unsure of its source or its processing.

ARROZ CON LOROCO

Aromatic Loroco Flower Bud and Carrot Rice

SERVES 4

Loroco is a delicacy of the Mesoamerican region. Popular in the cuisines of Guatemala and El Salvador, loroco buds or flowers are used whole, chopped, ground, or pureed in various preparations. Most commonly, loroco is used combined with cream sauces and in tamales, empanadas, and pupusas. My grandmother sometimes added it to her chicken and rice soup recipes. It has a delicious aroma and a unique flavor that pairs well with rice and other vegetables. The buds have a lively green color that sticks out in any dish you prepare with them. Pair Arroz con Loroco with any of the bean recipes in Chapter 3 (page 91).

1 cup long-grain white rice

1 teaspoon ground achiote

1 tablespoon canola oil

3 ½ tablespoons finely chopped yellow onion

1 teaspoon minced garlic

½ cup julienned carrots

1 ½ cups frozen (or fresh, if available) loroco flower buds, thawed and separated

¾ teaspoon kosher salt

Freshly ground black pepper

2 cups chicken or vegetable stock, store-bought or homemade (see page 198)

ADORNO (GARNISH)

Loroco flower buds or ½ cup chopped curly parsley

1. In a medium saucepan or skillet, sauté the rice and achiote in the oil for 1 minute over medium high heat. Add the onion and sauté an additional 1 minute. Add the garlic and sauté another 1 minute. Add the carrots and sauté 1 minute more. Finally, add the loroco, salt, black pepper to taste, and stock, and stir well. Bring to a quick boil over high heat, adjust the heat to medium low, and simmer, covered, until most of the liquid is absorbed, 15 to 20 minutes.

2. Fluff the rice and vegetables with a fork right before serving. Garnish with parsley.

RECIPE VARIATION

Arroz con Palmito (Rice with Hearts of Palm): Follow the recipe given, but substitute canned sliced or diced hearts of palm from 1 (14-ounce) can for the loroco.

AMALIA'S NOTE

- I don't rinse packaged fortified rice because water washes away the added nutrients. Rinsing doesn't speed the process or do anything that cooking wouldn't do. This recipe makes delicious and fluffy rice in minutes. Rinse rice only if you are unsure of its source or its processing.

ARROZ A LA MEXICANA
Mexican Tomato and Vegetable Rice

SERVES 4

1 cup long-grain white rice

1 tablespoon canola oil

½ cup finely chopped yellow onion

1 teaspoon minced garlic

½ cup julienned or shredded carrots

1 cup pureed Roma tomatoes

¾ teaspoon kosher salt

1 ¾ cups chicken or vegetable stock, store-bought or homemade (see page 198)

1 cup frozen baby peas

I am naturally fond of Mexican cuisine because so many staple ingredients are shared with Guatemalan and Mesoamerican cuisines. Guatemalan vegetable rice is similar to this recipe, yet it is noticeably different in looks and flavor, with spices in addition to vegetables. The combination of ingredients can make a difference in achieving authentic results. Dicing vegetables versus pureeing them can alter the flavor and looks of any dish, and that could be the difference between one dish and a very similar one. I love this rice because it's fuss free, the ingredients are readily available, and it goes well with saucy or bean dishes. It's home comfort food.

1 In a medium saucepan or skillet, sauté the rice in the oil for 1 minute over medium high heat. Add the onion and sauté for an additional 1 minute. Add the garlic and sauté for another 1 minute. Add the carrots and sauté for 1 minute more. Finally, add the tomato puree, salt, and stock, and stir well. Bring to a quick boil over high heat, adjust the heat to medium low, and simmer, covered, until most of the liquid is absorbed, 15 to 20 minutes.

2 Add the peas and distribute them on top of the rice, turn off the heat, cover, and steam the peas with the residual heat for 5 minutes. Fluff the rice and vegetables with a fork right before serving.

RECIPE VARIATIONS

Arroz Anaranjado (Orange Rice): Follow the Arroz a la Mexicana recipe, adding ½ cup cooked sliced chorizo sausage after the garlic. Garnish with chopped parsley and avocado slices.

Arroz Verde (Green Rice): Follow the Arroz a la Mexicana recipe, but omit the carrots and substitute pureed roasted poblanos for the tomato. Add ½ cup chopped flat-leaf parsley after the garlic. Garnish with avocado slices and more parsley leaves.

Arroz Guatemalteco (Guatemalan Vegetable Rice): Follow the Arroz a la Mexicana recipe, but omit the tomato puree, add ½ cup julienned red bell pepper, ½ cup diced Roma tomatoes after the garlic, 1 pinch ground cloves, and freshly ground black pepper to taste, and increase the chicken stock to 2 cups.

AMALIA'S NOTE

- I don't rinse packaged fortified rice because water washes away the added nutrients. Rinsing doesn't speed the process or do anything that cooking wouldn't do. This recipe makes delicious and fluffy rice in minutes. Rinse rice only if you are unsure of its source or its processing.

FIDEO CON POLLO
Soupy Cumin, Tomato, and Chicken Vermicelli

SERVES 2 to 4

This has been one of my favorite Mexican dishes because it is easy to make as well as delicious and comforting. Homestyle fideo is traditionally made either soupy or less saucy and with just a few vegetables, noodles, and chicken consommé powder. It can be a side or become the main meal by adding shredded chicken and more diced vegetables and even avocado chunks. This is my soupy version using mostly fresh ingredients that elevate the soup to a new level. Traditionally it's not spicy, but I am fond of all things spicy.

1. In a medium saucepan, cook the chicken thighs in the stock over medium low heat, covered, for 20 minutes. Remove the thighs from the stock and dice or shred them. Set the chicken aside. Reserve the stock.

2. In a wide yet deep skillet, sauté the vermicelli in the canola oil over medium high heat until medium brown, stirring constantly, about 2 to 3 minutes. Set aside.

3. In a blender, puree the onion, garlic, tomato puree, cumin, achiote, salt, black pepper to taste, and cilantro. Add the puree to the skillet with the vermicelli and sauté over medium heat for 2 minutes.

4. Add the chicken and broth to the skillet and stir well to combine. Cover and simmer over low heat until the vermicelli is tender, about 5 minutes.

5. Add the lime juice, stir well, and ladle the soup into individual bowls. Garnish with the indicated toppings as desired.

AMALIA'S NOTES

- The quickest way to steam peas while still frozen is to put them in a medium mesh colander over a medium pot of boiling water for 3 to 5 minutes, shaking the colander once during this process to allow for even steaming.

- Pasta will continue to absorb liquid if it's not all consumed in one sitting. Adjust any leftovers by adding more chicken stock. Add less or more stock according to taste.

- Increase the amount of cooked chicken or add cooked turkey if you want to increase the protein-to-pasta ratio. Then increase the liquid and seasonings as needed.

2 boneless, skinless chicken thighs
3 cups chicken stock, hot, store-bought or homemade (see page 198)

1 cup fideo (vermicelli or spaghetti) pasta, broken into 1-inch pieces
1 teaspoon canola oil

¾ cup finely chopped onion
2 teaspoons minced garlic
1 cup fresh tomato puree
½ teaspoon ground cumin
½ teaspoon ground achiote
½ teaspoon kosher salt
Freshly ground black pepper
2 tablespoons chopped cilantro

1 tablespoon freshly squeezed lime juice

ADORNO (GARNISH)

½ cup diced carrots, cooked al dente
½ cup frozen baby peas, steamed
Avocado slices
Thinly sliced serrano chile (optional)
Cilantro, in sprigs or chopped

TALLARINES CON PITOS Y CREMA

Spicy Tagliatelle with Pito Blossoms, White Beans, Jalapeño, and Latin Cream

SERVES 2

1 tablespoon butter

¾ cup diced yellow onion

1 tablespoon minced garlic

¼ cup diced Roma tomatoes

1 cup fresh or thawed frozen
pito blossoms

¾ cup julienned red bell pepper

1 thinly sliced jalapeño,
including seeds and veins,
or 1 tablespoon sliced
pickled jalapeños

2 store-bought corn tortillas,
torn into 2-inch pieces,
soaked in 1 cup hot chicken
stock, store-bought or
homemade (see page 198)

½ cup unsalted crema or
Mexican table cream

1 teaspoon kosher salt

Freshly ground white pepper

1 (15-ounce) can white
beans, drained

1 ½–2 cups cooked tagliatelle
pasta, al dente (see note)

ADORNO (GARNISH)

Cotija cheese, crumbled
Cilantro leaves, chopped
Jalapeño slices (optional)

The pito plant is native to Mesoamerica and some parts of South America. In Guatemalan and Salvadoran cooking, pito flowers are added to beans, soups, and stews. Pito means "whistle," and the elongated shape of the flower supported by a firm stem resembles a long pink or orange whistle. It also resembles a tiny machete in its sheath. Both flower and stem are edible, hold up well in cooking, and resemble green beans in texture and perhaps flavor. They are available frozen, and if using fresh pitos, you can steam them and serve atop salads or as a garnish for colorless dishes. White beans combine beautifully with this creamy pasta, adding yet another layer of flavor, texture, and even more nutrition. Use vegetable broth to make it a vegetarian dish, but you can also add cooked chicken or turkey for another outstanding combination.

1. Add the butter to a nonstick medium skillet and sauté the onions, garlic, tomatoes, and pito blossoms over medium high heat for 2 minutes. Add the bell pepper and jalapeño, reduce the heat to medium low, cover, and cook until the pito buds are tender, 4 to 5 minutes.

2. In a blender, puree the soaked tortillas and stock. Add the puree to the vegetable mixture. Add the crema to the skillet and stir well to blend the flavors, season with salt and white pepper to taste, and continue cooking until slightly thickened, about 2 minutes.

3. Add the beans and tagliatelle and stir well to combine. Garnish with Cotija, cilantro, and jalapeño slices, if using.

AMALIA'S NOTE

- Cook pasta in salted water. Use about ½ teaspoon kosher salt per 4 cups of water. Keep in mind other ingredients already contain salt in this recipe, such as the sauce, canned beans, and cheese.

CORBATAS EN ESCABECHE CON JAMÓN SERRANO
Serrano Ham, Garbanzo, and Vegetable Bow-Tie Pasta Salad

SERVES 4 to 6

I like easy, delicious, and lively foods. This recipe is all that and more. Escabeches come in many styles and forms on the Mesoamerican and Latin table. Escabeche is a technique and preparation method that can be adapted to many foods, hot or cold, including pasta. It came to Meso- and Latin America through Spain. This festive pasta salad is a hit at any gathering because it goes well with picnic menus, casual foods, or formal dinners. It can be presented in any style, from appetizer to side to main meal. Make it your own by adding other ingredients of choice.

1. In a large bowl, combine the pasta, ¼ cup julienned red onion, bell pepper, hearts of palm, green beans, garbanzos, carrots, celery, baby onions, olives, capers, jamón, and parsley. Set aside.

2. To make the sauce, add the oil to a medium skillet over medium low heat. Gently cook the ½ cup sliced red onion, garlic, bay leaves, thyme, salt, and black pepper to taste, until onion is translucent, 4 to 5 minutes. Turn the heat off and add the vinegar. Let the mixture cool to room temperature.

3. Add the sauce to the bowl with the pasta and vegetables. With a soft spatula, gently turn the ingredients with folding strokes to coat well with the sauce. Then repeat this procedure from time to time to allow for even marinating. Allow the ingredients to marinate in the refrigerator for 30 minutes or longer.

4. Serve in a bowl or on a platter lined with green leaf lettuce.

AMALIA'S NOTES

- Cook pasta in salted water. Use about ½ teaspoon kosher salt per 4 cups of water. Keep in mind that salt is already contained in other ingredients in this recipe, such as canned garbanzos, baby onions, olives, capers, jamón serrano, and the sauce.

- Cold dishes taste less salty when just out of the refrigerator. The pasta will continue to absorb flavors while it sits in the sauce. Add additional salt and vinegar according to taste.

- To make this the main dish, increase the number of legumes and add cooked chicken in addition to serrano ham.

- To make this dish vegetarian, leave out the jamón serrano and increase the legumes.

---

1 ½ cups cooked bow-tie pasta, al dente (see note)
¼ cup thinly julienned red onion
¼ cup 2-inch strips roasted red bell pepper
¼ cup thinly sliced palmito (heart of palm)
¼ cup French-cut green beans, cooked al dente
½ cup fresh or canned garbanzos
¼ cup thinly sliced carrots
¼ cup thinly sliced celery
¼ cup quartered pickled baby onions
¼ cup sliced Spanish olives stuffed with pimentos
1 ½ tablespoons Spanish capers
1 cup 2-inch strips jamón serrano (serrano ham)
½ cup roughly chopped curly parsley leaves

ESCABECHE (SAUCE)

¼ cup extra-virgin olive oil
½ cup thinly sliced red onion
1 tablespoon minced garlic
2 dried bay leaves
½ teaspoon dried thyme
¾ teaspoon kosher salt
Freshly ground black pepper
2 tablespoons champagne or white wine vinegar

Leaf lettuce to line the bowl or platter

MACARRONES VERDES
Fire-Roasted Guaque Chile and Tomatillo Cream Sauce Macaroni

SERVES 2

2 fresh guaque or poblano
chiles

1 medium tomatillo, husked

¼ cup sliced green onions

2 teaspoons minced garlic

¼ cup whole cilantro leaves
and stems

¼ cup whole parsley leaves
and stems

½ cup chicken stock,
store-bought or homemade
(see page 198)

1 tablespoon butter

1 fresh or dried bay leaf

⅛ teaspoon fresh or
dried thyme

½ teaspoon kosher salt

Freshly ground white pepper

¼ cup unsalted crema or
Mexican table cream

1½–2 cups cooked macaroni
pasta, al dente

ADORNO (GARNISH)

Unsalted crema or Mexican
table cream

Cotija cheese

Chopped cilantro and
parsley leaves

In Guatemala, fresh guaque is used for chiles rellenos or roasted in salads and can be medium hot. Poblano, commonly used in Mexican cuisine, can be used as a suitable substitute for this recipe; it is different in flavor profile but similar in texture. Interestingly, when dried, fresh guaque chile retains its original name, unlike poblano, which is called ancho when dried. Both dried guaque and ancho are widely used in moles, stews, soups, sauces, rubs, and other preparations in the cuisines of both Guatemala and Mexico. If you are lucky enough to find fresh guaques in the United States, you're in for a treat. Poblano is an equally delicious chile pepper in any style. For the sauce for this recipe, you could use a combination of fresh and dried guaque (or guajillo) (or Poblano and ancho) for a unique twist. This dish could be a side as is, or add cooked chopped chicken or pork for a heartier main dish.

1. Fire roast the chiles and tomatillo until charred all over and the peels can be easily removed, about 5 minutes. Peel the peppers with the help of damp paper towels. Do not rinse them. Remove the seeds and veins.

2. In a blender, puree the roasted chiles, tomatillo, green onions, garlic, cilantro, and parsley with the stock.

3. Add the butter to a skillet over medium low heat and pour in the green puree. Add the bay leaf, thyme, salt, and white pepper to taste. Simmer until bubbly, about 5 minutes.

4. Add the crema and stir to blend. Continue cooking until slightly thickened, about 2 minutes. Add the macaroni and stir well.

5. Garnish with crema, cheese, and chopped cilantro and parsley. Serve immediately.

AMALIA'S NOTE

- Cook pasta in salted water. Use about ½ teaspoon salt per 4 cups of water. Keep in mind that salt is already contained in other ingredients in this recipe, such as the sauce and cheese.

PAPAS ASADAS CON CREMA Y QUESO

Grilled Russet Potatoes with Chive Butter, Latin Cream, and Cotija Cheese

SERVES 2 to 4

In some of my favorite steak houses in Guatemala City, they serve a similar version of these potatoes. I like them so much because they are delicious, look good on the plate, and are super easy to make. I like all kinds of potatoes but prefer russet for this recipe because they are quite large, so you only need half of one per person. You can also use fingerlings, Yukon Gold, and other potatoes. All of them are delicious. Pair this dish with grilled meats, chicken, or seafood and a green salad.

1. In a medium bowl, combine the butter, lemon juice, and chives with a fork or whisk.

2. Slice the potatoes in half lengthwise. Brush with some oil and lay flat side down on a medium-hot nonstick griddle until light brown and a bit crispy, 3 to 5 minutes.

3. Transfer the potatoes to a platter or individual plates and dress them equally with the chive butter, crema, and Cotija cheese. Top with the parsley.

AMALIA'S NOTES

- Cook the potatoes al dente in salted water. Use about ¼ teaspoon salt per cup of water.

- To make the potatoes more stable on the plate, before slicing them in half, shave a strip off both sides of each potato to make them sit flat.

- For a plated dinner party, cook the potatoes ahead, grill them as needed, and dress them on each plate right before passing them to the table.

MANTEQUILLA DE CEBOLLÍN (CHIVE BUTTER)

4 tablespoons butter, at room temperature
2 teaspoons freshly squeezed lemon juice
2 teaspoons ⅛-inch-chopped chives

2 cooked unpeeled russet potatoes (see note)
Canola oil

¼ cup crema agria (Mexican, Guatemalan, Honduran, or Salvadoran sour cream)
4 teaspoons crumbled Cotija cheese
½ cup lightly chopped curly parsley

PAPAS A LA RANCHERA

Stewed Potatoes in Tomato and Guajillo Sauce

SERVES 2 to 4

1 guajillo chile, seeded,
  deveined

4 medium Yukon Gold
  potatoes, unpeeled, sliced
  ½ inch thick, cooked al dente

SALSA RANCHERA
(SAUCE)

1 tablespoon extra-virgin
  olive oil
½ cup diced yellow onion
1 teaspoon minced garlic
½ cup diced green bell peppers
1 ½ tablespoons minced
  pickled jalapeños
1 cup diced Roma tomatoes
¼ teaspoon dried thyme
½ teaspoon kosher salt
Freshly ground black pepper
¾ cup chicken stock,
  store-bought or homemade
  (see page 198)

2 tablespoons torn flat-leaf
  parsley leaves

Potatoes are delightful in this slightly spicy sauce. Ranchera sauce is used in Mexican and Guatemalan cooking to top sunny-side-up eggs and other dishes. It takes a few minutes to make and dresses dishes deliciously. While this recipe is traditionally made with corn or vegetable oil, olive oil enhances taste and texture and helps the sauce cling to the potatoes. Guajillo adds a scrumptious kick and color. For a twist in flavor, add cooked chorizo or other vegetables of choice. Serve with your favorite steak, grilled meats, or scrambled eggs.

1. Soak the guajillo in 1 cup hot water for 10 minutes. Puree the soaked guajillo and half of its soaking water with an immersion or small blender until smooth.

2. Add the oil to a skillet over medium heat and cook the onion, garlic, bell peppers, jalapeños, Roma tomatoes, guajillo puree, thyme, salt, black pepper to taste, and chicken stock, until the sauce is medium thick yet still chunky, about 6 to 8 minutes.

3. Add the potatoes to the skillet with the sauce and gently combine them with a soft heat-resistant spatula. Cook for 5 minutes just to reheat the potatoes, stirring carefully from time to time, being careful not to break the potatoes. Garnish with parsley.

AMALIA'S NOTES

- The potatoes will continue to absorb flavors while they sit in the sauce. Add additional salt according to taste.

- You can use other kinds of potatoes, such as fingerling or russet.

PAPAS A LA CREMA

Creamy Red Potatoes with Onion, Red Bell Peppers, Lime, and Parsley

SERVES 2

Papas a la crema is inspired by a dish my sister regularly makes for her family in Guatemala City. It's simple, it's tasty, and it takes minutes to make. When you are in a hurry to come up with a side, boil some potatoes, dice a few ingredients, and you have an awesome complement. It's that easy. Make it with a variety of potatoes or just one kind. Build it further with ingredients of choice. Pair it with seafood or meat and chicken dishes in Chapters 8 and 9, pages 223 and 253.

4 cooked red potatoes, unpeeled, in ¼-inch-thick slices

2 ½ tablespoons diced yellow onion or thinly sliced green onions

2 tablespoons red bell pepper finely diced, plus more for garnish

2 tablespoons chopped curly parsley, plus more for garnish

2 tablespoons crema agria (Mexican, Guatemalan, Honduran, or Salvadoran sour cream)

2 teaspoons freshly squeezed lime juice

½ teaspoon kosher salt

Freshly ground white pepper

1. Combine the onions, bell pepper, parsley, crema, lime juice, salt, and white pepper to taste in a medium bowl and stir well to blend the flavors.

2. Add the potatoes to the creamy mixture and gently mix them well. Allow the flavors to blend at least 30 minutes in the refrigerator before serving.

3. Garnish with the bell peppers, green onions, and parsley.

AMALIA'S NOTES

- Slice potatoes prior to cooking. This shortens the cooking time. For this recipe, cook them in lightly salted water for about 8 to 12 minutes.

- Cold dishes taste less salty when just out of the refrigerator. The potatoes will continue to absorb flavors while they sit in the sauce. Add additional salt and lime juice according to taste.

- You can also use three cooked, cubed, unpeeled Yukon Gold potatoes in this recipe.

- The longer the potatoes sit in the sauce, the more intense the flavors will be.

ADORNO (GARNISH)

¼ cup finely diced red bell peppers

1 teaspoon sliced green onions

1 sprig curly parsley

6

Ensaladas y Verduras
Salads and Vegetables

LA HUERTA

La huerta is the place where vegetables, greens, and herbs grow. Huertas are occasionally in people's backyards, especially in the Mesoamerican countryside. Favorable weather and economics contribute to this. It is less expensive and more convenient to have fresh ingredients readily available at home.

Although I am not a vegan or vegetarian, I am a big fan of vegetables and greens and often plan my menus around them. I crave salads and foods with lots of vegetables because I grew up enjoying high-quality fresh foods in Guatemala. In the Mesoamerican kitchen, this is easy to do. There are countless ways to integrate vegetables into delicious preparations.

Although there are many choices, I have chosen to concentrate my time and effort on the most popular vegetables in the region, many of which are also some of my favorites. Most are readily available in the United States at major grocery chains or online.

Here I highlight recipes I have enjoyed while living in my homeland and traveling throughout Mesoamerica that are simple, quick to prepare, and scrumptious. Vegetables are the stars of the Latin kitchen overall, but in this area, they are taken to a new level in preparation and use.

In the Mesoamerican kitchen, it is so easy to add flavor to vegetables or greens with just a few ingredients, many of which are likely already in your refrigerator or pantry. Lime, lemon, orange, tangerine, naranja agria (sour orange), vinegar, chiles, spicy sauces, ground pepita de ayote (pumpkin seeds), oregano, cumin, thyme, bay leaf, cilantro, culantro, parsley, epazote, and mint are some of my favorite go-to seasonings.

Vegetables and fruits that appear repeatedly in recipes in the Mesoamerican kitchen (many of which are native) are corn, beans, squash, tomatoes, tomatillos, peppers, avocados, yuca, chipilín, loroco, izote, and pito. With such a wide array of fresh foods available in the region, it is not coincidence but rather kitchen ingenuity that contributes to creating tasty dishes.

The recipes in this chapter are not only practical, healthy, nutritious, and delicious, but also they pair well with many of the recipes found throughout this book. They are gluten free, and many are naturally vegan and vegetarian. With an abundance of fresh fruits and vegetables, it is easier to make substitutions and adapt a dish to any eating style or special diet. Using pureed vegetables, corn tortillas, rice, or cornstarch or root-based starches, such as yuca, it can be more flavorful and more nutritious than using all-purpose flour for thickening soups and sauces, and just as effective.

I invite you to partake in a fresh adventure with la huerta in mind and discover a fresh bounty and new ways to add Mesoamerican zest to your table. With natural great taste, there's little you need to do to enhance high-quality seasonal favorites.

ENSALADA DE CHILES A LA LLAMA
Fire-Roasted Bell Pepper Salad with Garlic and Oregano Vinaigrette

SERVES 4 to 6

4 bell peppers (red, yellow, orange, and green)
3 whole medium yellow onions, skins on

VINAGRETA DE AJO Y ORÉGANO (GARLIC AND OREGANO VINAIGRETTE)

1 tablespoon fresh garlic puree or minced garlic
¾ teaspoon crumbled dried oregano
2 ½ tablespoons red wine vinegar
2 tablespoons extra-virgin olive oil
¾ teaspoon kosher salt
Freshly ground black pepper

¼ cup hand-torn flat-leaf parsley

If you like fire-roasted fresh peppers of any kind, you'll love this salad. The first time I had this salad was some time ago at a Guatemalan restaurant known for having delicious dishes to pair with grilled meats. I never forgot the flavor experience and kept it in my head to make it mine at home, and I enhanced it with fire-roasted onions and parsley. I am fond of peppers in any style, and this combination of roasted peppers and onions with the garlic-oregano vinaigrette is the bomb. It's simple and delicious. *Llama* means flame, and it's amazing the flavor depth fresh ingredients can acquire when charred. Serve this salad with grilled meat or build it into another dish by combining with cold cooked rice or pasta.

1. Fire roast the bell peppers on a gas stovetop with the flame on high until charred all over to loosen the skins. Use one or two 13-inch wire splatter guards set over the stovetop and put aluminum foil around the burners to catch the burnt pieces and any juices. This process may take 20 to 30 minutes. Allow them to cool slightly. Peel, seed, and devein the peppers but do not rinse them. Cut them into strips and place in a large bowl.

2. Simultaneously fire roast the onions in the same manner as the peppers, turning them with tongs to char them evenly. The onions are ready when they start steaming and juice starts oozing from the sides. The onions should be visibly translucent when you peel one or two layers. Remove the charred layers and trim on both ends. Cut the onions into eighths and add them to the large bowl with the pepper strips. Combine gently with a soft spatula and set aside.

3. To make the vinaigrette, add the garlic, oregano, vinegar, olive oil, salt, and black pepper to taste to a small bowl and whisk well to blend the flavors. Add it to the peppers and onions and gently fold the vinaigrette into the mixture with the spatula.

4. Serve immediately garnished with parsley, or hold the parsley and refrigerate until ready to use. Add the parsley right before serving. If refrigerating, repeat the folding procedure a few times prior to serving it to marinate the ingredients evenly.

RECIPE VARIATION

Chiles a la Llama y Palmitos a la Vinagreta (Fire-Roasted Bell Peppers and Hearts of Palm with Garlic and Oregano Vinaigrette): Follow the recipe given, except add, during step 3, 1 cup sliced, fresh cooked or canned hearts of palm from 1 (14-ounce) can. Hearts of palm (fresh or canned) are delicate, so either add them just cooked, or char them lightly in a similar fashion as the peppers and onions, but for less time, about 2 minutes per side. To compensate for adding another ingredient, add more oregano, salt, and/or vinegar to taste, as necessary.

AMALIA'S NOTES

• If you don't have a gas stove, you may alternatively char the peppers and onions on the grill. Follow the instructions above, but keep in mind that the timing will depend on the heat intensity of your grill.

• I recommend peeling the peppers and onions at the sink, where you can get rid of all the charred pieces. After peeling, use damp paper towels to wipe the remaining burnt bits from the peppers and onions.

• Cold salads tend to taste less salty when just out of the refrigerator. Also, the peppers will absorb the flavors around them the longer they sit in the sauce. Add more oregano, salt, and/or vinegar to taste, as necessary.

GUISO DE CHILOTES CON PIPIÁN
Baby Corn and Chayote Squash Stew

SERVES 4 to 6

Corn and squash are two ingredients that are delicious by themselves and together. Baby corn is known as chilote, shilote, and jilote in Mesoamerica; and chayote squash is known as güisquil and pipián. In this recipe, I combine two of my favorite Nicaraguan stews, guiso de chilote and guiso de pipián, which are made in a similar way. This stew is simple, delicious, and easy to make. Fresh baby corn is widely available in Nicaragua and Costa Rica and served as an appetizer, in soups, and in other preparations. This stew can be turned into a one-dish meal by adding cooked chicken.

1. Add the butter to a medium skillet and melt over medium low heat for 1 minute. Add the onion and cook until translucent, 2 to 3 minutes. Add the chiltomas and ⅔ cup tomatoes and cook for 2 minutes. Add the stock and stir well. Add the squash, baby corn, and salt, then cover and simmer for 4 minutes.

2. In a blender, combine the tortillas and milk and process to a creamy consistency, about 3 to 4 minutes.

3. Add the milk mixture to the vegetables, mix thoroughly, and cook 2 minutes to thicken. Add the crema, stir to blend thoroughly, and cook 1 additional minute.

4. Sauté the ½ cup vine-ripened tomatoes in the canola oil over medium high heat, stirring gently with a soft spatula for 2 minutes.

5. Garnish the stew with the sautéed tomatoes and serve immediately.

RECIPE VARIATION

Guiso de Chilote (Costa Rican Fresh Baby Corn Stew): In a medium skillet over medium high heat, sauté ⅔ cup small-diced yellow onion in 1 tablespoon butter for 2 minutes. Add 12 (1-inch-sliced) chilotes (baby corn) and cook for 2 minutes. Gradually add 1 tablespoon instant corn masa flour combined with ⅓ cup skim milk and ¼ teaspoon ground achiote, ½ teaspoon sugar, ¾ to 1 teaspoon kosher salt, and freshly ground white pepper to taste. Stir well, cook for 3 to 4 minutes, then serve immediately.

AMALIA'S NOTES

- Although fresh is always best, young baby corn also comes in cans and jars in a mild brine.

- Chayote squash is available at Latin markets and many major grocery stores.

- When reheating leftovers, add a little stock or water to bring back the creamy consistency of the sauce.

1 ½ tablespoons butter

⅔ cup small-diced yellow onion

¼ cup diced green chiltoma or green bell pepper

¼ cup diced red chiltoma or red bell pepper

⅔ cup small-diced vine-ripened tomatoes

¾ cup vegetable or chicken stock, store-bought or homemade (see page 198)

1 large pipián (chayote squash), peeled and sliced or diced

12 chilotes (fresh baby corn) or 1 (15-ounce) can baby corn, rinsed, in 1-inch slices

1 ¼ teaspoons kosher salt

2 store-bought corn tortillas, torn by hand

¼ cup skim milk

2 tablespoons unsalted crema or Mexican table cream

ADORNO (GARNISH)

½ cup seeded and very small-diced vine-ripened tomatoes

1 teaspoon canola oil

ESCABECHE DE VERDURAS
Marinated Vegetable Salad

SERVES 4 to 6

1 cup ¼-inch-sliced carrots

1 cup ¼-inch-sliced cauliflower
  florets

1 cup ¼-inch-sliced chayote
  squash

1 cup fresh French-cut
  green beans

1 cup julienned red bell pepper

1 cup frozen baby peas

ESCABECHE (SAUCE)

1 tablespoon extra-virgin
  olive oil

¾ cup thinly julienned
  red onion

1 teaspoon minced garlic

1 dried bay leaf

¼ teaspoon dried thyme

1 teaspoon kosher salt

Freshly ground black pepper

¼ cup champagne or
  white wine vinegar

1 ½ cups water

ADORNO (GARNISH)

Leafy greens

1 fresh or dried bay leaf

1 fresh thyme sprig

A simple yet refreshing way of preparing vegetables with a Mesoamerican flair, this salad is present at homes, restaurants, and parties and is served as a side with roast chicken or pork or with grilled seafood in the coastal areas of El Salvador and Guatemala. There are versions of this recipe in Mexico and a simpler version of escabeche made with jalapeños, carrots, and onions served as a delicious topping at eateries. Escabeche de verduras is colorful and tasty and can be prepared with a variety of vegetables or just a few. This combination is my favorite because the vegetables dress a plate nicely and hold up well during cooking and marinating. The key is to undercook them so they retain a nice crunch. Sometimes I slice just a few vegetables thinly and marinate them raw without the oil, turning the salad into a curtido (pickled vegetables).

1. In a medium saucepan, bring 2 cups of water to a quick boil over medium high heat. Insert a steamer basket in the pan and separately steam al dente each of the vegetables, except the red bell pepper, as follows. Steam uncovered, stirring gently from time to time: the carrots for 4 minutes, the cauliflower for 3 minutes, the chayote squash for 2 minutes, the green beans for 3 to 4 minutes, and the peas for 1 ½ minutes. Combine all the steamed vegetables in a mixing bowl and let them cool. Add the red bell pepper.

2. To make the sauce, add the oil to a medium skillet over medium low heat. Gently cook the red onion, garlic, bay leaf, thyme, salt, and black pepper to taste, until the onion is translucent, 4 to 5 minutes. Turn off the heat and add the vinegar and water. Let the mixture cool to room temperature.

3. Add the sauce to the bowl with the vegetables. Fold gently with a soft spatula to coat completely. Then repeat this procedure from time to time to allow for even marinating. Cover and marinate in the refrigerator for several hours.

4. When ready to serve, either serve the vegetables in the marinade or drain them and let them sit in a colander until completely dry. Then transfer them to an attractive bowl lined with leafy greens, a bay leaf, and a thyme sprig.

RECIPE VARIATION

Escabeche (Salvadoran Marinated Vegetable Salad): Follow the recipe given, except omit the red bell pepper and add 1 cup shredded cabbage. To the sauce, add 2 teaspoons mustard and ½ teaspoon sugar (or to taste). Add salt and black pepper to taste.

AMALIA'S NOTES

• While steaming the vegetables, add more water by the cup to the steaming saucepan to compensate for evaporation.

• The longer the vegetables sit in the marinade, the deeper the flavor will be. For best results, marinate the vegetables overnight.

• When cold, these vegetables tend to taste less salty or vinegary. Add more salt (or vinegar) to taste, if desired.

ENSALADA DE MANZANA Y PAPA

Apple, Grape, Celery, and Roasted Bell Pepper Potato Salad

SERVES 4 to 6

This simple and delicious salad brings back memories from dinner parties during the holidays at my sister's home in Guatemala City. The festive salad goes well with roast turkey, fresh ham, or any roast. A word of caution: this scrumptious creamy delight could become your go-to side for barbecues and picnics. Make it with all the ingredients in this recipe, with just a few, or add other ingredients of choice.

1. In a wide bowl, combine the apples, potatoes, grapes, celery, bell peppers, onions, 2 tablespoons chopped parsley, and ham, if using.

2. In a small bowl, mix the vinegar with the mayonnaise, egg yolks, salt, and white pepper to taste, and mash well with a fork to make a smooth and homogenous mixture.

3. Add the mayonnaise to the fruits and vegetables and blend with a soft spatula to coat them thoroughly. Refrigerate for 1 hour or longer.

4. Garnish with the parsley leaves or chives, 2 grapes, roasted bell pepper bits, and sliced egg and serve.

AMALIA'S NOTES

- This salad can include mini marshmallows. If you are a fan, add them.

- Refrigerated foods may taste less salty than room-temperature foods. Before serving, taste and add more salt, if desired.

- Add more mayonnaise if you like your salad creamier, and add additional vinegar if you like it more tart.

1 ¼ cups peeled diced tart or sweet crisp red apples of choice
1 ¼ cups diced Yukon Gold potatoes, peeled, cooked al dente
¾–1 cup red or green grapes, halved lengthwise
½ cup minced celery
½ cup diced roasted red bell peppers
¼ cup thinly sliced green onions or shaved red onions
2 tablespoons roughly chopped curly or flat-leaf parsley
¼–½ cup diced boiled ham (optional)

3 tablespoons white wine vinegar
¼ cup olive-oil mayonnaise
2 hard-boiled large egg yolks, passed through a colander
½ teaspoon kosher salt
Freshly ground white pepper

ADORNO (GARNISH)

2 tablespoons curly or flat-leaf parsley leaves or chives
2 whole grapes
1 tablespoon roasted red bell pepper bits or strips
1 hard-boiled egg, sliced

ESQUITES NICAS

Nicaraguan Spicy Buttery Corn and Epazote Skillet

SERVES 2

1 ½ cups fresh corn kernels
  (from about 2 ears of corn)
1 tablespoon butter
1 teaspoon freshly squeezed
  lime juice
1 tablespoon chopped epazote
¼ teaspoon kosher salt
¼ teaspoon Congo chile
  powder, piquín chile powder,
  or Cobán chile powder
Freshly ground black pepper

ADORNO (GARNISH)

Epazote leaves, sliced or
  chopped
Chile powder

Esquites—izquitl in Nahuatl—is a fresh-corn-based dish made in varying styles. The food is popular in Mexico City and elsewhere in Mexico during street fairs and community celebrations, where it is traditionally served in a portable cup. The dish originated in Mexico and quite possibly traveled in some form to Nicaragua with the Nahuatl-speaking cultures that inhabited the west side of the country prior to Spanish colonization, so esquites is also popular in Nicaragua. Corn snacks, whether in kernels or on the cob, are also present in other Mesoamerican countries with distinctive touches and presentations. Esquites can be an appetizer, snack, side, or salad. Adapt esquites to your menu or gathering and serve it warm, at room temperature, or cold.

1. In a medium skillet, pan fry the corn in the butter over medium low heat until the corn is tender, 4 to 5 minutes.

2. Add the lime juice, epazote, salt, chile powder, and black pepper to taste. Mix well, and cook for 2 minutes.

3. Garnish with sliced or chopped epazote leaves and a sprinkle of chile powder. Serve it as a snack on fresh corn leaves or as a side.

RECIPE VARIATIONS AND OTHER CORN RECIPES USING SIMILAR PREPARATION

Esquites (Mexican Corn Snack): Follow the recipe given, except add 2 teaspoons minced yellow onion and pan fry with the corn. Garnish with Cotija cheese. You can also cook 2 whole fresh ears of corn in salted water with the onion, cut off the kernels with a sharp knife, and combine the kernels with the epazote and butter and a little of the corn cooking water in a medium saucepan. Simmer for 5 minutes to reduce the liquid and dress with lime, Cotija cheese, and chile powder. Top with a dollop of either crema or mayonnaise.

Elotes Locos (Corn on the Cob with Butter, Mayonnaise, Cheese, and Chile): In a large pot, cook 4 ears of corn in salted boiling water until tender, about 8 minutes. Using a pastry brush, slather each ear with butter and mayonnaise, and sprinkle with Cotija cheese and ground spicy chile to taste.

GÜICOYITOS MIGADOS
Baby Squash with Herbed Corn Tortilla Crumbs

SERVES 2

Baby squash is one of my favorite vegetables because it is delicious and easy to prepare. In Guatemala, güicoyitos are very small green squash that resemble a pumpkin in shape and have a similar flavor and texture to zucchini. The equivalent of this squash in Mexico is calabacitas, elongated pear-shaped squash with light green skin and a slightly firmer texture. Güicoyitos and calabacitas can be steamed, sautéed, roasted, creamed, made into soups, or breaded. This Guatemalan recipe traditionally uses bread crumbs, but as a twist for flavor and to make it more inclusive of all diets, I use corn tortilla crumbs instead. I have relatives who have celiac disease, and when they visit me, I gladly adapt many of my recipes to be gluten free. With Mesoamerican cuisine, this is easy to do, as it also is to make it vegan or vegetarian.

2 tablespoons butter

3 tablespoons diced yellow onion

½ teaspoon kosher salt

Freshly ground black pepper

4 güicoyitos (baby squash) or 2 calabacitas, trimmed, unpeeled, and sliced ¼ inch thick

ADORNO (GARNISH)

2 tablespoons corn tortilla crumbs or seasoned bread crumbs (see note)

1 tablespoon chopped flat-leaf or curly parsley

1. Melt the butter over low heat in a deep nonstick skillet. Add the onion, salt, and black pepper to taste, and cook until the onion is translucent, about 2 minutes.

2. Add the squash and gently combine ingredients with a soft heat-resistant spatula. Cover and cook over medium heat until the squash is tender, about 4 minutes. Stir with folding strokes at least once during this cooking time to allow for even cooking.

3. Transfer the cooked squash to a serving dish and sprinkle with the tortilla crumbs and parsley.

AMALIA'S NOTES

- To make tortilla crumbs, take 1 store-bought corn tortilla, tear it into smaller pieces, and pulse in a food processor until it resembles crumbs. Season with ¼ teaspoon salt and dry pan toast the crumbs in a skillet until medium brown. One tortilla makes a little over 2 tablespoons of crumbs.

- Other vegetables that can be prepared in a similar way are chayote squash, carrots, peruleros (Guatemalan white chayote), potatoes, any roots (yuca, salsify, malanga, ichintal)—anything that would hold up well during cooking.

ENSALADA DE PEPINO Y TOMATE
Cucumber, Tomato, Red Onion, Corn, and Lime Salad

SERVES 4 to 6

1 English cucumber, sliced
¼ inch thick
½ cup thinly sliced red onion
2 vine-ripened tomatoes,
sliced ¼ inch thick
⅓ cup freshly squeezed
lime juice
½ teaspoon kosher salt
Freshly ground black pepper

ADORNO (GARNISH)

½ cup cooked corn kernels
Curly parsley sprigs
1 lime, thinly sliced

If pressed for time, this quick and delicious salad can be a side or the main item on your salad plate. I often ate this salad for lunch after school, except my mom made it with just cucumbers and onion. Tomato adds another texture and nice touch and is delicious combined with cucumber. Corn makes it pop. Guatemalans use limes in many dishes, from beer and tamales to soups, stews, and fruits. Ensalada de Pepino y Tomate is so simple that you could make it on the spot right before a picnic or dinner gathering. Acidic dishes like this go well with grilled foods. Add more color and zest to your table with this salad and other fruit and vegetable combinations that are as easy as this one (see variations below).

1. Arrange attractively to taste, or alternate layers of cucumber, onions, and tomatoes on a platter and repeat until all the vegetables are used. You can also mix all the ingredients in a bowl.

2. In a small bowl, combine the lime juice with the salt and mix well to dissolve the salt. Drizzle it on the vegetable mixture and add black pepper to taste. For best results, add the lime juice ½ hour before serving.

3. Garnish with the corn kernels, parsley, and lime slice. Serve immediately.

RECIPE VARIATIONS AND OTHER RECIPES USING SIMILAR PREPARATION

Ensalada de Pepino (Cucumber Salad): Follow the recipe above, except leave out the tomatoes, corn, and parsley. Garnish with 1 tablespoon chopped mint.

Ensalada de Remolacha con Sal de Mar (Fresh Beets with Onion, Lime, and Sea Salt): Combine 2 ½ cups fresh cooked diced beets with ¼ cup julienned yellow onion and ⅓ cup freshly squeezed lime juice. Add sea salt to taste.

AMALIA'S NOTE
- Use white wine vinegar instead of lime juice for a twist in flavor.

FLOR DE IZOTE GUISADA
Yuca Blossoms with Tomato Chirmol

SERVES 2

Flor de izote comes from a type of yuca plant native to Mesoamerica and is a delicacy in Guatemala and El Salvador (and is their national flower). It's not unusual to see this plant grown in people's backyards along with other ornamental plants. The meaty core is slightly bitter, while the petals are mild yet delicious. Remove the pistils if using fresh flowers. Flor de izote is great in fritters or salads, stewed, or added to rice and soups. This preparation is simple and allows for a deeper level of appreciation for tasting the flowers. It can be great as an appetizer alongside corn or vegetable chips. It also can be a salsa-like garnish to top grilled meats. Izote blossoms are best fresh, but they are also available frozen or in jars with a mild brine. A key characteristic of these flowers is their bitterness—no matter how long you cook or soak them, they will still be slightly bitter. Lime, vinegar, and acidic sauces containing tomatoes pair well and tame the bitterness somewhat. In Guatemala and El Salvador the izote core (or buttons) and blossoms are pickled and sold commercially in grocery stores.

1 tablespoon canola oil

¼ cup diced yellow onion

½ teaspoon minced garlic

¾ cup diced Roma tomatoes

¾ cup vegetable or chicken stock, store-bought or homemade (see page 198)

¾ teaspoon kosher salt

1 (6-ounce) package frozen yuca blossoms

2–3 teaspoons freshly squeezed lime juice

1. Add the oil to a large skillet over medium high heat. Add the onion, garlic, tomatoes, stock, and salt, and bring to a quick boil over high heat, adjust the heat to low, and cook until it looks like a cooked salsa, about 5 minutes. Mash the sauce ingredients lightly with a flat potato masher to create a chunky sauce consistency.

2. Add the frozen yuca blossoms and lime juice and stir gently to combine. Cook over low heat, covered, for 3 to 5 minutes. Serve.

RECIPE VARIATIONS AND OTHER RECIPES USING YUCA BLOSSOMS

Flor de Izote Guisada con Huevo (Yuca Blossoms with Tomato Chirmol and Scrambled Egg): Follow the recipe above. After the yuca blossoms are cooked, make a well in the center of the skillet and add 1 beaten egg. Cook the egg, stirring constantly until it appears scrambled, then combine with the rest of the mixture in the pan. Omit the lime juice.

Flor de Izote con Limón (Yuca Blossoms with Lime and Sea Salt): Cook the frozen yuca blossoms over medium heat in ½ cup cold water, covered, until soft, about 5 minutes. Add sea or kosher salt to taste and 2 tablespoons freshly squeezed lime juice.

Curtido de Flor de Izote (Pickled Yuca Blossoms): Follow the Flor de Izote con Limón recipe, except omit the lime juice and add 1 ½ tablespoons white wine vinegar, increase the water to ¾ cup, and add kosher salt to taste, ½ dried bay leaf, and a pinch dried thyme to the mixture.

AMALIA'S NOTE

- Frozen or fresh (if available) yuca blossoms are best for this recipe. They can be purchased at Latin markets and online.

SANCOCHO DE HOJAS VERDES
Stewed Greens with Bell Peppers, Tomatoes, Onions, and Lime

SERVES 2

1 cup vegetable or chicken stock, store-bought or homemade (see page 198)

½ cup diced vine-ripened tomatoes

½ cup red bell pepper cut into 2-inch-long strips

½ teaspoon minced garlic

½ cup shaved yellow onion

1 cup roughly chopped equal amounts of fresh herbs: culantro, cilantro, epazote, mint, marjoram, and parsley

½ teaspoon kosher salt

1 tablespoon freshly squeezed lime juice, or a combination of equal parts lime and orange juice

1 thinly sliced serrano chile (optional)

8 ounces (about 7–8 cups) single or mixed greens such as spinach, kale, or collard greens

I have vivid memories of eating yerba mora (a Mesoamerican native leafy plant) as a little girl in my grandmother's home in Guatemala. This simple yet flavorful preparation can be made with a variety of greens. Although hers contained fewer ingredients, the recipe lends itself to modifications to include other flavors that are part of the Latin culture. I favor lime, fresh or dried chiles, and lots of herbs to provide a subtle background for any fresh greens geared for poaching or stewing. This sancocho can be even turned into a soup by adding more stock and pieces of cooked chicken.

1. In a saucepan, combine the stock, tomatoes, bell pepper, garlic, onion, herbs, salt, lime juice, and serrano, if using. Bring to a quick boil over high heat, adjust the heat to medium low, and simmer, covered, for 2 minutes.

2. Add the greens and let them stew in the flavorful broth, pushing them down with a spatula from time to time to submerge them. Simmer, covered, for 3 to 4 minutes. Serve.

RECIPE VARIATION

Torta de Hojas Verdes (Skillet Greens Cake): In a large bowl, combine all the ingredients from left, omitting the stock, and mix thoroughly with 3 beaten eggs seasoned with ¼ teaspoon kosher salt. Heat a nonstick skillet, add 2 tablespoons extra-virgin olive oil, and add the greens mixture to the skillet, pushing down the greens with a spatula to make it into a compact cake. Cook over low heat until the egg is almost fully cooked, 4 to 5 minutes. With the help of a platter, invert the cake onto the platter, add 1 tablespoon olive oil to the hot skillet, and slide the cake back on the skillet to cook the other side, about 2 additional minutes. The cake should be light brown on both sides. Serve it cut into wedges, topped with **Salsa Salvadoreña** (Salvadoran Basic Quick Tomato Sauce). Find this recipe in variations under Salsa Criolla Fría (Quick Homestyle Sauce, page 316), or use any of the other sauce variations within that recipe.

AMALIA'S NOTE

- Instead of stewing, try sautéing the greens in a little olive oil using all the ingredients above without the stock, plus 1 teaspoon shredded fresh ginger.

ENSALADA DE REPOLLO

Spicy Cabbage Slaw with Lime

SERVES 4 to 6

This salad, or a version of it, appears throughout the cuisines of the Mesoamerican region. Everyone makes it their own (with fewer or varying ingredients) and uses it in unique ways. This is my version. Use it as an appetizer or starter, or build it into the main meal by topping it with grilled shrimp or fish or roasted pork. Use it to top tacos, yuca, and anything to which you want to add a nice limey crunch. It is one of my favorites when I entertain because it lends itself to so many uses. Make it with just a few or all the ingredients in this recipe. Ensalada de Repollo has a beautiful texture and color, adds volume on the plate, and is delicious.

3 cups shredded cabbage

1 cup shredded carrots

1 cup green bell pepper cut into 2-inch long-strips

1 cup red or multicolored grape or cherry tomatoes, whole or halved

¾ cup shaved red onion

1 serrano chile, thinly sliced, veins and seeds included

½ cup chopped parsley leaves

½ cup chopped cilantro leaves

1 ½ teaspoons kosher salt

Freshly ground black pepper

¼ cup freshly squeezed lime juice

1 Combine the cabbage, carrots, bell pepper, tomatoes, onion, serrano, parsley, and cilantro in a large bowl. Add the salt, black pepper to taste, and lime juice right before serving. Mix well and serve immediately.

RECIPE VARIATIONS

Ensalada de Repollo Tica (Costa Rican Cabbage-Cilantro Slaw): In a medium bowl, thoroughly mix 2 cups shredded cabbage, 1 cup diced Roma tomatoes, 2 tablespoons chopped culantro or cilantro, 3 teaspoons fresh lime juice (or to taste), and kosher salt and freshly ground black pepper to taste. Serve immediately.

Curtido Crudo (Guatemalan Spicy Lime-Cabbage Slaw): In a large bowl, thoroughly mix 3 cups shredded cabbage, ½ cup shredded carrots or julienned red bell pepper, ½ cup julienned yellow or red onion, 1 thinly sliced serrano or jalapeño, 3 tablespoons freshly squeezed lime juice, and kosher salt to taste. Serve immediately.

Curtido con Rábanos (Guatemalan Spicy Radish-Cabbage Slaw): Follow the Curtido Crudo recipe, but substitute ½ cup chopped radishes for the carrots or red bell pepper and add 1 tablespoon chopped cilantro. Serve immediately.

Curtido (Salvadoran Slaw): In a large bowl, combine 3 cups shredded cabbage with 1 cup shredded carrots, ½ cup julienned yellow onion, 1 thinly sliced jalapeño or serrano chile, 2 dried bay leaves, 1 teaspoon crumbled dried oregano, ½ teaspoon sugar, 1 to 1 ½ teaspoons kosher salt, ¼ cup white vinegar, and 1 ½ cups hot water. Mix well and allow to marinate in the refrigerator for several hours or overnight.

AMALIA'S NOTES

• For optimum flavor and texture, eat fresh curtido salads with lime the day you make them. If you have leftovers, eat them within a day or two. Discard when the vegetables no longer taste fresh or start breaking down.

• Curtidos made with vinegar keep in the refrigerator for weeks.

• The volume of shredded cabbage will go down once mixed with lime juice or vinegar; acids and other liquids make the cabbage more compact. The flavor will still be fabulous, but be aware of this when deciding when to plate your food.

• Marinated and pickled foods taste less salty when they're cold. Taste the salad for seasoning at the temperature it will be when you serve it and add more seasoning if desired.

GUACAMOL NICA

Nicaraguan Guacamole

SERVES 2

1 ripe avocado, diced

2 hard-boiled eggs, peeled and diced

2 tablespoons minced yellow onion

1 ½ tablespoons freshly squeezed lime juice

½ teaspoon kosher salt

Lettuce leaves and tomato slices, for serving (optional)

This refreshing version of guacamole is more of a chunky avocado salsa than the guacamole from other parts of Mesoamerica. Hard-cooked eggs complement and add a new texture to this salad. In Guatemala and Nicaragua, we refer to this salad as guacamol without the *e*. Within Mesoamerica, everyone makes guacamole with varying ingredients and styles. Guatemalan avocados are creamy and do not oxidize easily after cut. Guatemalan and Mexican avocados make an excellent guacamole. The key to a delicious guacamole lies in the quality of the avocados and proper seasoning. Serve with El Diablito (Shredded Chicken and Vegetable Stew, page 258) or Gallo Pinto Nica (Nicaraguan Red Bean and Cilantro Fried Rice, page 247) for an authentic Nicaraguan meal and complement it with fresh Tlaxcalli (Mesoamerican Corn Tortillas, page 97).

1 Combine the avocado, eggs, onion, lime juice, and salt in a small bowl and mix gently with a soft spatula.

2 Serve as is or on a plate lined with lettuce leaves and tomato slices.

RECIPE VARIATIONS

Guacamol Chapín (Guatemalan Guacamole): In a medium bowl, mash 3 ripe avocados to a chunky texture and add 2 tablespoons freshly squeezed lime juice, 1 tablespoon shredded yellow onion, ½ teaspoon crumbled dried oregano, and ½ teaspoon kosher salt. Mix well and serve.

Guacamole Guanaco (Salvadoran Guacamole): Follow the recipe for Guacamol Chapín, adding 1 clove garlic mashed to a paste, extra-virgin olive oil to taste (optional), and freshly ground black pepper to taste. Garnish with chopped hard-boiled eggs and shredded queso fresco, and serve.

Guacamole Tico (Costa Rican Guacamole): In a medium bowl, mash 2 ripe avocados to a chunky texture and add ½ cup diced Roma tomatoes, 1 ½ tablespoons freshly squeezed lime juice (or to taste), 1 tablespoon shredded onion, kosher salt to taste (keeping in mind the seasoning sauces that follow already

contain salt), 2 tablespoons chopped culantro or cilantro, and Worcestershire and Tabasco sauce to taste. Mix well and serve.

Guacamole Mexicano (Mexican Guacamole): In a medium bowl, mash 2 ripe avocados to a chunky texture and add pico de gallo: 2 tablespoons minced onion, 3 tablespoons chopped cilantro, 1 teaspoon minced serrano or jalapeño, ½ cup small-diced Roma tomatoes, 1 tablespoon freshly squeezed lime juice (or to taste), and ¼ to ½ teaspoon kosher salt. Mix well and serve immediately.

Guacamole Catracho (Honduran Guacamole): To a medium bowl, add 3 diced ripe avocados, 2 diced hard-boiled eggs, 1 tablespoon mayonnaise or extra-virgin olive oil (optional), 1 tablespoon chopped cilantro (optional), 2 tablespoons lime juice, and kosher salt and black pepper to taste. Combine all ingredients carefully with a soft spatula and serve immediately.

FIAMBRE ROJO

Marinated Vegetables, Meats, Cold Cuts, Seafood, and Cheeses

SERVES 6 to 8

Fiambre is one of the most unique and distinctive dishes in Guatemalan cuisine. Deeply cultural and symbolic, it is a salad that contains all the food groups. Eaten as a one-dish meal honoring the dead on All Saints' Day on November 1, it is so substantial that one bowlful is often plenty for one person. Fiambre's origin is uncertain; born during colonial times, this syncretic dish mixes local customs with those that started Guatemalan cuisine's transformation since Spanish contact. Fiambre is a lunchtime feast that follows visits to the cemetery to decorate, deliver treats, and pay respects to the departed and culminates with a traditional fruit dessert. The preparation often begins days before, and it can involve family, friends, and relatives, who take the opportunity to visit and create something this special in the company of good cooks. Every family makes fiambre their own (red, white, or green), so it varies by maker (see recipe variations on page 190), yet one thing is certain: the secret of a good fiambre is in the caldillo, the vinaigrette, which every creator modifies to their taste. It is a delightful experience that will leave you waiting for next year's fiambre adventure.

Continued on page 190

VERDURAS (VEGETABLES)

2 ½ cups shredded cabbage
2 cups julienned green beans
2 cups quartered cauliflower florets
2 cups julienned carrots
8 asparagus spears
¼ cup frozen baby peas
2 cups julienned beets

CALDILLO (VINAIGRETTE)

¼ cup Guatemalan Sharp brand vinegar, champagne vinegar, or white wine vinegar
½ cup water (left over from cooking the vegetables)
1 tablespoon Spanish capers
½ cup extra-virgin olive oil, or to taste
½ tablespoon grated fresh ginger
1 tablespoon minced garlic cloves
¾ teaspoon mustard seed
¾ teaspoon black peppercorns
2 dried bay leaves
¾ teaspoon dried thyme
½ teaspoon crumbled dried oregano
1 ½ teaspoons sugar
2 teaspoons kosher salt
¾ cup chicken stock, store-bought or homemade (see page 198)

1 cup finely chopped flat-leaf parsley leaves
1 cup thinly sliced red onion

ENLATADOS/BOTES (CANNED/JARRED INGREDIENTS)

¼ cup thinly sliced palmito (hearts of palm)
10 pickled baby onions
¼ cup thinly sliced baby pickles
10 Spanish olives stuffed with pimentos, sliced
1 tablespoon Spanish capers
¼ cup jarred roasted red bell pepper strips
4 pacaya flowers in brine

POLLO, MARISCOS Y CARNES FRÍAS (CHICKEN, SEAFOOD, AND COLD CUTS)

½ cup shredded rotisserie chicken
½ cup ham strips
½ cup thinly sliced Spanish chorizo
½ cup Serrano ham strips
½ cup cooked Latin chorizo slices
½ cup cooked shrimp, tuna, or sardines (or other proteins)

PROTEÍNAS VEGETALES (VEGETABLE PROTEINS)

¼ cup fava beans (optional)
¼ cup garbanzos (optional)

QUESOS (CHEESES)

¼ cup cubed queso fresco
1 ¼ cup American or mild cheddar cheese, cut into 2-inch-long strips

ADORNO (GARNISH)

Butter lettuce
1 (2-ounce) jar baby corn
2 hard-boiled eggs, cut into wedges
3 radishes, cut into flowers
¼ cup thinly sliced yellow onion
¼ cup sliced sautéed mushrooms
¼ cup dried Cotija cheese, crumbled
Chamborote chile or manzano chile (or cut a small red bell pepper into a flower)

Day 1

1. Bring 4 cups salted water to a boil in a saucepan. One at a time, cook the cabbage, green beans, cauliflower, carrots, asparagus, and peas in the same water, al dente. When finished cooking, reserve ½ cup cooking water for preparing the vinaigrette.

2. In a separate saucepan, cover the beets with water and bring to a quick boil over high heat, reduce the heat to low, and cook until tender, about 40 minutes. Peel the beets under cold running water, then julienne them. Combine the beets, cabbage, green beans, cauliflower, carrots, and peas in a large nonreactive bowl and let them cool. Set the asparagus aside for use as a garnish.

3. To make the vinaigrette, combine the vinegar, leftover cooking water, capers, olive oil, ginger, garlic, mustard seed, peppercorns, bay leaves, thyme, oregano, sugar, and salt in a blender. Blend until very creamy. Add the chicken stock and blend again to combine. The vinaigrette will have a strong taste; this is necessary to marinate all the cooked vegetables.

4. Add the vinaigrette to the bowl with the cooked vegetables and stir in the parsley and red onion. With a soft spatula, gently push all the vegetables down to fully submerge them in the vinaigrette. Let the vegetables marinate in the refrigerator overnight. Taste the next day and add more seasonings, if needed.

Day 2

1. Open all the canned and jarred ingredients. Combine a little of each of the juices in a measuring cup to make ¼ to ⅓ cup. Add the juices to the marinated vegetables and mix well.

2. Place all the canned/jarred ingredients, chicken, seafood, and cold cuts, vegetable proteins, cheeses, and garnishes in individual bowls, line them up on a table right next to the marinated vegetables, then begin assembling the fiambre.

3. To assemble, on attractive salad plates or in bowls, layer all the ingredients, starting with butter lettuce, followed by some marinated vegetables, some canned/jarred ingredients, some chicken, some seafood, some cold cuts, some vegetable proteins, and some of the cheeses. Repeat these layers until you've used up all the ingredients. Make sure the last layer shows a little of every ingredient used.

4. Finish the servings with the garnishes. Start with the baby corn, then use the egg wedges, radishes, yellow onion, mushrooms, asparagus spears, Cotija cheese, and chamborote chile.

RECIPE VARIATIONS

Fiambre Blanco (White Fiambre): Follow the recipe above, omitting the beets.

Fiambre Verde (Green Fiambre): Follow the recipe for Fiambre Rojo, except leave out the beets and carrots. Add 1 cup roughly chopped celery to the vinaigrette. Add ½ cup finely chopped flat-leaf parsley leaves to the garnishes.

AMALIA'S NOTES

- Marinated and pickled foods taste less salty when they're cold. Taste the fiambre for seasoning at the temperature it will be when you serve it and add more seasoning if desired.

- Fiambre Rojo should look medium pink. It keeps for 3 days after assembly, or you can freeze it in small portions.

7

Caldos, Sopas y Sancochos
Broths and Light and Hearty Soups

LATIN SECRET SAUCE

I grew up cooking with who I consider the master cooks of my childhood and time in Guatemala. These women included my maternal grandmother, mother, sister, aunts, and friends, who had a secret sauce in common: innate cooking skill and, most importantly, sazón.

Sazón is the ability to know the right seasoning for the right dish. This is learned by doing and taking note, the reason why tradition is so important for us Latin Americans. None of the people I learned from and continue to learn from have been professional cooks. They have been women who cook because of need or passion and do it well.

In Meso- and Latin America, many women (and some men) grow up bonding with family members in the kitchen. It is the place where one spends a great deal of time creating family heirloom recipes from scratch, either routinely or during special times and holidays.

When I went to chef school, I started learning new techniques for making recipes better and cooking easier. To pass my exams, I had to relearn how to cook, as the cooking I learned during my upbringing was purely based on adding, stirring, tasting, and adjusting. At first I found it tedious and time consuming to have to stop to do *mise en place* (recipe and kitchen organization), as I felt it slowed me down, but once I got used to my new routine, I embraced it wholeheartedly without forgetting my cultural roots.

Soup-making in Latin America, like many other types of cooking except baking, still happens as a result of doing and redoing. The ancient recipes that we pass from generation to generation are an inherent part of our heritage and who we are. They bring us together during happy and sad times.

Recados or Recaudos

Recados are thin or thick sauces or broths produced by stewing meat with vegetables.

They can also be the resulting broth from cooking meats such as chicken in a pan along with sofrito, or sauces made for tamales. Or they can be seasoning pastes for marinating meats.

It is interesting that the better cooks without formal training are skilled at throwing ingredients into a soup pot without following any learned professional techniques, yet they have developed their own ways that work for what they do. Eateries at open markets and mom-and-pop restaurants distinguish themselves because they follow tradition. Tradition is what attracts people to visit these places to enjoy a cozy chat and comfort food.

Spanish-influenced soups throughout Meso- and Latin America are often the same soup under the same or different names with varying ingredients and seasonings. One of the most common, puchero (also known as cocido, caldo de res, olla de carne, and sancocho), is basically a hearty soup or stew containing many vegetables, tubers, and herbs, as well as beef bones and meat or chicken.

As a professional chef, I have devised my own way of creating and writing recipes by following my roots and traditions, which I blend with professional cooking techniques. As a result, recipes are more concise and focus on big flavor and quality. Everyone likes to eat a delicious soup, and some are even enticed to make it if it looks good and easy to make. That is my goal with this chapter and book.

A Word about Stock

Latin Americans have not traditionally cooked with stocks, as simmering proteins and vegetables produce a broth that is often enhanced with sofrito, herbs, spices, vegetables, and sometimes bouillon. Homemade stock is time consuming and requires technique to make it right. In the United States, stocks are conveniently packaged and widely available at supermarkets, eliminating the need for bouillon, which was part of American home cooking in the past (and selectively in the present). While now frowned upon by some, bouillon is still alive in some parts of Meso- and Latin America.

CONSOMMÉ A LA AMALIA
Aromatic Homestyle Soup

MAKES 5 ¾ cups

LA BALSA (THE RAFT)

3 jumbo egg whites,
  slightly beaten

½ cup ground lean chicken,
  turkey, or beef

½ cup finely diced yellow onion

½ teaspoon minced garlic

¼ cup finely diced
  Roma tomatoes

¼ cup finely diced green
  bell peppers

¼ cup chopped cilantro
  leaves and stems

¼ cup chopped culantro
  leaves and stems

¼ cup chopped mint leaves
  and stems

½ teaspoon kosher salt

¼ teaspoon freshly ground
  black pepper

6 cups cold homemade stock
  or store-bought chicken,
  turkey, or beef stock
  (see page 198)

Consommé does not translate the same across all cultures. In Guatemala and Mesoamerica, consommé is a cloudy broth that is served as is or combined with just a few vegetables, and oftentimes it also is served as a nurturing soup to the sick and at funeral homes during visiting time. During my time studying at Le Cordon Bleu, my perception of consommé changed from the cloudy soup I knew to a deeply flavored clear soup that can be elegantly dressed in any style. The secret is in the raft, a combination of lean proteins, vegetables, and egg whites used to enhance flavor and give the stock a clear appearance. I use a combination of ingredients I have on hand in my kitchen to add Latin flavor and authenticity to my consommé. The difference between stock and consommé is twofold: consommé has a deeper flavor and a translucent look. The process of making consommé from scratch can be long with homemade stock, so here is a way to shorten the cooking time with similar delicious results. If you wish to make the stock from scratch, the recipe is on page 198.

1. Add the egg whites, ground chicken, onion, garlic, tomatoes, bell peppers, cilantro, culantro, mint, salt, and black pepper to a bowl. With a soft spatula, mix well to combine all ingredients thoroughly with the egg whites.

2. Add the raft mixture to a medium soup pot. Add the stock you are using. With the same spatula, stir gently to combine. Over medium low heat, bring the soupy chunky mixture, uncovered, to a gentle simmering point, stirring from time to time, about 10 to 15 minutes. As soon as you see steady simmering bubbles, stop stirring and do not stir from here on. Adjust the heat to low. As it gently cooks, the chunky mixture will start to float, creating a raft on top of the stock. With a small ladle, make a small hole at the center of the raft. From time to time, scoop hot stock through the hole and gently pour it back in around the raft.

3. Continue cooking, uncovered, for 45 to 50 minutes. During this time, the bubbling stock will come to the surface gently through any openings in the raft. This is expected and required to clarify the stock. Keep a close eye on it; the consommé should simmer gently at all times for the raft technique to be effective.

4. With a large ladle, carefully remove the clarified stock while pushing gently down on the raft. Strain and filter the consommé through a paper grease (or coffee) filter cone to degrease it.

5. Use the consommé as is, add diced vegetables or pasta cooked al dente, use as a base for some recipes in this chapter (see Pavesa, page 201), or freeze it for later use.

Continued on page 198

RECIPE FOR STOCK TO USE AS A BASE FOR CONSOMMÉ OR OTHER RECIPES IN THIS BOOK

Fondo Base (Amalia's Basic Stock): In a soup pot, combine 8 cups water, 1 pound oven-roasted beef bones, ¼ pound beef trimmings or stew meat, ¼ cup chopped celery, ¾ cup diced yellow onion, 3 sliced green onions, ½ teaspoon minced garlic, 1 quartered Roma tomato, ½ cup diced green bell pepper, ½ cup diced carrot, 1 bunch cilantro, and a sachet d'épices (spice bag) that includes 3 peppercorns, 3 whole cloves, and 1 dried bay leaf. Bring to a quick boil over high heat, reduce the heat to medium low, and simmer, covered, for 2 ½ to 3 hours. Skim the foam or impurities that rise to the surface from time to time. Strain out the solids, cool the stock in an ice bath, and add salt to taste when you use it in a recipe.

AMALIA'S NOTES

- For fish, shrimp, or seafood consommé, follow the same procedure for Consommé a la Amalia, using the bones and heads of 2 non-oily fish (such as Dover sole or flounder), 2 cups shrimp shells, or a combination of fish and shrimp; seafood stock as a base; and 1 tablespoon chopped lime or lemon zest (or half of each).

- To make chicken or turkey stock, follow the same recipe as Fondo Base, except use raw bones (carcass, feet, neck, and head) or roast them and simmer the stock for 2 hours.

- To make vegetable stock, follow the same recipe as Fondo Base, except omit all animal protein.

- Commercial stocks are usually made by simmering roasted bones in water with a few vegetables or mirepoix (a combination of onion, celery, and carrots) and some herbs and spices, including bay leaf, parsley stems, and peppercorns, for longer periods of time. This recipe produces a delicious homestyle basic stock without any preservatives and can be frozen in small freezer bags to use when needed.

PAVESA

Poached Egg on Toast and Queso Seco Soup

SERVES 2

4 cups chicken or beef bone broth or stock, store-bought, or homemade stock or consommé (see pages 197 and 198)

½ cup cilantro leaves and stems
½ cup mint leaves and stems

½ cup vermicelli pasta, cooked al dente
2 slices French or bread of choice, toasted
2 eggs

ADORNO (GARNISH)

Crumbled queso seco (dried Guatemalan cheese) or Cotija cheese
1 recipe **Salsita de Chile Guaque** (Guatemalan Guajillo Tomato Sauce, page 316)
Curly parsley, chopped

Pavesa reminds me of some restaurants in Guatemala City that prepare this soup well. Of Pavia, Italy, origin, the soup likely came to Guatemala and the rest of Latin America through Spain and has remained a favorite. It is one of my sister's and my favorite soups. It is easy to make, and although it looks light, it can be hearty as the egg and the bread combined with the soup are quite filling. This makes it a good soup choice for weekdays when cooking time is short for families. Pavesa varies by maker; my version incorporates flavor depth and gourmet style.

1. In a small soup pot, combine the bone broth, stock, or consommé with the cilantro and the mint. Simmer over medium low heat, covered, until very aromatic, about 8 minutes. Remove and discard the herbs from the soup. Keep hot at low heat.

2. Preheat an oven or toaster oven on the broiler setting.

3. Select two dishes or ceramic bowls that are oven and broiler safe. Place the half of the vermicelli on the bottom of the bowl and a slice of toasted bread on top. Make an indentation in the center of the bread with your fingers and carefully break an egg into it. Ladle half of the hot soup directly over the yolk. Repeat for the second bowl.

4. Place each bowl under the broiler to cook the egg a bit more, about 2 to 3 minutes. The egg whites should look cooked yet tender, and the yolk a bit cloudy and runny.

5. Garnish with the cheese, sauce, and parsley.

AMALIA'S NOTE

- If using consommé, omit the cilantro and mint.

SOPA CALDOSA CON ALBÓNDIGAS DE PAVO
Turkey Meatball and Fidelini Soup

SERVES 4 to 6

Albóndigas soup, or meatball soup, was one of my dad's favorite soups. It is popular at the Mesoamerican table with varying ingredients per country and home. Typically, it is made with beef meatballs. Albóndigas, of Arab origin, came to Latin America through Spain. Sopa caldosa, or rich broth, combined with the meatballs is a hearty one-dish meal that is usually served during lunch. Not all versions are made with the rich broth or have pasta; some contain diced vegetables. This is my version using turkey with equally delicious results. For a twist, add pork and beef meatballs to the mixture. I like to add avocado chunks and hot sauce to my soups, and this one would be delicious with them too.

1 To make the broth, combine the turkey thighs, 1 cup diced yellow onion, 1 teaspoon minced garlic, carrot, bell pepper, celery, tomatoes, cilantro, 1 ½ teaspoons salt, and stock in a soup pot. Bring to a quick boil over high heat, adjust the heat to medium low, and simmer, covered, for 30 minutes.

2 To make the meatballs, combine the ground turkey, diced ½ cup onion, ¾ teaspoon garlic, mint, eggs, 1 teaspoon salt, black pepper to taste, and 6 tablespoons masa flour in a medium bowl and mix well with your hands (wear disposable gloves). Form meatballs with a ¾-ounce scoop to make 1 ½-inch meatballs and then round them by hand. Use the additional 2 tablespoons flour for dusting and to prevent the meatballs from sticking to your hands. Set the formed meatballs aside.

3 Remove the turkey or chicken pieces from the stock and save them for another recipe. With a strainer, remove all the vegetables from the stock, discard the cilantro, and puree the vegetables in a blender, using some of the stock as needed for the mixture to blend. Strain the pureed mixture through a fine-mesh sieve back into the soup pot.

4 In a small skillet, combine the fidelini with the oil and brown the pasta over medium high heat, stirring constantly, to a medium brown, 3 to 5 minutes. Add it to the soup pot.

5 With the help of a spoon, carefully immerse the meatballs into the soup and simmer gently over low heat, covered, until thoroughly cooked, about 20 to 25 minutes.

6 Ladle the soup and pasta into bowls. Add four to five meatballs per bowl. Garnish with parsley.

AMALIA'S NOTES

- You can make this recipe in steps. Make the broth one day and the meatballs the next day. Use all or some of the meatballs. Freeze raw meatballs until solid on a baking sheet and store them in the freezer in a resealable plastic bag if you will not cook them all at once.

- The pasta will continue to absorb liquid as it sits. Add more stock to the soup as needed. Taste and add salt if needed.

- For a gluten-free version, use gluten-free pasta. The meatballs are made with corn flour, so they are already gluten free.

SOPA CALDOSA (RICH BROTH)

¼ pound bone-in skinless turkey thighs or 2 bone-in skinless chicken thighs and 2 skinless legs, visible fat removed

1 cup diced yellow onion

1 teaspoon minced garlic

1 medium carrot, diced

½ red bell pepper, diced

2 celery stalks, diced

2 vine-ripened tomatoes, diced

1 ½ cups whole cilantro leaves and stems (roughly 1 bunch)

1 ½ teaspoons kosher salt

6 cups turkey or chicken stock, store-bought or homemade (see page 198)

ALBÓNDIGAS DE PAVO (TURKEY MEATBALLS) (MAKES 28–30 MEATBALLS)

1 pound ground turkey

½ cup finely diced yellow onion

¾ teaspoon minced garlic

3 tablespoons finely chopped mint leaves

2 eggs

1 teaspoon kosher salt

Freshly ground black pepper

8 tablespoons instant corn masa flour, divided

½ cup fidelini, fideo, or vermicelli pasta

¼ teaspoon canola oil

½ cup chopped flat-leaf parsley leaves

SPECIAL EQUIPMENT

Disposable gloves

DELICIA DE GÜICOY
Creamy Acorn Squash Soup

SERVES 2 to 4

1 tablespoon butter
¾ cup diced yellow onion
1 teaspoon minced garlic
1 dried bay leaf
⅛ teaspoon dried thyme
¼ cup chopped cilantro leaves
and stems
1 ½ teaspoons kosher salt
Freshly ground white pepper
¼ cup diced Roma tomatoes
4 ½ cups peeled and diced
güicoy (or acorn squash)
(from about 1 squash)
3 cups chicken or vegetable
stock, store-bought or
homemade (see page 198)
1 tablespoon unsalted crema
or Mexican table cream

ADORNO (GARNISH)

Crema
Chopped cilantro leaves
Toasted acorn squash seeds
(see note)

As an elegant starter or a light lunch, Delicia de Güicoy is a delicate yet flavorful soup that takes only a few minutes to make. This Guatemalan delicacy is typically made with güicoy sazón, a squash similar to acorn squash. (Güicoy is also known as ayote in Mesoamerica.) Young and mature squash in many shapes and forms is often present in kitchens throughout the region. Serve this creamy delight in ceramic soup bowls or clear cups rimmed with chile powder for a fun twist. Delicia de Güicoy is a crowd pleaser.

1. In a saucepan over medium low heat, melt the butter and cook the onion and garlic until translucent, about 2 to 3 minutes.

2. Add the bay leaf, thyme, cilantro, salt, white pepper to taste, and tomatoes, and cook for 2 minutes. Add the squash and stock, bring to a quick boil over high heat, adjust the heat to medium low, and simmer, covered, until the squash is tender, about 10 minutes.

3. Puree with an immersion or regular blender until very smooth. Add the crema and stir well.

4. Garnish with crema, chopped cilantro leaves, and toasted squash seeds as desired.

AMALIA'S NOTES

- To peel acorn squash, cut it in half lengthwise. Using a soup spoon, remove the core and seeds. Put the seeds in a colander and separate them from the core under running water. Discard the core. Spread the seeds flat on a paper towel and allow them to dry until you're ready to pan toast them. Cut the squash into wedges, following the natural indentations of the squash. You will end up with many wedges that will be easier to peel with a peeler.

- To pan toast the seeds, heat a small skillet over medium high heat, add the seeds, and move them around the pan with a spatula until medium brown, about 3 to 5 minutes.

- This soup is also delicious when made with Guatemalan güicoyitos or Mexican calabacitas (baby squash).

PINOL DE MARRANO CON CHATATE

Toasted Dried Corn, Pork Rib, and Chaya Leaf Stew

SERVES 4 to 6

This simple and scrumptious recipe is my special version of bisabuelita (maternal great-grandmother) Carmen's pinol. As a little girl, I often visited her home in Quezaltepeque, Chiquimula, to play in her large patio, where she grew tamarind, pomegranates, avocados, limes, and leafy plants, including chatate (chaya leaves), which she added to her stew. The flavors and textures I remember are of a heavenly soupy combination of creamy corn bits, fall-off-the-bone pork pieces, and chaya leaves. Chaya leaves are native to the Mesoamerica region. They're delicate, somewhat similar to the texture of swiss chard, with a unique flavor. An ancestral food, pinol is made in the central, north, and southwestern Mayan highlands of Guatemala. Pinol (see Pinol de Conejo, Toasted Dried Corn, Roasted Tomato, Cilantro, and Rabbit Stew, page 111) is a national symbol and was declared intangible cultural patrimony (heritage) by the Guatemalan government along with four other Mayan stews (Jocón, Pepián, Kaqik, and Mole). Within the stew, there are simple and more elaborate preparations ranging from coarse to smooth textures and various colors, with few to many ingredients. Pinol is made with turkey, beef, pork, hen (adult female chicken), and chicken in Guatemala, El Salvador, and Nicaragua. At its base, pinol is made with toasted white or yellow dried corn, which is either broken into bits or stone ground to a coarse powder.

1 cup maíz trillado blanco (cracked white hominy corn)

2 ½ cups vegetable stock, store-bought or homemade (see page 198)

2 boneless country-style pork ribs, cut into 1 ½-inch cubes

½ pound pork shoulder, visible fat removed, cut into 1 ½-inch cubes

1 small Roma tomato, cut into 8 wedges

1 ½ cups roughly chopped yellow onion

1 teaspoon minced garlic

¾ cup whole cilantro leaves and stems

3 cups vegetable stock, store-bought or homemade

1 ½ teaspoons kosher salt

Freshly ground black pepper

1 cup chatate (chaya leaves) or swiss chard leaves, washed, trimmed, sliced into 1-inch-wide ribbons or torn by hand into about 2-inch pieces

Cilantro sprigs

1. Pan toast the corn in a medium skillet over medium high heat until medium brown, about 5 minutes, flipping it constantly or moving it around with a soft spatula. Keep a close eye on it, as it can burn easily if left unattended. In a medium soup pot, combine the corn with the 2 ½ cups stock. Bring to a quick boil over high heat, adjust the heat to low, and simmer gently, covered, stirring from time to time until the corn is partly cooked, about 1 hour.

2. Add the pork ribs, pork shoulder, tomato, onion, garlic, cilantro, 3 cups stock, and salt and black pepper to taste to the corn pot, and bring to a quick boil over high heat. Adjust the heat to low and simmer, covered, until the pork and corn are fully cooked, about 2 to 2 ½ hours.

3. Add the chaya leaves or swiss chard and stir well. Cover and simmer 5 to 8 minutes longer.

4. Garnish with cilantro sprigs and serve.

RECIPE VARIATION

For a smoother texture, prepare this recipe using whole grain coarse-grind stone-ground cornmeal, using the cooking technique and recipe in Pinol de Conejo (Toasted Dried Corn, Roasted Tomato, Cilantro, and Rabbit Stew, page 111).

AMALIA'S NOTES

• White and yellow cracked hominy corn is available at Latin stores, major grocery chains, and online.

• Chaya leaves are available at Latin farmers' markets, Asian markets, or online.

• Hominy corn doubles in size during cooking. As it sits, pinol continues to absorb liquid. Add more stock as needed to any leftovers.

SOPA DE POLLO CON ARROZ Y VERDURAS
Grandma's Chicken, Rice, and Vegetable Soup

SERVES 4 to 6

2 bone-in skinless chicken
thighs, visible fat removed
4 skinless chicken drumsticks,
visible fat removed
1 medium yellow onion,
peeled and t-scored
1 teaspoon minced garlic
2 small dried bay leaves
1 ½ cups whole cilantro leaves
and stems
6 cups chicken stock,
store-bought or homemade
(see page 198)

RECADO (SOFRITO)

1 teaspoon canola oil
¼ cup finely chopped onion
¾ cup finely diced
Roma tomatoes
Smidgen ground cloves
1 ½ teaspoons kosher salt
Freshly ground black pepper

¼ cup long-grain white rice
½ cup julienned carrots
½ cup julienned red bell pepper
½ cup julienned chayote squash
½ cup frozen baby peas

ADORNO (GARNISH)

Avocado chunks
Chopped cilantro leaves

This is my special tribute to my grandmother. When I think of chicken soup, memories come to mind of her so-very-special chicken and rice soup. Hers had fresh-killed pollo criollo (patio chicken), which surpasses the flavor of any chicken I have had anywhere after I left Guatemala. This tasted so especially good; maybe it is my taste buds longing for her soup, but I know a good-tasting chicken when I taste one. The closest I have come to the flavor I crave is tree-range organic chicken (see note). My grandmother had the chickens in her patio for several weeks and fed them grain and clean water and allowed them to roam freely. She used to tell me and my siblings she wanted to "clean" them before we ate them, implying that their drinking water, diet, or environment may not have been the best before the chickens came to her home. Curiously, this is eons ago, and she was already conscious about clean food. Serve with avocado chunks, hot sauce, and warm freshly made corn tortillas (see page 97).

1. In a soup pot, combine the chicken, t-scored onion, garlic, bay leaves, cilantro leaves and stems, and stock. Bring to a quick boil over high heat, then adjust the heat to medium low and simmer, covered, for 30 minutes.

2. Meanwhile, make the sofrito. Heat the oil in a medium skillet and add the chopped onion, tomatoes, cloves, salt, black pepper to taste, and ½ cup hot stock from the soup pot. Cook until the sofrito has a chunky consistency, about 3 minutes. Mash the sofrito with a flat potato masher to thicken it to a puree consistency.

3. Remove the chicken from the soup pot and keep warm. Remove the onion, roughly chop it, and reserve. Remove the bay leaves and cilantro leaves and stems and discard. Shred the chicken using two forks. Return the chopped onion and shredded chicken to the soup pot. Add the sofrito and the rice and stir well. Simmer, covered, for 10 minutes.

4. Add the carrots, bell pepper, chayote squash, and peas. Stir well, cover, and simmer for 10 minutes.

5. Serve the soup garnished with avocado chunks and cilantro with warm corn tortillas on the side.

RECIPE VARIATION

Sopa de Pollo con Lorocos (Loroco Flower Bud Soup): Follow the recipe given, omitting the cloves. Substitute the rice with 1 cup diced cooked potatoes and add 1 cup loroco flower buds in step 3.

AMALIA'S NOTES

- This soup is chunky and substantial. If you like it less chunky or want to stretch it to feed more people, add more stock. Taste and add additional seasonings if needed.

- As an option, use certified organic tree-range chickens. They are raised outdoors under the canopy of trees and roam around, freely pecking on sprouted grain and a diversity of forages, including perennial medicinal herbs. The chickens are fed a balanced organic-certified feed. Tree-range chickens are better for the environment, farmers, people, and the planet, as they are raised under regenerative farming standards. On top of it all, they are leaner and taste delicious. They are available through local farmers and online.

CALDO DE GALLINA
Grilled Hen Soup with Vegetables

SERVES 4 to 6

While traveling in the Cobán, Alta Verapaz, region of Guatemala, I had this delicious soup more than once by different cooks. My grandmother used to make it for our family in Quezaltepeque, Chiquimula, adding the egg yolks that came with the hen. Caldo de gallina is a scrumptious homestyle soup. What is unique here in flavor is the gallina criolla (tree-range patio hen) and that the hen is grilled after it is cooked in the soup. The hen acquires a unique taste and look when grilled. Hens are leaner than chickens and can be smaller and a bit tougher, depending on age. As simple as it sounds, once on the table, the soup is a feast for the senses when served with all the traditional pairings. Caldo de gallina is a delightful soup that will leave you and your guests thoroughly satisfied.

1. Combine the hen, onion, green onion, garlic, bell pepper, tomatoes, mint, cilantro leaves and stems, and stock in a medium soup pot. Bring it to a quick boil over high heat. Adjust the heat to medium low and simmer, covered, for 30 minutes. Skim off any impurities (foam) that rise to the top from time to time.

2. Remove the hen from the pot and keep warm. Mash the vegetables in the soup with a flat potato masher. With a slotted spoon, fish out all the visible vegetable solids from the soup and put them into a mesh colander. With a soft spatula, press the vegetable solids over the pot to squeeze out any liquid left, and discard the solids.

3. Add the carrots and potatoes and cook 10 minutes. Add the squash and green beans and cook until all vegetables are al dente, about 10 to 15 minutes more. Add the chopped cilantro, chopped mint, achiote, salt, and black pepper to taste. Stir well. Keep warm on the lowest heat setting.

4. Grill the hen pieces on the stovetop on a preheated griddle over medium high heat until medium brown, about 1 minute per side, right before serving.

5. To assemble, either serve the soup in a heat-resistant large dish and put the grilled hen in it and arrange all the garnishes around it, or place a bowl on top of a large plate. Serve the soup and vegetables in the bowl. The chicken, garnishes, and pairings go right next to the bowl on the plate.

RECIPE VARIATION

Sopa de Gallina (Salvadoran Hen Soup): Follow the recipe given, except leave out the green onions and increase the diced onion quantity to 1 ½ cups. Omit the mint and substitute with celery leaves, parsley, and culantro, or cilantro. Leave out the green beans and substitute with 6 baby corn cut in thirds, and add 3 tablespoons rice with the carrots and potatoes. Serve the soup, vegetables, and hen in the soup. Do not grill the hen.

AMALIA'S NOTES

• Hens are available through local farmers.

• As an option, use certified organic tree-range chickens. They are raised outdoors under the canopy of trees and roam around, freely pecking on sprouted grain and a diversity of forages, including perennial medicinal herbs. The chickens are fed a balanced organic-certified feed. Tree-range chickens are better for the environment, farmers, people, and the planet, as they are raised underregenerative farming standards. On top of it all, they are leaner and taste delicious. They are available through local farmers and online.

• Find the recipe for Arroz con Verduras (Vegetable Rice) in recipe variations under Arroz con Remolacha (Beet and Vegetable Rice) on page 143.

1 tree-range organic hen or chicken, cut into 8 to 10 pieces (see note)
1 cup diced yellow onion
5 green onions, trimmed and cut into 2-inch pieces
1 tablespoon minced garlic
½ cup diced green bell pepper
2 ½ Roma tomatoes, cut into wedges
½ cup mint leaves and stems
1 cup cilantro leaves and stems
6 cups chicken stock (see page 198)

3 medium carrots, peeled and sliced ¼ inch thick on the bias
5 medium Yukon Gold potatoes, peeled and halved lengthwise
2 chayote squash, peeled and sliced ¼ inch thick on the bias
1 ½ cups trimmed 2-inch-cut green beans

SAZÓN (SEASONINGS)

½ cup chopped cilantro leaves
½ cup chopped mint leaves
¾ teaspoon ground achiote
1 ½ teaspoons kosher salt
Freshly ground black pepper

ADORNO Y ACOMPAÑANTES (GARNISH AND PAIRINGS)

Arroz con Verduras (Vegetable Rice) (see note)
Avocado slices
Warm corn tortillas
Hot chile sauce

SOPA DE PANQUEQUITOS
Chicken Broth with Parslied Mini Crepes

SERVES 2 to 4

¾ cup whole cilantro leaves
and stems

¾ cup whole parsley leaves
and stems

½ cup minced yellow onion

½ teaspoon minced garlic

¾ cup shredded carrots
(optional)

4 cups chicken bone broth
or stock, store-bought,
or homemade stock or
consommé (see pages
197 and 198)

**PANQUEQUITOS
(MINI CREPES)
(MAKES 37)**

¼ cup skim milk

1 large egg

1 tablespoon water

2 teaspoons melted butter

2 tablespoons all-purpose flour

¼ teaspoon baking powder

¼ teaspoon kosher salt

1 tablespoon minced onion

1 tablespoon finely chopped
curly parsley leaves

¼ cup finely chopped
cilantro leaves

Sopa de panquequitos, also known as sopa de tartaritas or sopa de tortitas de harina, is a delightful soup that takes me back to my childhood. My mom used to make it, and I thought it was the cutest thing because of the mini crepes. This experience remained with me when I moved to live with my grandmother in Quezaltepeque, Chiquimula, as a little girl and played "a la comidita" (little cooking) with my school girlfriends, making mini dishes consisting of little fried eggs, pancakes, and more. My brother Juan (who as an adult went to the university to study architecture) used to "build" makeshift mini houses for us so that we could eat our comidita inside. On rainy days, my friends and I would go inside the little house and listen to the noise the rain made on the tin roof. Precious times!

1. In a medium soup pot, combine the cilantro and parsley leaves and stems, ½ cup onion, garlic, carrots (if using), and broth, stock, or consommé. Bring to a quick boil over high heat. Adjust the heat to medium low and simmer, covered, until aromatic, about 5 minutes. Keep the heat on low.

2. In a blender, or in a bowl with a whisk, blend together the milk, egg, water, butter, flour, baking powder, salt, and 1 tablespoon onion. Add the chopped parsley and blend well.

3. Preheat a nonstick wide skillet over medium low heat. Drop teaspoons of the batter mixture on the skillet to make mini crepes, keeping a little distance between spoonfuls, and flip them when the sides turn a bit dry, about 30 seconds per side. The mini crepes should be light brown on both sides. This is a quick process, so you must stand by the skillet until all the batter is used. Transfer each crepe to a small bowl, cover, and keep warm.

4. When ready to serve, remove and discard the cilantro and parsley leaves and stems from the soup pot. Add the ¼ cup chopped cilantro and stir well.

5. To serve, add the mini crepes to the bottom of a soup tureen or divide among individual bowls and ladle the hot broth on top. The mini crepes should rise to the top.

AMALIA'S NOTES

- You can make the mini crepes ahead and freeze them in one layer, separated by parchment paper in freezer bags to use when needed.

- Typically, this soup is only a broth flavored with herbs and then served with the mini crepes. I choose to add more texture, flavor, and color with the onion, cilantro, and carrots. The vegetables are in the background, yet visible, and give the soup a better look. Opt to use all the vegetables, use just a few, or leave them out.

SANCOCHO PANAMEÑO
Panamanian Chicken and Root Vegetable Soup

SERVES 4 to 6

There are many versions of sancocho throughout Mesoamerica and the Latin Caribbean, and likely the concept came from Spain's Canary Islands. Kirchhoff's Mesoamerica didn't include Panama, but I include it in my kitchen because it is in the same territory and some of its cuisine has synergy with Mesoamerica's cuisine. This sancocho is one example. During several trips to Panama City and the countryside, I grew fonder of this soup. It is hearty, delicious, nutritious, and comforting. It is a one-dish meal that can be made easily during a weekday when time is short. Depending on region, Sancocho Panameño is made with hen or chicken and just a few ingredients or a combination of zapallo (squash) and a variety of root vegetables, such as yuca, ñame (yam), and otoe (taro root, also known as malanga and yautia), which act as thickeners once they start falling apart in the soup. This is my favorite version because the combination of the many vegetables gives the soup more character. For an amazing experience, serve it for lunch as is or for dinner paired with white rice.

4 to 6 bone-in skinless chicken
  thighs and legs
1 ½ cups diced yellow onion
1 teaspoon minced garlic
¼ cup diced green bell pepper
¼ cup diced red bell pepper
½–1 ají chombo (native pepper)
  or habanero chile, seeded
  and minced
¾ cup whole cilantro leaves
  and stems
6 cups chicken stock,
  store-bought or homemade
  (see page 198)

1 ear corn, shucked and
  in quarters
2 (2-inch) chunks yuca,
  halved lengthwise
2 (2-inch) chunks ñame (yam),
  halved lengthwise
¾ teaspoon crumbled dried
  oregano
1 ½ teaspoons kosher salt
Freshly ground black pepper

ADORNO (GARNISH)

Cilantro sprigs and leaves,
torn by hand

1. Combine the chicken, onion, garlic, bell peppers, chile, whole cilantro leaves and stems, and stock in a soup pot and bring to a quick boil over high heat. Adjust the heat to medium low and simmer, covered, for 10 minutes.

2. Add the corn, yuca, ñame, oregano, salt, and black pepper to taste and simmer gently over low heat, covered, for 30 minutes. The root vegetables should be almost falling apart; if not, cook a bit longer, checking in 5-minute increments. The soup should be a bit cloudy and slightly thick. Remove and discard what is left of the cilantro leaves and stems.

3. Ladle into individual bowls, garnish with the cilantro, and serve.

AMALIA'S NOTES

• Latin root vegetables are available in Latin markets and online, fresh and frozen. Yuca, fresh and frozen, is available at major grocery stores.

• When I don't have all the root vegetables handy, I use a combination of yuca and potatoes in the soup. Once soft, potatoes will have the same effect as the other root vegetables. Although not part of the traditional recipe, potatoes are a root vegetable too and go well in this delicious soup.

• Yuca has a stringy inner core that must be removed prior to eating. This becomes more visible when the yuca is cooked and split in half lengthwise.

• As an option, use tree-range organic chickens, which are raised under regenerative farming practices.

CREMA DE ELOTE
Cream of Corn Soup

SERVES 2

1 tablespoon butter
¾ cup diced yellow onion
1 teaspoon minced garlic

2 cups frozen corn kernels
¾ cup chicken bone broth
  or stock, store-bought,
  or homemade stock
  (see page 198)
¾ cup skim milk
1 ½ teaspoons kosher salt
Freshly ground white pepper

ADORNO (GARNISH)

2 teaspoons unsalted crema or
  Mexican table cream, divided
2 teaspoons queso fresco
  (fresh Latin cheese), divided

This delightful Costa Rican soup is one of my favorites. It's easy, delicious, and nutritious and can be made with just a few ingredients. I keep many vegetables in my freezer at all times, and corn is one of them. This soup could also be made with frozen peas instead of corn. For a twist of flavor, add sliced fresh hot peppers at the same time as the corn. Serve in attractive ceramic bowls or clear cups to better appreciate the soup's beautiful yellow color. Kids and adults alike love crema de elote.

1. In a saucepan over medium low heat, melt the butter and cook the onion and garlic until translucent, about 2 to 3 minutes.

2. Add the corn and cook for 3 minutes, stirring constantly. Add the stock, milk, 1 ½ teaspoons salt, and white pepper to taste, and bring to a quick boil over high heat. Adjust the heat to medium low and simmer, covered, until the corn is tender, about 10 minutes.

3. Puree with an immersion blender or in a regular blender until very smooth.

4. Garnish each serving with 1 teaspoon each crema and queso fresco.

RECIPE VARIATION

Sopa Crema de Elote (Guatemalan Cream of Corn Soup): Follow the recipe given, adding a smidgen of nutmeg with the salt and pepper. Garnish with crema and croutons instead of the queso fresco.

AMALIA'S NOTE

- If you have access to fresh corn, use it instead of frozen corn. You may have to simmer the soup a bit longer as it may be more runny, or compensate by adding an additional ½ cup corn.

SOPA MEIN DE CAMARÓN
Shrimp and Vegetable Noodle Soup

SERVES 4

This soup is not a traditional Mesoamerican recipe, but it is popular in Guatemala City, where there are many Chinese immigrants. Made with shrimp, fish, or chicken, a few vegetables, and lo mein noodles, it's a true delight. Sopa mein, along with other typical Chinese dishes like chow mein, is a favorite in Guatemalan homes. It's delicious and easy to make. I like that by combining a few dry and fresh ingredients and seafood or meat of choice, one can have a hearty and delicious soup in a matter of minutes. Make it your own by adding other vegetables that cook quickly and hold up well to quick simmering.

1. Peel and devein the shrimp. Put the shells in a soup pot and set aside the peeled and deveined shrimp. Add the diced celery, tomatoes, 1 cup green onions, garlic, ½ teaspoon ginger, peppercorns, cloves, salt, and stock to the shells in the soup pot. Bring to a quick boil over high heat, then adjust the heat to medium low and simmer, covered, for 30 minutes. Strain out and discard the solids from the soup base and keep the soup base hot.

2. Return the soup base to a quick boil over high heat. Reduce the heat to medium low, add the noodles, and cook 2 minutes. Add the shrimp and cook 1 minute. Season with the soy sauce, ¼ teaspoon ginger, and black pepper to taste. Stir well. Use caution when adding salt. Keep in mind that commercial stock already contains salt and soy sauce is highly salted, so taste the broth before adding salt to determine if it needs any.

3. Add the sprouts, sliced celery, cabbage, and carrots. Stir well, cover, and simmer gently over low heat for 2 minutes. The shrimp should be firm yet tender, not rubbery, and the vegetables should be cooked al dente.

4. Serve the soup in a tureen or in individual bowls. Garnish with the remaining green onions and the head-on shrimp.

RECIPE VARIATIONS

Sopa Mein de Pescado (Fish and Vegetable Noodle Soup): Follow the recipe given, except use a non-oily fish (such as Dover sole or flounder), instead of shrimp. Use the head and bones instead of shrimp shells in the soup base and slices of the meat in place of the shrimp.

Sopa Mein de Pollo (Chicken and Vegetable Noodle Soup): Follow the recipe for Sopa Mein de Camarón, except use 4 bone-in, skinless chicken thighs in the soup base instead of the shrimp shells and chicken stock instead of the seafood stock. Add the shredded meat from the cooked chicken thighs in place of the shrimp.

AMALIA'S NOTE

- I use a handheld mandoline to slice all the vegetables thinly. This helps cook the vegetables to al dente quickly.

SOPA BASE (SOUP BASE)

20 medium shell-on shrimp
¾ cup diced celery
½ cup diced vine-ripened tomatoes
1 cup sliced green onions
1 teaspoon minced garlic
½ teaspoon freshly grated ginger
8 black peppercorns
4 whole cloves
½ teaspoon kosher salt
6 cups fish or seafood stock, store-bought, or homemade seafood consommé (see pages 197 and 198)

1 (6-ounce) package lo mein or chow mein stir-fry noodles

SAZÓN (SEASONINGS)

1 tablespoon Chinese soy sauce, or to taste
¼ teaspoon freshly grated ginger
Freshly ground black pepper
Kosher salt (optional)

1 cup soybean sprouts
¾ cup thinly sliced celery
¾ cup thinly sliced cabbage
½ cup thinly sliced carrots

ADORNO (GARNISH)

¼ cup thinly sliced green onions
4 cooked medium (50–70 count) shrimp, unpeeled, heads on

SOPA DE FRIJOLES BLANCOS CON CHANCHO
White Bean and Pork Vegetable Soup

SERVES 4 to 6

1 pound pork loin, cut into
  2 (½-inch) pieces
½ cup diced yellow onion
1 teaspoon minced garlic
½ cup diced bell peppers
  (red, green, or a combination
  of both)
1 teaspoon kosher salt
Freshly ground black pepper
2 cups vegetable or chicken
  stock, store-bought or
  homemade (see page 198)

2 cups cooked white
  beans (see page 100)
  or 1 (15.5-ounce) can
  white beans

1 cup diced Yukon Gold
  potatoes
1 cup sliced carrots

2 teaspoons Worcestershire
  sauce

A Costa Rican and Central American classic, pork and beans made with a variety of beans and vegetables is a delicious addition to any menu. It's a quick and easy dish to make and can constitute a main meal for lunch or dinner. It can be modified according to taste. Turn this soup into a stew by simmering it longer or by pureeing some of the beans to thicken it. What is unique about sopa de frijoles con chancho is seasoning it with English sauce (Worcestershire), which gives the broth a distinctive flavor when combined with typical ingredients. Commonly this soupy stew is made with pork ribs, but pork loin is leaner and more tender, and cooks faster. Lizano, a sauce from Costa Rica, and Worcestershire sauce are key seasonings in many Costa Rican dishes, including Gallo Pinto Tico (see page 248), a traditional rice and beans dish, and a staple not only in Costa Rica but in Nicaragua as well (although with varying ingredients).

1. Combine the pork, onion, garlic, bell peppers, salt, black pepper to taste, and stock in a soup pot and bring to a quick boil over high heat. Adjust the heat to medium low and simmer, covered, for 10 minutes.

2. Add the beans, stir well, and simmer, covered, for 10 more minutes.

3. Add the potatoes and carrots, stir well, cover, and simmer until the vegetables are cooked al dente, about 5 to 10 minutes.

4. Add the Worcestershire sauce, stir well, and simmer for 5 more minutes. Serve immediately.

8

Delicias Costeñas
Coastal Delights

COCINA TROPICAL

Undoubtedly, Mesoamerica is a region where many cultures converge and where cuisines fuse in delicious ways. On the Caribbean coast, Garifuna, Belizean, and Yucatecan flavors meld seamlessly with the traditional Central American cuisines as if it was meant to be. In this chapter, I present my take and modern adaptation of some of my favorite dishes of the region.

Garifuna cuisine fuses native ingredients, flavors, and techniques to create Afro-Caribbean-influenced dishes. Popular dishes are rice and beans and tapado (a coconut seafood chowder with yuca and plantains). The cuisine is centered around cassava (yuca) and other key ingredients such as plantains, coconut, and seafood, all of which are abundant in tropical climates.

Garifuna or Garinagu

A culture of their own, the Garifuna are a group of Afro-Caribbean people descended from Arawaks, Caribs, and West Africans. They live mainly on the Caribbean coast of Central America in Guatemala, Belize, Honduras, and Nicaragua. A small population lives in the United States.

Belize (a British commonwealth realm) has an interesting mix of many cultures unlike those of its neighbors. Next to Guatemala to the east and Mexico to the north, Belize has commonalities with the cuisines of Central America but is connected to the Maya and Garifuna culture only, and as such they share some dishes that are popular in each of these cuisines, like ceviche, tamales, seafood chowders, and stews.

In the Yucatán Peninsula, native Maya (plus Spanish, Portuguese, French, Dutch, Lebanese and the Levant, Cuban and the Caribbean, and African) influences create a unique yet familiar cuisine centered around the local fauna and flora and many of the staples that unify the Mesoamerican region, with unique twists on cooking techniques (pibs) and flavor base combinations (recados). Costa Rica, the area of convergence in Central America, is where the local and indigenous cultures of Mesoamerica (Aztec and Maya) and South America (Peru) once came together. This cultural mix created a unique culinary fusion centered around the regional staples and subsequent cultural influences.

Panama's cuisine has traits of native, African, Spanish, Afro-Antillian, Colombian, and, to some extent, American cuisine. There is a synergy of Panama's cuisine with the rest of Central America's that it has made its own.

Tropical cuisine relies heavily on unique seafood from both the Pacific Ocean and the Caribbean Sea. There are native local fish, shellfish, and others. Fresh seafood preparation is often simple yet delicious.

Creativity is high in seafood cocktail creations, with raw and cooked seafood and many styles of fried fish. Conch is a delicacy of the cultures of the Caribbean coast; oysters and conchas (curiles), black clams from the Pacific, can be eaten raw on the half shell or in ceviches.

On the Pacific coast of Guatemala and Central America, despite their endangered status, sea turtle eggs are considered an exotic and aphrodisiac food, and they're prepared at street food stands in a matter of minutes. Passersby stop to have a beer with a boquita (appetizer) prepared with these delicacies.

Soups and chowders, fried fish with plantain chips, rice and beans, and casados (another form of rice and beans) are some of the most popular and traditional foods, as some are one-dish meals consisting of not only a variety of seafood but vegetables too. Some of these identify the cultures where they belong, namely tapado in Livingston, Guatemala, sopa de caracol in Honduras, and gallo pinto in Costa Rica and Nicaragua (with black and red beans, respectively).

Cocina tropical is a feast for the palate as well as the soul and senses. It grabs and seduces you much like the beauty of the scenery with palm trees, warm weather, and sea breezes.

CHUPE DE LANGOSTINOS
Baby Lobster Tomato Chowder

SERVES 1 to 2

2 teaspoons canola oil
½ cup diced yellow onion
½ teaspoon minced garlic
½ cup small-diced green
  bell pepper
1 cup small-diced vine-ripened
  tomatoes
1 cup clam juice, store-bought,
  or homemade seafood
  consommé, divided (see
  page 198)

¼ cup tomato sauce
2 tablespoons dry white wine
1 ½ tablespoons chopped
  cilantro leaves
½ cup petite-diced Yukon Gold
  potatoes
1 small dried bay leaf
¼ teaspoon hot chile powder
1 teaspoon kosher salt
Freshly ground black pepper

6 ounces cooked langostinos
  or salad shrimp, or a
  combination of both

ADORNO (GARNISH)

Cilantro sprigs

Belizean chupe de langostinos is one of my go-to quick starters for a dinner gathering. It's scrumptious and takes only a few minutes to make. It's perfect for a light lunch or can become the main meal when accompanied by bread and a salad. The traditional soup is made with shrimp, but I am fond of langostinos because they are deliciously delicate. Sometimes I make it with a combination of the two, and the experience is just as amazing.

1. In a medium saucepan, combine the oil, onion, garlic, bell pepper, tomatoes, and ½ cup clam juice or stock. Simmer over medium high heat, covered, for 3 minutes. Mash the mixture with a flat potato masher until slightly smooth, and cook about 2 more minutes.

2. Add the remaining ½ cup clam juice or stock, tomato sauce, wine, chopped cilantro, potatoes, bay leaf, chile powder, salt, and black pepper to taste. Simmer over medium low heat, covered, for 8 minutes.

3. Add the langostinos or shrimp and simmer over low heat, covered, 3 to 5 more minutes.

4. Serve and garnish with cilantro sprigs.

AMALIA'S NOTE
- Langostinos are available frozen at wholesale stores and online.

BROCHETAS DE LANGOSTA
Flambéed Lobster Skewers with Lime, Garlic, and Coconut Butter Sauce

SERVES 2

Lobster in any style is a luxurious dish, and you'll love this easy grilled lobster flambé with flavors from the Central American tropics. I like to use good-quality rums to flambé, such as award-winning Zacapa Centenario from Guatemala or Flor de Caña from Nicaragua. The rum combined with the coconut butter sauce elevates this dish to a gourmet level that you can dress elegantly for a special dinner. Or make it for a casual barbecue on the patio. Paired with Belizean red beans and coconut rice and green plantain chips, this dish is a winner in my book and may become a favorite of yours too. Another good pairing would be Ensalada de Repollo (Spicy Cabbage Slaw with Lime, page 184) or Ensalada Mixta (Mixed Salad, page 236).

1 Assemble the skewers beginning with a piece of lemon, followed by a piece of lobster, 1 piece of fresno pepper, another piece of lobster, 1 piece of jalapeño pepper, and ending with another piece of lobster. Repeat the procedure for the other skewer. Brush the skewers generously with olive oil. Season with ¼ teaspoon salt and black pepper to taste.

2 Preheat a nonstick griddle skillet over medium high heat while you make the sauce.

3 Add the butter to a small skillet and melt over medium low heat. Add the garlic and sauté until aromatic, about 2 minutes. Add the coconut milk and stir well, then add the lime juice, cilantro, ½ teaspoon salt, and black pepper to taste. Stir well and sauté 1 minute.

4 Place the lobster skewers on the hot griddle and grill for 5 minutes on one side and 2 minutes on the other side. Pour the rum on top and set aflame using a candle lighter. Transfer the skewers to a serving plate, drizzle the sauce on top, and serve with red beans and coconut rice and green plantain chips.

AMALIA'S NOTES

• Adjust the size of the pepper pieces to the size of lobster chunks.

• Zacapa Centenario and Flor de Caña rums are available at wholesale liquor stores or online.

• Make the red beans and coconut rice the day before. Make the plantain chips before you grill the lobster.

• Use 9-inch skewers for larger chunks of lobster.

• For safety, follow the flaming directions carefully. Never pour rum directly from the bottle into the pan with high flames, as the bottle could explode. Flaming with rum or other high-alcohol-content liquor can be dangerous if not done properly and safely. Do not allow children to be close while flaming.

BROCHETAS (SEAFOOD SKEWERS)

1 (½-inch-thick) slice lemon, quartered into 4 wedges
2 (5-ounce) lobster tails, shelled and cut into 3 pieces each
2 (1-inch-sliced) fresno pepper pieces
2 (1-inch-sliced) jalapeño pepper pieces
Olive oil
¼ teaspoon kosher salt
Freshly ground black pepper

SALSA DE COCO Y AJO (LIME, GARLIC, AND COCONUT BUTTER SAUCE)

1 tablespoon butter
2 teaspoons minced garlic
¼ cup coconut milk
1 tablespoon freshly squeezed lime juice
1 tablespoon chopped cilantro leaves
½ teaspoon kosher salt
Freshly ground black pepper

1 ½ tablespoons good-quality rum

ACOMPAÑANTES (PAIRINGS)

1 recipe **Arroz con Frijoles Rojos y Coco** (Belizean Red Bean and Coconut Rice, page 247)
1 recipe **Tajadas** (Green Plantain Chips, page 74)

SPECIAL EQUIPMENT

2 (7-inch) bamboo skewers

SOPA DE CARACOL
Conch and Coconut Chowder
SERVES 4

¾ pound fresh or frozen conch, thawed (about 3 medium fillets)

½ cup petite-diced red and green bell peppers
1 teaspoon butter

SOFRITO (QUICK BASE SAUCE)

1 tablespoon butter
¾ cup diced yellow onion
1 ½ teaspoons minced garlic
½ cup julienned green bell pepper
½ cup julienned red bell pepper
1 cup diced vine-ripened tomatoes
½–¾ teaspoon cayenne pepper
½ teaspoon condimented achiote paste
1 ½ teaspoons kosher salt
Freshly ground white pepper

1 cup clam juice, store-bought
1 (13.5-ounce) can coconut milk
2 (3 ½-inch) pieces frozen yuca, thawed, halved or quartered lengthwise
2 (3 ½-inch) pieces peeled green plantains or bananas (or a combination), halved or quartered lengthwise

This Honduran soup is so delicious and popular that it even has its own bilingual song, "Sopa de Caracol" ("watanegui consup" for "I want to eat soup" in the Garifuna language), written by a Belizean singer and translated into Spanish and made famous by Honduran band Banda Blanca. This soup has cousins throughout the Garifuna region of Central America. Close relatives are tapado costeño and tapado de pescado con coco in Honduras and tapado from Livingston, Guatemala. Caracol (conch, pronounced *konk*) is a delicacy and delightful mollusk native to the Bahamas, Turks and Caicos Islands, Florida Keys, and surrounding regions. Used for ceviches, sushi, soups, and chowders, as well as grilled and stewed, conch needs only a few minutes of cooking time. In Spanish, caracol is also the name of the sea and freshwater smaller snails, and to differentiate them, people often refer to them as caracol de mar (sea conch).

1. Slice the conch as thinly as possible into several layers, then cut it into 1 ½- to 2-inch strips.

2. Sauté the ½ cup petite-diced bell peppers in 1 teaspoon butter over medium high heat, stirring gently with a soft spatula for 2 minutes. Set aside.

3. To make the sofrito, combine the butter, onion, garlic, julienned bell peppers, tomatoes, cayenne pepper, achiote paste dissolved in a little of the clam juice, salt, and white pepper to taste. Cook over medium heat, covered, for 3 minutes.

4. Add the clam juice and coconut milk. Stir well to blend flavors. Add the yuca and plantains or bananas. Cover and cook over medium low heat until the vegetables are soft, about 6 to 8 minutes.

5. Add the conch and stir well. Cover and cook for 3 to 5 minutes. Serve immediately, garnished with the petite-diced sautéed bell peppers.

AMALIA'S NOTES

- Conch has a natural chewy yet tender texture when raw and cooked, similar to clams. Cooking makes it tougher, so it's best to cook it lightly. I like serving my conch either raw in ceviche or in a soup when it has cooked for just a few minutes so the texture is still tender. I use sushi-grade conch when I eat it raw.

- I prefer not to pound my conch to tenderize it; rather, I slice it as thinly as possible into several layers, then cut it into strips. This works well whether you eat it raw or add it to soup.

- Conch is available frozen by ordering it through your local fishmonger or online. In some major grocery stores and Asian markets in Florida, it is available fresh.

- Condimented achiote (annatto) paste is available at major grocery stores, Latin stores, and online under the El Yucateco brand.

- Yuca is available fresh and frozen at major grocery stores.

- Yuca has a stringy inner core that must be removed prior to eating. This becomes more visible when the yuca is cooked and split in half lengthwise.

ASADO MAR Y TIERRA
Chilean Sea Bass and Filet Mignon Grill

SERVES 2

Stray away from the usual barbecue menu of hamburgers and hot dogs and venture into this Asado Mar y Tierra, a sea-and-land grill that could turn your patio barbecue into a delicious rendezvous or fiesta. I am a big fan of this combination pairing buttery Chilean sea bass and juicy, tender filet mignon with easy-to-make fresh sauces. This menu includes flavors from Mexico, Guatemala, and Costa Rica for a delightful dining experience. Preparation is quite simple and can include other sides, such as Guacamol Nica (Nicaraguan Guacamole, page 187) and other dishes of personal choice. All you need to add is Guatemalan or other Central American beer, or choose a variety of drinks and cocktails from Chapter 1, page 31, and let the party begin.

1. In a medium bowl, whisk together the sour orange juice, onion, oregano, olive oil, ½ teaspoon salt, and black pepper to taste. Pour half into another medium bowl. Add the fish and filet mignon to separate bowls and marinate in the refrigerator for 30 minutes. Skewer the fish and filet separately, two fish skewers and two filet skewers, and set aside.

2. Preheat the grill over medium high heat. Season the grill to prevent sticking by rubbing the grates with a terry cloth towel (or rag) coated with canola oil. Hold the towel with grill tongs to prevent burns.

3. Grill the fish 3 minutes on one side and 2 minutes on the other side. The fish is done when it's opaque and flakes easily. Grill the filet for 4 minutes on one side and 2 minutes on the other side (or to your desired doneness). Keep the fish and filet mignon warm.

4. To make the grilled corn, grill the corn on high heat until charred all over and cooked, about 3 to 5 minutes. Turn the corn constantly as soon as popping begins for even grilling. Dip half a lime in sea salt and rub it generously on the corn.

5. Serve the fish topped with the green sauce and the filet topped with the red sauce with the rice and corn on the side.

AMALIA'S NOTES

- Cutting the fish and the filet mignon into same-size pieces will make it easier to marinate, skewer, and cook.

- Make the rice a few hours before or the day before.

- Find the recipe for Chirmol Chapín (Charred Tomato and Mint Salsa) in recipe variations under Chirmoles (Mayan Sauces) on page 301, and Arroz con Frijoles Rojos y Coco (Belizean Red Bean and Coconut Rice) and Gallo Pinto Tico (Costa Rican Black Bean and Cilantro Fried Rice) on page 247 and 248, respectively.

SALMUERA (MARINADE)

¾ cup fresh sour orange juice (jugo de naranja agria) or equal parts fresh orange and lemon juice
½ cup shaved yellow onion
½ teaspoon crumbled dried oregano
2 tablespoons olive oil
½ teaspoon kosher salt
Freshly ground black pepper

½ pound Chilean sea bass fillets or cod or mahi mahi fillets, cut into 3-inch pieces
½ pound filet mignon, cut into 2-inch-thick cubes

ELOTE ASADO CON LIMÓN Y SAL MARINA (GRILLED CORN ON THE COB WITH LIME AND SEA SALT)

1–2 ears corn, shucked
½ lime
Sea salt

ACOMPAÑANTES (PAIRINGS)

1 recipe **Salsa de Miltomate y Aguacate** (Tomatillo, Avocado, Serrano, and Cilantro Sauce, page 308)
1 recipe **Chirmol Chapín** (Charred Tomato and Mint Salsa) (see note)
1 recipe **Gallo Pinto Tico** (Costa Rican Black Bean and Cilantro Fried Rice) (see note)

SPECIAL EQUIPMENT

4 (7- or 9-inch) bamboo skewers

HUDUTU CON MACHUCA
Coconut Seafood Soup with Mashed Plantain Dumplings

SERVES 2 to 4

MACHUCA (MASHED PLANTAINS)

1 ripe plantain, cut into
   2-inch slices
1 green plantain, cut into
   2-inch slices
¾ teaspoon kosher salt

HUDUTU (SOUP)

1 teaspoon canola oil
½ cup finely diced yellow onion
1 teaspoon minced garlic
½ cup julienned green
   bell pepper
½ cup julienned red bell pepper
½–1 teaspoon minced
   habanero chile
2 tablespoons chopped cilantro
¾ teaspoon crumbled
   dried oregano
¼ teaspoon ground achiote
1 ½ teaspoons kosher salt
Freshly ground white pepper

1 cup clam juice, store-bought,
   or homemade seafood
   consommé (see page 198)
1 (13.5-ounce) can
   coconut milk

2 (4-ounce) flounder fillets
2 (4-ounce) sole fillets
8 medium (50–70 count)
   shrimp, deveined, peeled,
   tails off
4 clams, scrubbed and
   debearded
4 mussels, scrubbed

ADORNO (GARNISH)

Cilantro sprigs

Hudutu is a delightful Garifuna soup popular on the Central American Caribbean coast. There are many versions of the soup and machuca (mashed plantains) too. These are my versions based on my experiences in Garifuna country in Livingston, Guatemala, the Belize Cayes, and Roatán, Honduras. What makes the soup complete is the machuca, a typical side. *Machuchar* in Spanish means "to mash." In the Garifuna culture, sometimes they use green plantains only or a combination of ripe and green. As simple as it is, machuca is a delicious pairing for coconut-based soups and pan-fried fish. Traditionally, the plantains are mashed with a large, tall, and deep wood mortar and pestle called hana. The soup is so easy to prepare and can be made with fish only or a combination of seafood. I enjoy making it with what is fresh and available at the fishmonger. This soup is worthy of celebration and is a nice starter or complete meal for any gathering with family or friends.

1. In a medium saucepan, cook the plantains in 3 cups boiling water until soft but not mushy, about 20 to 25 minutes. Peel. In a stand mixer with the paddle attachment, beat the plantains with ¾ cup of the cooking water and the ¾ teaspoon of salt until doughy and the dough no longer sticks to the sides of the bowl, about 4 minutes. Form the dough into a ball with your hands, then pinch off and form golf-ball-size dumplings. Cover and keep warm.

2. In a medium soup pot, combine the canola oil, onion, garlic, bell peppers, habanero, cilantro, oregano, achiote, 1 ½ teaspoons salt, and white pepper to taste, and sauté over medium high heat until the onion is translucent, about 3 minutes. Add the clam juice or stock and the coconut milk. Cover and simmer over medium low heat for 2 minutes. Add the flounder, sole, shrimp, clams, and mussels. Cover and simmer until the clams and mussels open, about 4 to 5 minutes more. Discard any clams or mussels that do not open.

3. Serve in bowls garnished with cilantro sprigs and the machuca dumplings on the side.

RECIPE VARIATION

Angú (Costa Rican Mashed Plantains with Onion and Bell Peppers): Follow the recipe for machuca and add ¾ cup chopped onion and ¾ cup diced green bell peppers sautéed in 1 tablespoon canola oil to the mixture.

AMALIA'S NOTE

- If you have leftover dumplings, freeze them in deep plastic disposable storage boxes or containers with a lid for another time. This ensures they retain their shape.

MACARELA ESPAÑOLA ASADA AL HORNO CON TAJADAS
Oven-Roasted Spanish Mackerel and Green Plantain Chips

SERVES 4 to 6

Pescado frito con tajadas (fried fish with plantain chips) is prepared from the Caribbean coast of Belize to Costa Rica and beyond. The seasonings, preparation, and presentation vary by country and region. Inspired by the scrumptious meal, oven roasting the fish instead of pan frying it creates an equally amazing experience, especially when combined with some of my favorite flavors and sides. While in Garifuna country in Guatemala, Belize, and Honduras, I had the local fish, each time pan fried instead of oven roasted, including a delicious mixed salad. For a fun twist, pair the dish with traditional sides, such as Arroz con Frijoles Rojos y Coco (Belizean Red Bean and Coconut Rice, page 247), Encurtido de Cebolla (Spicy Pickled Onions and Carrots, page 293), and a delicious Ensalada Mixta (Mixed Salad, see below).

1. To make the marinade, whisk together the ½ cup sour orange juice, garlic, oregano, cilantro, 1 teaspoon salt, and black pepper to taste. Brush the fish with the marinade on both sides, from head to tail, in the scored areas, and inside the cavity. Let the fish marinate for 30 minutes. Do not refrigerate.

2. Preheat the oven to 350°F.

3. Line a rimmed baking sheet with parchment paper and brush the paper lightly with olive oil. Put the fish on top. Drizzle the fish with ½ cup olive oil divided equally on one side only. Pour the marinating juices around the fish. Roast for 20 minutes, then rotate the baking sheet around 180 degrees to ensure even roasting. Continue roasting the fish until it flakes easily, about 10 minutes more.

4. Meanwhile, make the salad and dressing. Combine the lettuce, tomatoes, cucumber, and onion in a large bowl and chill. To make the dressing, whisk together the mayonnaise, ketchup, mustard, ¼ cup sour orange juice, 1 teaspoon salt, and black pepper to taste in a small bowl. Serve the salad with the dressing on the side.

5. Serve the fish on the baking sheet with the tajadas and chosen sides placed right next to the fish, or carefully lift the fish with a wide spatula to prevent breaking the fish and place it on a platter. Coat the orange and lemon slices with the chopped cilantro and lay them out attractively around the fish. Arrange the sides on the platter as desired.

AMALIA'S NOTES

- Other types of fish that hold well during oven roasting and look beautiful on the plate are red snapper, sea bass, and mahi mahi. Visit your local fishmonger to buy the freshest fish. Fish will vary in size, so choose carefully for the number of people you are serving.

- The fish can also be dredged in whole grain coarse-grind stone-ground cornmeal and pan fried.

SALMUERA (MARINADE)

½ cup fresh sour orange juice (jugo de naranja agria) or equal parts fresh orange and lemon juice
2 teaspoons minced garlic
1 teaspoon crumbled dried oregano
1 ½ tablespoons chopped cilantro leaves
1 teaspoon kosher salt
Freshly ground black pepper

2 whole, head-on fresh Spanish mackerels (about 2 pounds each), scored on the bias four times on each side
½ cup Spanish extra-virgin olive oil

ENSALADA MIXTA (MIXED SALAD)

3 cups torn romaine lettuce, washed and spun dry
1 cup grape tomatoes, halved lengthwise
1 cup thinly sliced English cucumber
¾ cup julienned red onion

SALSA ROSA CON NARANJA AGRIA (SOUR ORANGE MAYONNAISE DRESSING)

½ cup olive oil mayonnaise
¼ cup ketchup
½ teaspoon Dijon mustard
¼ cup fresh sour orange juice (jugo de naranja agria) or equal parts fresh orange and lemon juice
1 teaspoon kosher salt
Freshly ground black pepper

ACOMPAÑANTES (PAIRINGS)

1 recipe **Tajadas** (Green Plantain Chips, page 74)

ADORNO (GARNISH)

6 (¼-inch-thick) orange slices
4 (¼-inch-thick) lemon slices
1 tablespoon chopped cilantro leaves

SOPA DE CANGREJO

Crab, Tomato, and Guajillo Chile Soup

SERVES 2 to 4

1 cup diced vine-ripened
tomatoes

½ cup diced tomatillos

⅔ cup large-diced yellow onion

1 teaspoon minced garlic

½ guajillo chile, seeded and
torn into small pieces

1 teaspoon condimented
achiote paste

1 tablespoon ground dried
shrimp

1 ½ store-bought corn tortillas,
torn into small pieces

2 cups clam juice,
store-bought, or homemade
seafood consommé
(see page 198)

¼ cup chopped cilantro leaves

1 tablespoon chopped
epazote leaves

1 tablespoon freshly squeezed
lime juice

1 cup diced potatoes

1 cup diced chayote squash

½ cup French-cut fresh
green beans

1 ½ teaspoons kosher salt

Freshly ground black pepper

3 tablespoons unsalted crema
or Mexican table cream

1 ½ cups premium crab meat

ADORNO (GARNISH)

¼ cup chopped cilantro leaves

2 teaspoons chopped
epazote leaves

This soup, popular throughout Central America, is near and dear to my heart, as it reminds me of a soup my grandmother used to make when I was little. This is my kicked-up version. She had a store that catered to the needs of her town where we lived. She gave people thirty-day credit terms for the items they could not pay for immediately, and sometimes people would pay her back with freshly caught river crabs, live chickens, fresh eggs, freshly harvested vegetables, and more, in appreciation for the credit extension or in place of money. The crabs were closely tied up next to each other vertically with long strips of banana leaves to secure the legs in place. I always got excited each time I saw the crabs tied up this way; they were still able to move their legs somehow. I anticipated the delicious soup each time. We paired it with warm corn tortillas.

1 In a soup pot, combine the tomatoes, tomatillos, onion, garlic, guajillo, achiote paste, dried shrimp, corn tortillas, and clam juice or stock. Bring to a quick boil over high heat. Adjust the heat to medium low and simmer, covered, for 5 minutes. Puree with an immersion blender or in a regular blender until smooth.

2 Add the ¼ cup cilantro, 1 tablespoon epazote, lime juice, potatoes, chayote squash, green beans, salt, and black pepper to taste, and simmer, covered, until the vegetables are al dente, about 5 to 8 minutes.

3 Add the crema and stir well. Add the crab and blend gently with the soup ingredients. Cover and simmer gently over low heat for 3 minutes.

4 For the garnish, combine the remaining ¼ cup cilantro and 2 teaspoons epazote in a small bowl. Serve the soup garnished with the mix.

AMALIA'S NOTES

- Condimented achiote (annatto) paste is available at major grocery chains, Latin stores, and online under the El Yucateco brand.

- Premium crab meat is available at your local fishmonger, at major grocery chains, or online.

COCTEL DE CAMARONES Y AGUACATE
Spicy Shrimp and Avocado Cocktail

SERVES 2

This cocktail brings back memories of when my parents used to have family reunions at our home. It was one of the starters on the menu. Sometimes my mom made it with just shrimp or just avocado, but I like combining the two, as they pair well. Although shrimp is the classic, langostinos, lobster, conch, calamari, and other seafood would be great in this sauce. Soda crackers are a traditional side for cocktails and ceviches in Guatemala City, but corn tostadas would be delicious too.

1. In a medium bowl, combine the V-8 juice, ketchup, lime juice, onion, tomatoes, cilantro leaves, chile pepper, salt, and black pepper to taste and mix well.

2. Add the shrimp and avocado balls. Gently mix with the sauce with folding strokes using a wide, soft spatula.

3. Refrigerate until needed or serve immediately in shrimp cocktail cups or short or tall glasses. Garnish with cilantro sprigs and saltine crackers.

RECIPE VARIATION

Campechano (Yucatán Shrimp and Oyster Cocktail): Follow the recipe given, except omit the V-8 juice and substitute ¼ cup tomato juice. Add 1 tablespoon freshly squeezed lime juice instead, ½ teaspoon Worcestershire sauce, 2 teaspoons Spanish extra-virgin olive oil, and ½ teaspoon white wine vinegar. Use equal parts shrimp and freshly shucked or canned oysters. Add a splash of orange soda right before serving. Serve with nacho chips.

AMALIA'S NOTE

- For best results, serve and eat this cocktail the day you make it.

¼ cup V-8 juice
2 tablespoons ketchup
1 ½ tablespoons freshly squeezed lime juice
1 ½ tablespoons minced yellow onion
¼ cup small-diced seeded vine-ripened tomatoes
2 tablespoons chopped cilantro leaves
½–1 teaspoon minced fresh hot chile (chiltepe or piquín, habanero, or serrano)
½ teaspoon kosher salt
Freshly ground black pepper

12 medium (50–70 count) shrimp, deveined, peeled, and tails off
1 ripe avocado, scooped out with a melon baller

ADORNO (GARNISH)

Cilantro sprigs
Saltine crackers

CALDO DE PESCADO
Spicy Fish Soup
SERVES 2 to 4

SOFRITO (BASE SAUCE)

1 teaspoon canola oil
⅔ cup diced yellow onion
1 teaspoon minced garlic
⅔ cup julienned green
 bell pepper
½–1 thinly sliced Fresno chile
⅔ cup thinly sliced carrots
1 cup chopped vine-ripened
 tomatoes

2 cups clam juice,
 store-bought, or
 homemade seafood
 consommé (see page 198)
1 tablespoon anchovy paste
1 tablespoon chopped
 flat-leaf parsley
1 teaspoon crumbled dried
 oregano
2 small dried bay leaves
½ teaspoon ground achiote
½–1 teaspoon Cobán chile
 powder or other dried hot
 chile powder
1 tablespoon freshly squeezed
 lime juice
1 teaspoon kosher salt
Freshly ground black pepper

2 medium Yukon Gold
 potatoes, peeled, sliced
 ¼ inch thick
1 pound fish cut into 2 ½-inch
 chunks (sole, cod, halibut,
 flounder, corvina, mahi mahi,
 or other fish of choice)

ADORNO (GARNISH)

¼ cup chopped flat-leaf parsley
½ teaspoon crumbled dried
 oregano
1 lime, cut into 4 to 6 wedges

The coastal regions of Central America (Caribbean and Pacific) boast a wide variety of seafood preparations that are delicious and super simple, such as this Caldo de Pescado. It can be made in a matter of minutes once you have all the ingredients prepped. It is perfect for a weekday as a one-dish meal. It pairs well with warm soft or crispy corn tortillas or toasted French bread slices. It can be built into a bigger soup by adding more seafood, such as shrimp, clams, or mussels, and to give it a Spanish touch, add some saffron during the third step. I added Cobán chile powder, a smoky and very tasty spicy chile native to Cobán, Alta Verapaz, Guatemala.

1. In a soup pot, make a sofrito with the oil, onion, garlic, bell pepper, Fresno chile, carrots, and tomatoes and cook over medium heat, covered, for 3 minutes.

2. Add the clam juice or stock and the anchovy paste dissolved in a little clam juice or stock, 1 tablespoon parsley, 1 teaspoon oregano, bay leaves, achiote, chile powder, lime juice, salt, and black pepper to taste. Cover and simmer over medium low heat for 3 minutes to blend flavors.

3. Gently nestle the potatoes and fish chunks in the hot soup and simmer, covered, until the potatoes are cooked al dente and the fish is opaque and flakes easily, about 5 to 7 minutes.

4. Carefully ladle the soup into bowls, distributing vegetables and fish chunks evenly. Combine the ¼ cup parsley and ½ teaspoon oregano in a small bowl and garnish the soup with the herb mix and lime wedges.

AMALIA'S NOTE

- Use fresh fish, if available, from your fishmonger, or frozen fish from major grocery stores.

CEVICHE DE CARACOL
Conch Ceviche

SERVES 4 to 6

Ceviche is one of the easiest and most delicious dishes there is on the seafood menu. I often make it a meal, especially if it contains conch. From the Yucatán Peninsula and Guatemala to the rest of the Central American Isthmus and beyond, there is a version of this recipe. To change the recipe a bit from time to time, I like to add a variety of citrus juices, coconut milk, and avocado to give my ceviche a new flavor and texture dimension. I've had ceviche in many styles, and one of the most surprisingly delicious was a Belizean ceviche with cucumber, shredded carrots, and celery dressed with vinegar. All ceviche is unique and exquisite. Serve it with soda crackers, corn tostadas, or any crunchy side you wish.

1. Slice the conch lengthwise two or three times so that it is as thin as possible. Then cut it into 1 ½- to 2-inch strips.

2. In a medium bowl, combine the conch with the lemon juice, orange juice, lime juice, red onion, salt, and black pepper to taste, and let marinate for 15 minutes.

3. Add the coconut milk and blend well. Add the habanero, bell pepper, tomatoes, and chopped cilantro, and gently fold them in with the rest of the ingredients.

4. Garnish with cilantro sprigs and avocado slices, and serve with soda crackers on the side.

RECIPE VARIATIONS

Ceviche Mixto (Seafood Ceviche): Follow the recipe given, using a combination of seafood, such as conch, cooked shrimp, cooked calamari rings, cooked octopus, abalone, or any other firm seafood of choice. Omit the coconut milk.

Ceviche de Ostras y Almejas y Conchas Negras (Oyster and Cherrystone and Black Clam Ceviche): Follow the recipe for Ceviche de Caracol, using freshly shucked oysters and cherrystone and black clams. Keep the oysters whole and dice the clams if they are too large for one bite. Omit the coconut milk.

Ceviche de Pescado (Honduran Fish Ceviche): Combine in a medium bowl 1 cup lightly cooked cubed corvina, 2 tablespoons diced red or yellow onion, 1 teaspoon minced habanero, ¼ cup lime juice, ¼ cup orange juice, ½ teaspoon minced garlic, 1 teaspoon olive oil, 2 tablespoons chopped cilantro, and kosher salt and freshly ground black pepper to taste. Mix well and serve immediately.

¾ pound fresh or thawed frozen sushi-grade conch (about 3 medium fillets)
3 tablespoons freshly squeezed lemon juice
3 tablespoons freshly squeezed orange juice
⅓ cup freshly squeezed lime juice
¾ cup thinly sliced red onion
1 teaspoon kosher salt
Freshly ground black pepper

2 tablespoons coconut milk
2 teaspoons seeded and deveined minced habanero chile
½ cup thinly julienned green bell pepper
1 cup diced and seeded vine-ripened tomatoes
½ cup chopped cilantro leaves

ADORNO Y ACOMPAÑANTE (GARNISH AND PAIRING)

Cilantro sprigs
Avocado slices
Soda crackers

AMALIA'S NOTES

• I use sushi-grade conch, fish, or shrimp if I plan to eat it raw. If I don't have access to fresh sushi-grade seafood, I immerse cubed fish or whole shrimp in salted boiling water until the fish is opaque and the shrimp turns pink, about 2 minutes. Then I chill it in the refrigerator to stop the cooking and add it to the rest of the ingredients.

• Conch is available frozen through your local fishmonger or online. In some major grocery stores and Asian markets in Florida, it is available fresh.

• Conch has a natural chewy yet tender texture when raw and cooked, similar to clams. Cooking makes it tougher, so it's best to cook it lightly. I like serving my conch either raw in ceviche or in a soup when it has cooked for just a few minutes so the texture is still tender.

• I prefer not to pound my conch to tenderize it; rather I slice it as thinly as possible into several layers and then cut it into strips. This works well whether you eat it raw or add it to soup.

• For best results, serve and eat this ceviche the day you make it. Adjust the lime juice or salt and spice level to your taste.

ARROZ CON FRIJOLES ROJOS Y COCO

Belizean Red Bean and Coconut Rice

SERVES 2 to 4

2 teaspoons canola oil
½ cup finely diced yellow onion
½ teaspoon minced garlic
¼ teaspoon minced
  fresh thyme
1 cup long-grain white rice
1 cup canned red beans
½ cup red bean broth
  (from a 15-ounce can
  of beans)
1 ¼ cup chicken or vegetable
  stock, store-bought or
  homemade (see page 198)
¼ cup coconut milk
½ teaspoon kosher salt
Freshly ground black pepper

Beans and coconut rice is a traditional pairing in tropical cuisines, especially of the Garifuna culture that inhabits the Caribbean coast of the Mesoamerican region. This Belizean dish has cousins throughout the area with varying ingredients and cooking techniques. Some are quick sautés, and others are quick simmering preparations. Throughout Mesoamerica, there are also other variations of rice-and-bean dishes that do not contain coconut; they are similar, yet they also differ by the color of beans used, either red or black. From coconut rice and beans and gallo pinto (Nicaragua and Costa Rica) to casamiento (El Salvador and Honduras), all are basic and typical sides for grilled seafood and beyond. Easy to make and delicious, rice and beans of any kind are quite possibly the perfect meal for any diet, as they constitute a whole protein. Any other ingredients you add to the dish are a bonus. This dish is naturally vegan when you use vegetable stock and gluten free to boot.

1. Add the oil to a medium skillet and sauté the onion, garlic, and thyme for 1 minute over medium hight heat. Add the rice and sauté until the rice is well coated with the oil, about 1 minute.

2. Add the red beans, bean broth, stock, coconut milk, salt, and black pepper to taste. Bring to a quick boil over high heat, then adjust the heat to medium low and simmer, covered, until rice has absorbed most of the liquid, 15 to 20 minutes. Serve.

RECIPE VARIATIONS

Arroz con Frijoles (Guatemala Garifuna Coconut Red Beans and Rice): Follow the recipe given, adding ¼ cup diced red bell peppers and 1 dried bay leaf to the skillet with the onion, garlic, and thyme.

Gallo Pinto Nica (Nicaraguan Red Bean and Cilantro Fried Rice): Sauté in 1 tablespoon canola oil over medium high heat 1 cup finely chopped onion, ¾ cup diced chiltomas (or substitute with green or multicolored bell peppers), ¾ cup canned red beans, ½ cup broth (from can of beans), and ½ teaspoon (or to taste) kosher salt (freshly ground black pepper is optional) for 3 minutes. Gradually add 1 ½ cups cooked long-grain white rice, using a firm spatula to break up any large clumps of rice. Sauté until the rice has absorbed the liquid, about 2 to 4 minutes more. Garnish with ¾ cup finely chopped culantro or cilantro leaves (see note).

Continued on page 248

Gallo Pinto Tico (Costa Rican Black Bean and Cilantro Fried Rice): Sauté in 2 tablespoons canola oil over medium high heat 1 cup finely chopped onion, ¾ cup diced multicolored bell peppers, ½ cup finely chopped cooked bacon, ¾ cup cooked black beans (see page 100), and ¾ cup finely chopped cilantro stems and leaves, for about 3 minutes. Season with 1 ½ tablespoons Lizano sauce (or Worcestershire sauce), ½ teaspoon Tabasco sauce, and kosher salt to taste, keeping in mind that the seasoning sauces already contain salt (freshly ground black pepper is optional). Sauté for 2 minutes more. Gradually add 1 ½ cups cooked long-grain white rice, using a firm spatula to break up any large clumps of rice. Sauté until the rice has absorbed the liquid, about 2 to 3 minutes more. Garnish with ½ cup roughly chopped cilantro leaves. Serve immediately.

Casamiento (Salvadoran Black Beans and Rice): Sauté in 1 tablespoon canola oil 1 cup finely chopped onion and ½ cup diced green bell pepper for 1 minute. Add ½ cup diced Roma tomatoes and sauté 1 minute. Add ¾ cup canned black beans and ½ cup broth (from a 15-ounce can), and ½ to ¾ teaspoon (or to taste) kosher salt. Gradually add 1 ½ cups cooked long-grain white rice, using a firm spatula to break up any large clumps of rice. Sauté until the mixture has absorbed the liquid, about 2 to 4 minutes more. Serve immediately.

AMALIA'S NOTES

- I don't rinse packaged fortified rice because water washes away the added nutrients. Rinsing doesn't speed the process or do anything that cooking wouldn't do. This recipe makes delicious and fluffy rice in minutes. Rinse rice only if you are unsure of its source or its processing.

- Alternatively, for fresher results, use freshly cooked beans instead of canned beans. See Frijoles (Favorite Bean Traditions, page 100).

- Gallo Pinto Nica should have a red hue. Mashing some of the beans in the broth before adding them to the vegetable and rice mixture can help achieve this color, or use freshly cooked red beans (see page 100).

TORTITAS DE CAMARÓN
Shrimp Cakes with Ancho-Guajillo Sauce and Grilled Cactus

MAKES 10 to 12 tortitas

Tortitas de camarón are a Lent season favorite food in Mexico. There are many versions by region with more or fewer ingredients. This is my version based on my trip to Oaxaca, Mexico, where I cooked with great local chefs. The main ingredient of the traditional recipe is dried ground shrimp, but I elevated them to a crab-cake-like status by adding fresh cooked shrimp to the mixture. They turn out even more fluffy and delicious. I kicked them up with a little piquín chile powder for another flavor dimension. I like to make them for entertaining guests during a cocktail party or serve them as a starter during a multicourse elegant dinner gathering. No matter the occasion, these cakes are delicious in the ancho-guajillo sauce and with cactus. I like grilling the whole cactus paddle and cutting it into long strips just before serving.

1 Combine the onion, garlic, tomatoes, tomatillos, ancho chile, guajillo chile, water, oregano, cumin, cloves, 1 teaspoon salt, and black pepper to taste in a saucepan and bring to a quick boil over high heat. Adjust the heat to medium low and simmer, covered, until all ingredients are soft, about 5 to 8 minutes. With an immersion blender or regular blender, puree the mixture until smooth.

2 With two layers of paper towels, squeeze as much water as possible out of the chopped shrimp. Do this at least three times. Combine the chopped and ground shrimp, chile powder (if using), and masa flour in a medium bowl and mix well. Set aside.

3 In a stand mixer with the whisk attachment or in a large bowl with a hand mixer, beat the egg whites at medium speed until stiff peaks form, about 5 minutes. Add the yolks. Beat 1 minute. With a soft spatula, gradually fold in the shrimp mixture with the beaten eggs until well incorporated and the batter looks crumbly.

4 Line a plate with paper towels. In a deep medium skillet, heat the oil until very bubbly at medium heat. It's ready when many bubbles form around the head of a wooden spoon. Drop tablespoons of the batter into the hot oil, flatten them slightly with a small spatula, and fry until golden, about 1 minute per side. Transfer the cakes to a paper-towel-lined plate to absorb excess oil.

5 Brush the cactus lightly with canola oil and season lightly with salt and black pepper to taste. Heat a nonstick griddle for 2 minutes over medium high heat. Place the cactus paddle on the hot griddle and grill until lightly charred, about 3 minutes per side.

6 To assemble the dish, place the grilled cactus paddle on a cutting board and cut it in half lengthwise, then slice it on the narrow side to end up with ½-inch-thick slices. Keep the slices close together to maintain the paddle shape. Arrange the paddle slices and the cakes on a platter, garnish with cilantro sprigs and lime wedges, and serve the sauce on the side.

AMALIA'S NOTE

- Dried shrimp is very strong and salty on its own, so it helps to combine it with the instant corn masa flour to mellow out the salt and add another layer of flavor. Dried shrimp and ground shrimp are available at Latin markets and online.

SALSA DE CHILE (ANCHO-GUAJILLO SAUCE)

⅓ cup diced yellow onion
1 ½ teaspoons minced garlic
¾ cup diced vine-ripened tomatoes
⅓ cup diced tomatillos, husked
1 ancho chile, seeded and deveined
1 guajillo chile, seeded and deveined
½ cup water
⅛ teaspoon crumbled dried oregano
Smidge ground cumin
Smidge ground cloves
1 teaspoon kosher salt
Freshly ground black pepper

6 ounces cooked salad shrimp, lightly chopped
¼ cup dried ground shrimp
¼–½ teaspoon hot piquín (pequin) chile powder (optional)
1 ½ tablespoon instant corn masa flour
2 large eggs, separated

⅓ cup canola oil

1 fresh cactus paddle, thorn free, washed, patted dry
Canola oil, for brushing
Kosher salt
Freshly ground black pepper

ADORNO (GARNISH)

Cilantro sprigs or chopped cilantro
Lime wedges

9

Carne, Aves y Cerdo
Beef, Poultry, and Pork

HOME SWEET HOME COOKING

In my kitchen, when I have the usual "what to make for dinner" dilemma, I often think of home and what gives me comfort. Home cooking is at the core of who I am as a mother and chef.

The flavors that I learned to appreciate in my homeland give me that sense of coziness and connection. At this stage of my life and career, what I continue to value is family, spirituality, and my calling to recreate the delicious flavors I grew up with and beyond to feed my incessant hunger to learn more.

Guisos and Tamales, Corn and Nixtamal

Guisos (stews) and corn in raw form or dried and transformed into masa (nixtamal) have been an integral part of indigenous cooking.

After the sixteenth century, the native dishes became blended with nonnative ingredients that came with the colonists. New stews also emerged.

Corn is either a main ingredient in a stew or a thickener and flavor enhancer, or it is made into mini tamales or tortillas that serve as bread to accompany the stews.

Nixtamalized corn (fresh masa) is also the main element for larger tamales, which often constitute a one-meal dish.

While my core is deeply Guatemalan, I am not foreign to the intricate connection of the cuisines I love with those of Guatemala's closest neighbors. After all, the flavors are so similar in a sense because we have many unifying forces.

People often ask me if Guatemalan cuisine is like Mexican. I say yes and no. We have commonalities in terms of ingredients (native and transplants), somewhat similar dishes, and colonial influences, but the differences lie in traditions and different multicultural indigenous roots, seasonings, and unique preparation styles. Guatemalan cuisine is vibrant and milder, and so are the rest of the cuisines of today's Mesoamerica.

It is likely that some of the obvious culinary similarities are connected to the trade routes and migrations of early indigenous peoples that swept from south-central Mexico and Guatemala to the southern regions of El Salvador, Honduras, Nicaragua, Costa Rica, and perhaps beyond.

Often one of our strongest connections to food is that which gives us comfort and which we have learned to appreciate throughout our lives. Those cozy meals connect us to our past and present. It is that sense of connection to family, celebration, and tradition that is a unifying force at the table. After all, food has been as common a denominator in our culture as it has been in past ones.

Sofrito

Sofrito, beyond being a base for cooking, forever changed Mesoamerican cuisine from indigenous to hybrid.

Sofrito, or refrito, is the mixture of native and imported ingredients that arrived in Latin America during the Exchange.

Sofrito is to Latin Americans what mirepoix is to the French, the cooking essence that often starts as a simple sauté of onions, garlic, and bell peppers built into a bigger sauce according to tradition, personal taste, and ingredient availability.

Modern Mesoamerican sofrito is used for building many of the recipes in this chapter and this book, often starting as a simple combination of ingredients and customized from there on for each dish.

CARNE GUISADA
Beef and Pork Stew

SERVES 4 to 6

½ pound pork loin, cut into
  1 ½-inch cubes
½ pound beef loin, cut into
  1 ½-inch cubes
2 teaspoons minced garlic
¼ cup fresh sour orange juice
  (jugo de naranja agria) or
  equal parts fresh orange
  and lemon juice
1 ½ teaspoons kosher salt
Freshly ground black pepper
2 tablespoons canola oil

1 cup finely diced yellow onion
½ teaspoon dried thyme
1 dried bay leaf
¼ teaspoon ground achiote
1 ½ cups finely diced vine-
  ripened tomatoes
2 cups beef stock, store-
  bought or homemade (see
  page 198)

1 cup Yukon Gold potatoes,
  unpeeled, halved or
  quartered
1 cup carrots, sliced ¼ inch
  thick on the bias

SPECIAL EQUIPMENT

Disposable gloves

Carne guisada has been one of my and my dad's favorites. It's just plain comfort food. In the Central American area, it is usually made with tougher and fattier cuts of meat, thus needing longer cooking time. This is my simplified and healthier version using pork and beef loin to lessen the fat and cooking time. In El Salvador, Guatemala, and elsewhere, the recipe varies, sometimes having more or fewer ingredients and seasonings. For a superb meal, pair it with Arroz con Chipilín (Chipilín Leaf and Red Bell Pepper Rice, page 140) and Escabeche de Verduras (Marinated Vegetable Salad, page 171).

1 Add the pork and beef to a large bowl. Wearing disposable gloves, use your hands to thoroughly coat the two meats with garlic, sour orange juice, salt, black pepper to taste, and oil. Marinate for 15 to 20 minutes.

2 In a medium nonstick skillet over high heat, sear the meats in two batches, stirring often, until brown all over, about 5 to 7 minutes. Adjust the heat to medium high. Add the onion, thyme, bay leaf, and achiote, and sauté for 2 minutes, stirring often. Add the tomatoes, stir well, and sauté for 2 minutes. Add the stock and bring to a quick boil over high heat, adjust the heat to medium low, and simmer, covered, for 15 minutes.

3 Either cook the potatoes and carrots first and serve them nestled in the stew, or add them to the stew, cover, and continue simmering until the vegetables are cooked al dente, about 10 to 15 minutes. Serve.

RECIPE VARIATIONS

Pollo o Pavo Guisado (Chicken or Turkey Stew): Follow the Carne Guisada recipe, except substitute the pork and beef with chicken or turkey dark meat. Add ½ cup medium-diced green bell pepper in step 2. Add ½ cup diced chayote squash in step 3. Adjust seasonings to taste.

Carne Guisada Guatemalteca (Guatemalan Pork Stew): Follow the Carne Guisada recipe, except substitute the beef with more pork loin. Omit the sour orange juice. Adjust seasonings to taste.

Carne Guisada Chapina (Guatemalan Beef Stew): Follow the Carne Guisada recipe, except substitute the pork with beef loin or beef stew meat. Omit the sour orange juice and substitute with 1 tablespoon red wine vinegar. Add ¼ teaspoon cinnamon with the thyme and bay leaf, and omit the carrots. Add ½ cup baby peas just before serving, and thicken the sauce with 1 tablespoon bread crumbs or instant corn masa flour dissolved in 2 tablespoons cold water during step 2, after the tomatoes. Adjust seasonings to taste.

AMALIA'S NOTE

• Achiote is available as fresh paste, dried seeds, and ground at most Latin stores, some major grocery stores, and online.

EL DIABLITO
Shredded Chicken and Vegetable Stew

SERVES 4 to 6

While in Granada, Nicaragua, I once had a meal I'll never forget. I was served this simple stew of pollo desmenuzado (shredded chicken) in a clay pot on top of an urn in the shape of a devil (hence the name El Diablito, which means "the little devil") with sides that included guacamole, chile criollo, queso seco, gallo pinto, crema agria (sour cream), and tortillas. I have been making the dish ever since. You will love it too, not only because it's easy, but also because it's nutritious, homey, and truly delicious. In Managua, this stew includes fewer vegetables and can be made in less than thirty minutes. El Diablito is a culinary experience paired with traditional sides that will leave you deliciously satisfied.

1 ½ tablespoons canola oil
2 cups julienned yellow onion
2 teaspoons minced garlic
1 cup diced Roma tomatoes
1 cup julienned green bell pepper
1 cup julienned carrots
1 cup julienned chayote squash

2 tablespoons tomato paste
½ cup chicken stock, store-bought or homemade (see page 198)
¼ cup fresh sour orange juice (jugo de naranja agria) or equal parts fresh orange and lemon juice
1 pound (about 3 cups) cooked shredded chicken
2 teaspoons kosher salt
Freshly ground black pepper

1 recipe **Gallo Pinto Nica** (Nicaraguan Red Bean and Cilantro Fried Rice) (see note)
1 recipe **Guacamol Nica** (Nicaraguan Guacamole, page 187)
1 recipe **Chile Criollo** (Nicaraguan Spicy Tomato and Cucumber Salsa) (see note)
Warm corn tortillas

1. Add the oil to a hot skillet over medium high heat and sauté the onion until it is translucent, about 3 minutes. Add the garlic and sauté 1 minute more. Add the tomatoes, bell pepper, carrots, and chayote squash and sauté another 2 minutes.

2. In a small bowl or measuring cup, stir together the tomato paste and chicken stock. Add it to the skillet with the sour orange juice, shredded chicken, salt, and black pepper to taste. Cover, reduce the heat to medium low, and simmer until the vegetables are cooked al dente, about 6 to 8 minutes.

3. Serve with the Gallo Pinto Nica, Guacamol Nica, Chile Criollo, and warm corn tortillas.

AMALIA'S NOTES

- For a twist on this recipe, use store-bought rotisserie chicken or cooked shredded beef or pork.

- Find the recipes for Gallo Pinto Nica (Nicaraguan Red Bean and Cilantro Fried Rice) and Chile Criollo (Nicaraguan Spicy Tomato and Cucumber Salsa) in recipe variations under Arroz con Frijoles Rojos y Coco (Belizean Red Bean and Coconut Rice) on page 247 and Salsa Criolla Fría (Quick Homestyle Sauce) on page 316, respectively.

CARNE PICADA CON VERDURAS

Chopped Beef and Vegetable Hash

SERVES 4 to 6

1 pound flank steak
  (about 3 cups cooked
  chopped steak)
2 cloves garlic
1 yellow onion, quartered
1 Roma tomato, quartered
2 cups beef stock,
  store-bought or homemade
  (see page 198)

1 ½ tablespoons canola oil
1 cup finely diced yellow onion
1 teaspoon ground achiote
2 teaspoons minced garlic
1 cup petite-diced Roma
  tomatoes
½ teaspoon dried thyme
2 small dried bay leaves
2 teaspoons kosher salt
Freshly ground black pepper

1 cup petite-diced carrots
1 cup petite-diced Yukon Gold
  potatoes
1 cup French-cut green beans
¾ cup baby peas

Carne picada (chopped meat) is a scrumptious picadillo-like preparation that can include beef, pork, chicken, or just vegetables. Every country in modern Mesoamerica makes its own. This Guatemalan version includes a sofrito as well as traditional vegetables. This preparation can be the protein on the plate, a topping for tostadas, a filling for tacos or chiles rellenos, or an appetizer with chips. As a main dish, pair it with Gallo Pinto Nica (Nicaraguan Red Bean and Cilantro Fried Rice, page 247) and tajadas (green plantain chips, page 74) for a delicious combination of flavors.

1. In a medium saucepan, combine the flank steak with the 2 garlic cloves, quartered onion, and quartered Roma tomato in the beef stock. Bring to a quick boil over high heat, adjust the heat to medium low, cover, and simmer for 30 minutes. Remove the meat from the stock and place it on a cutting board. Reserve the stock and vegetables. When the meat has cooled slightly, cut it into chunks, then chop it in a food processor using the pulse function or with a cleaver until it looks like medium-coarse chopped meat. Set aside. Puree the vegetables and stock with an immersion blender or regular blender and reserve in a separate bowl.

2. Heat the oil over medium high heat in the saucepan used to cook the beef. Add the finely diced onion and sauté until translucent, about 3 minutes. Add the achiote and sauté 1 minute more. Add the minced garlic, petite-diced tomatoes, thyme, bay leaves, salt, and black pepper to taste. Cook for 2 minutes. Add the chopped beef, carrots, potatoes, green beans, and reserved puree. Stir well and simmer, uncovered, to let the flavors blend and reduce the liquid, about 35 to 40 minutes. Stir from time to time. Turn off the heat and add the peas. Stir well, cover, and let the residual heat cook them, about 5 minutes. Serve.

RECIPE VARIATION

Carne Molida con Verduras (Salvadoran Ground Beef with Vegetables): Follow the recipe given, except use 3 cups cooked ground beef, omit all the tomatoes, and add ½ cup diced green bell pepper, ½ cup diced chayote squash, and 3 tablespoons tomato paste diluted in ½ cup stock during step 2. Season with 1 tablespoon Worcestershire sauce and reduce the kosher salt to 1 teaspoon (or to taste). Stir well to combine, cover, and simmer as indicated in step 2. Omit the peas.

AMALIA'S NOTE

• Achiote is available as fresh paste, dried seeds, or ground at most Latin stores, some major grocery stores, and online.

PIERNA CON PIÑA
Braised Spiced Fresh Ham with Roasted Pineapple
SERVES 10 to 12

While growing up in Guatemala, my dad used to take me and my siblings on long holiday weekends to the beach. When we stayed at one of my dad's friends' beach house, we always brought our meals, as there were no restaurants around. This was a pristine and secluded place. Waking up around 6 a.m. each day, my brother and I would run to the black sand beach before sunrise to chase the small crabs that were only visible at that time. At lunchtime, sometimes we had panes con pierna (sandwiches with fresh ham), and up to this day, I still remember the flavors together with the warm weather and the briny ocean breeze. Pierna con piña can also be the centerpiece of a nice holiday meal. This is my tribute to my childhood days with my dad and also my special rendition of the dish using farm-raised Mangalitsa pork from Minnesota. Mangalitsa pigs have been called the Kobe beef of pork, and the meat is absolutely melt-in-your-mouth delicious.

1. Prepare the ham 1 day before eating it. Combine the garlic, fresh ginger, thyme, 2 teaspoons Cobán chile powder, mustard, Maggi sauce, Worcestershire, 1 tablespoon panela, 1 tablespoon kosher salt, and black pepper to taste in a bowl and mix well until pasty. Rub the mixture all over the ham to coat it evenly. Cover with plastic wrap and refrigerate overnight.

2. The next day, pull the ham out of the refrigerator, remove the plastic, and let it sit on the kitchen counter for 1 hour.

3. Preheat the oven to 400°F.

Continued on page 264

SALMUERA (RUB)

2 teaspoons minced garlic
2 tablespoons shredded fresh ginger
1 ½ teaspoons dried thyme
2 teaspoons Cobán chile powder or guajillo chile powder
2 tablespoons Dijon mustard
2 teaspoons Maggi sauce
4 teaspoons Worcestershire sauce
1 tablespoon panela (piloncillo) or dark brown sugar
1 tablespoon kosher salt
Freshly ground black pepper

1 (12-pound) Mangalitsa fresh ham (farm raised or store-bought)

SALSA (BRAISING SAUCE)

2 cups petite-diced Roma tomatoes
1 cup petite-diced yellow onion
3 dried bay leaves
1 teaspoon ground canela (Ceylon cinnamon)
1 ½ teaspoons kosher salt
Freshly ground black pepper
½ cup raisins
½ cup sliced prunes

4 cups chicken stock (plus more for braising as needed), store-bought or homemade (see page 198)
3 cups fresh or bottled pineapple juice

MIEL (GLAZE)

2 cups panela (piloncillo) or dark brown sugar (see note on page 264)
2 teaspoons kosher salt
¼ teaspoon ground cloves
½ teaspoon ground canela (Ceylon cinnamon)
½ teaspoon Cobán chile powder or guajillo chile powder
2 cups fresh or bottled pineapple juice

1 fresh pineapple, peeled and cored in 1-inch slices
1 stick cold butter
Cherry tomatoes and curly parsley sprigs, for garnish

4 Transfer the ham to a braising pan. In a bowl, thoroughly combine the tomatoes, onion, bay leaves, 1 teaspoon cinnamon, 1 ½ teaspoons salt, black pepper to taste, raisins, and prunes and surround the ham with the mixture. Pour the stock around the ham on top of the mixture (not directly on the ham). Put the braising pan on the next-to-lowest rack of the oven and braise for 20 minutes. Lower the temperature to 350°F and continue braising. During the braising time, add half the pineapple juice and add the rest gradually to prevent the sauce ingredients from getting dry (add additional stock in 1-cup increments, as needed). Braise until the thermometer registers 145°F, about 2 ½ hours.

5 While the ham braises, make the glaze. Combine the 2 cups panela, 2 teaspoons salt, cloves, ½ teaspoon cinnamon, ½ teaspoon chile powder, and 2 cups pineapple juice in a saucepan. Bring to a quick boil over high heat, adjust the heat to medium low, and simmer, uncovered, until syrupy, about 15 to 17 minutes. With a wide silicone brush, baste the ham with about half the glaze halfway through the cooking time, then glaze lightly again at the end, saving any leftover glaze for serving. As the glaze cools down, it will thicken a bit more.

6 Preheat a nonstick griddle over medium high heat. Unwrap one end of the butter stick and rub it on the hot griddle to coat it thoroughly yet lightly. Roast the pineapple slices until medium brown, about 3 minutes per side. Do this in batches, adding more butter between batches as needed. Save the leftover butter for another recipe. Reserve the pineapple slices.

7 When it's done, transfer the ham to a cutting board and let it rest, covered with foil, until the temperature reaches 155°F to 160°F, about 10 minutes. Meanwhile, transfer the pan sauce to a clear heat-resistant glass bowl and degrease it. Slice the ham and brush the slices with the remaining glaze. Serve topped with the sauce (or serve the sauce on the side) and roasted pineapple slices, cherry tomatoes, and parsley sprigs.

AMALIA'S NOTES

• Mangalitsa pork is available from your local farmer or online. Pork shoulder can be a good substitute for the fresh ham and makes for a smaller-quantity meal.

• Panela is very hard and must be broken for measuring or melting. To break it, put it in a double layer of resealable bags, wrap it twice in a kitchen towel, and pound it with the smooth side of a metal meat mallet until the panela is almost powdery.

TAMALES DE ARROZ Y PAVO
Guatemalan Red Chile Sauce and Turkey Rice Tamales

MAKES 8 tamales

1 recipe **Recado** (Roasted Tomato, Guajillo, Mulato, Ancho, and Pumpkin Seed Sauce, page 307)

MASA (DOUGH)

2 cups white rice, soaked for 24 hours in 5 cups water

3 ½ cups chicken stock, divided

1 cup instant corn masa flour

1 ½ teaspoons kosher salt

6 tablespoons (3 ounces) canola oil

½ cup (4 ounces) melted butter

16 (14x11-inch) pieces banana leaves, wiped on both sides with a damp cloth

8 (25-inch-long) pieces cibaque (natural fiber) or kitchen twine, soaked, for tying

RELLENO (FILLING)

16 (3x1-inch) strips boneless, skinless turkey thighs, seasoned with kosher salt and freshly ground black pepper

16 (½-inch-wide) strips jarred roasted red bell pepper

16 Spanish olives stuffed with pimentos

8 prunes

40 raisins

ADORNO (GARNISH)

1 lime, cut into wedges

Tamales de arroz bring memories of when my mom used to make these special tamales for Christmas. They are delicate, festive, and delicious when drizzled with fresh lime juice and paired with Pan Francés (Guatemalan French Bread, page 325). Guatemala's most common tamales are tamales colorados (red tamales) and paches (potato tamales). Tamales colorados are Guatemala's national dish. In Guatemala City, people eat them every Saturday. They eat paches every Thursday. Tamale vendors place a red light outside their casa or tienda (home or neighborhood store) to signal to passersby that they have tamales for sale. Guatemalan tamales are special treats with a velvety texture containing a saucy and meaty core traditionally wrapped in a combination of banana and maxán leaves. Maxán (pronounced *mashán*), native to Mesoamerica, means "salt leaf" in Quiché Maya.

1. Drain the soaked rice. In a food processor with the blade attachment, process the rice to a fine consistency with 1 cup stock. Stop the food processor and scrape the sides as needed. Add another cup of stock and process again for 1 minute. Add the masa flour and the salt and process again to blend. As the mixture becomes doughy, gradually add the rest of the stock through the tube feeder to make a runny dough.

2. Add the oil and butter to a medium nonstick preheated skillet over medium low heat. Add the dough, and using a whisk, stir well to combine it with the fat. Cook, stirring constantly to keep the dough from forming lumps and from sticking to the skillet. Switch to a soft spatula when it becomes too hard to stir with the whisk. The dough is ready when the spoon starts leaving heavy tracks, the oil and butter are well integrated into the dough, and the dough starts lifting from the edges and has thickened to a soft paste, about 15 minutes. Let the dough cool slightly. Divide the dough into 8 equal portions.

3. For each tamale, lay one piece of banana leaf (matte side up) on top of another piece of banana leaf in a crisscross way. Place one dough portion at the center of the banana leaves, make a small well with a spoon, and top with 2 pieces of turkey, 3 tablespoons sauce, 2 pepper strips, 2 olives, 1 prune, and 5 raisins. Wrap the tamale and seal it tightly: Bring together the corners of the bottom leaf and make three small folds beginning at the top. Then press the leaves flat, from the outside in, to hold the ingredients in the center. Make one fold at each of the unsealed leaf edges so they overlap to form a rectangular tamale. Tie with cibaque or kitchen twine.

4. Fill a deep pot with 10 cups water. Place all the tamales vertically in a steamer basket and put the basket in the pot. Bring the water to a boil over high heat, cover the pot, and reduce the heat to medium low. Steam the tamales until they're cooked, about 1 ½ hours. When the tamales are done, the dough should hold the shape of the package and should be shiny and slightly translucent, not opaque. Let the tamales sit in the pot, covered, with the heat off for at least 1 hour before serving them. This resting time will bring the temperature down, and the tamales will firm up a bit.

5. Serve the tamales garnished with lime wedges.

Continued on page 267

RECIPE VARIATION

Tamales Colorados (Guatemalan Red Chicken or Pork Tamales in Banana Leaves):
Combine in the bowl of a mixer with the paddle attachment, at speed 2, 2 cups instant corn masa flour and 4 cups chicken stock to make soft, moist dough. Add ¾ cup plus 1 tablespoon vegetable shortening, and kosher salt to taste. Fluff the dough for 3 minutes at speed 4. Taste and adjust the salt, if needed. Fluff again for 1 additional minute. Transfer the dough to a nonstick skillet and cook it over low heat, stirring constantly with a whisk to keep it from forming lumps and from sticking to the skillet, switching to a soft spatula when it becomes too hard to stir with the whisk, and cook until the dough is ready, about 15 minutes. The dough is ready when the whisk starts leaving tracks and the dough starts lifting from the edges. Let the dough cool slightly. Divide the dough into 8 equal portions. Then use the same sauce, fillings (use chicken or pork or both instead of turkey), garnishes, banana leaves, and cibaque or twine, and follow steps 3 to 5 on page 265.

AMALIA'S NOTES

- I use an 8-quart pasta pot with a deep steamer basket to make this recipe.

- You can use cooked shredded chicken, pork, or a combination.

- If the dough is lumpy at any given point during cooking, use the whisk to break up the lumps. Then go back to using the soft spatula. As the dough thickens, it will be harder to stir with a whisk.

- Tamales freeze well. To reheat them, steam them for 20 to 30 minutes. Reheat refrigerated tamales by steaming them for 15 to 20 minutes.

- Banana and maxán leaves are available frozen at Latin stores and some major grocery stores.

PAN CON ENSALADA DE POLLO Y PAPA
Chicken and Potato Salad Roll

SERVES 2 to 4

These sandwiches are nostalgic for me, as they remind me of my childhood when I used to go to piñata parties. After playing with other children, breaking the piñata, and grabbing as many candies and small toys as we could, we often were served ice cream, cake, and petite chicken salad sandwiches paired with a refreshing natural drink made with seasonal fruits or toasted ground pumpkin seeds. I have all these flavors in my head and tongue. They are cozy. Make this salad for your next special gathering and serve it elegantly on its own surrounded by French bread croutons, or make gourmet sandwiches with a French baguette, bolillo bread, or any other bread of preference. Serve them for lunch or make mini rolls for a casual gathering.

1. In a small bowl, with a soft spatula, combine the potatoes with the vinegar and marinate for 30 minutes. Gently mix them from time to time to ensure even marinating.

2. Combine the crema, mayonnaise, lime juice, salt, and white pepper to taste in a medium bowl and stir well. Add the celery, onion, roasted bell peppers, cilantro, and chicken. Add the marinated potatoes and mix well. Cover and refrigerate for at least 30 minutes to blend flavors.

3. Split the bolillo roll at the top, leaving the bottom attached. Line the bread with one or two pieces of lettuce, fill with the salad, and garnish with the bell pepper strips. Serve.

AMALIA'S NOTE
- Make this salad with cooked roasted turkey, cooked shrimp, or any other cooked seafood of choice.

ENSALADA DE POLLO Y PAPA (CHICKEN AND POTATO SALAD) (MAKES ABOUT 3 CUPS SALAD)

1 cup petite-diced Yukon Gold potatoes, peeled, cooked

2 tablespoons white wine vinegar

2 tablespoons crema agria (Guatemalan, Salvadoran, Honduran, or Mexican sour cream)

2 tablespoons olive oil mayonnaise

2 teaspoons freshly squeezed lime juice

1 teaspoon kosher salt

Freshly ground white pepper

3 tablespoons finely chopped celery

3 tablespoons finely chopped yellow onion

3 tablespoons finely diced jarred roasted bell peppers

3 tablespoons finely chopped cilantro leaves

1 ½ cups shredded store-bought rotisserie chicken

3 bolillo rolls or 1 French baguette sliced into 6-inch pieces

1 head butter lettuce

¼ cup roasted bell peppers, cut into ¼-inch-wide strips

CARNE MECHADA

Braised Eye of Round Larded with Bacon, Ham, and Garlic

SERVES 4 to 6

2 pounds eye of round roast

3 slices cooked bacon, cut into
1-inch pieces

2 slices cooked ham, cut into
1-inch pieces

½ link Spanish chorizo, cut into
½-inch slices

1 tablespoon Spanish capers

8 cloves garlic

¼ teaspoon dried thyme

¼ teaspoon crumbled
dried oregano

1 teaspoon kosher salt

Freshly ground black pepper

1 tablespoon canola oil

½ cup diced yellow onion

½ cup diced vine-ripened
tomatoes

½ cup diced tomatillos, husked

¼ teaspoon ground canela
(Ceylon cinnamon)

1 dried bay leaf

1 ½ cups beef stock

2 tablespoons thinly
sliced chives

Carne mechada is a traditional dish in Central and Latin America, but not all dishes are created equal. The technique *mechar* is to lard a lean meat with pork fat, and in Latin America, this translates into inserting various other ingredients into the meat. In some Latin countries, carne mechada is shredded stewed meat, but the original recipe of inserting fat into the meat came to us via Spain, quite possibly from Andalucía. Larding adds bits of fat and flavor. Braising the meat achieves a dual purpose: cooking the meat slowly to tenderize it and yield a delicious sauce. It's a relatively simple yet delicious preparation that anyone can make their own with just a few steps. This delightful dish is the Guatemalan version. Serve it with rice or potatoes and a nice salad (for inspiration, go to Chapters 5 and 6, pages 135 and 163, respectively).

1. With a paring knife, make 2-inch-deep slits into the roast with the grain, about 1 inch apart. For a 2-pound roast, you will need to make four to five rows of slits in a checkered pattern. Insert your index finger into the slits to make them wider and visible.

2. In a food processor, pulse each of the following separately: bacon, ham, chorizo, capers, and garlic. Combine them in a bowl. Fill each slit in the roast with about ½ teaspoon of this mixture, pushing it with your finger as far as it will go. Repeat until all holes are filled. Use any remaining mixture to top off the deeper holes. Rub the roast with thyme, oregano, salt, and black pepper.

3. Preheat a braising pan over medium high heat, add the canola oil, and sear the meat about 1 ½ minutes per side, making sure it's seared all around, including the sides. Use tongs to help you turn the meat or to hold it in place when needed.

4. Remove the meat from the pan, and using the residual oil and brown bits, build the base of the sauce. Add the onion and sauté until translucent, about 3 minutes. Add the tomatoes, tomatillos, cinnamon, bay leaf, and stock. Bring to a quick boil over high heat, adjust the heat to medium low, and braise, covered, until the thermometer registers 145°F for medium rare, about 40 to 45 minutes.

5. Remove the roast from the pan and transfer it to a cutting board. Tent with foil to keep warm. Reduce the sauce by half over medium high heat, about 6 to 8 minutes. To serve, slice the roast against the grain and spoon the sauce over it and top with the chives.

AMALIA'S NOTES

- You can use other cuts of beef, such as chuck roast and brisket. Brisket can also be shredded, if desired.

- Before adding any salt to the sauce, taste it first, as there is already salt from the roast, capers, and stock.

PICADILLO DE PLÁTANO Y CARNE
Green Plantain Beef Hash

SERVES 4

Picadillos are popular throughout Mesoamerica, especially in Costa Rica, where a large variety are made with just vegetables or combined with proteins (see recipe variations on page 274). Picadillos can be at the center stage of the table or become stuffing for turkey, chicken, chiles rellenos, or rolled tacos. Or they can become Costa Rican gallos, the equivalent of Mexican tacos sometimes topped with Ensalada de Repollo Tica (Costa Rican Cabbage-Cilantro Slaw, page 184) as in Gallo de Picadillo de Plátano y Carne (Fresh Corn Tortillas Topped with Green Plantain Beef Hash and Cabbage-Cilantro Slaw, page 69). Corn tortillas are a staple in the predominant corn cultures of the Americas that can be a side or the actual vessel for eating anything from picadillo and grilled meats to beans and cheese.

1 ½ cups peeled, small-diced green plantains (see note)

½ pound 80% lean ground beef

1 cup diced yellow onion
½ teaspoon ground achiote
1 teaspoon minced garlic
1 cup small-diced Roma tomatoes
¼ cup chopped cilantro
2 teaspoons Worcestershire sauce
1 teaspoon Tabasco sauce
1 teaspoon kosher salt
Freshly ground black pepper

1. In a medium saucepan, cook the plantains in salted boiling water until al dente, about 5 minutes. Drain and set aside.

2. In a deep skillet, cook the beef over medium high heat thoroughly until lightly browned, stirring constantly and breaking up the clumps, about 8 to 10 minutes.

3. Add the onion and cook until translucent, about 3 minutes. Add the achiote, stir well, and cook until the meat turns medium orange, about 1 minute. Add the garlic and cook 1 minute. Gradually add the plantains, tomatoes, cilantro, Worcestershire, Tabasco, salt, and black pepper to taste. Stir well, cover, and simmer over medium low heat to blend flavors, about 5 minutes. Serve.

AMALIA'S NOTES

- To peel green plantains or bananas, slice off the two ends with a sharp paring knife. Score the peel carefully, making sure not to cut the plantain. Carefully lift a piece of the skin and slowly run your finger under it to remove it.

- Add 2 teaspoons of canola oil (or to taste) if you are using the leanest ground beef available. Otherwise, the oil is not needed, as there's enough fat in the meat to prepare this dish.

- Find other picadillo recipes throughout the book by searching the index.

Continued on page 274

Picadillo de Chayote y Carne (Costa Rican Chayote and Beef Hash): Follow the recipe on page 272 but omit the plantains and substitute with 1 ½ cups small-diced chayote squash.

Picadillo de Chayote y Elote (Costa Rican Chayote and Corn Hash): In a medium skillet over medium high heat, warm 2 tablespoons canola oil. Add the following ingredients in the order listed, sautéing each for 1 minute before adding the next ingredient: ¾ cup diced yellow onion, 1 teaspoon minced garlic, 1 tablespoon minced celery, 1 cup small-diced chayote squash, ½ cup corn kernels, ½ cup milk (optional), 2 tablespoons chopped cilantro, and kosher salt and freshly ground black pepper to taste.

Picadillo de Papaya Verde (Costa Rican Green Papaya Hash): In a medium skillet over medium high heat, warm 2 tablespoons canola oil. Add the following ingredients in the order listed, sautéing each for 1 minute before adding the next ingredient: ½ cup diced yellow onion, 1 teaspoon minced garlic, ½ teaspoon ground achiote, ½ cup diced red or green bell pepper, 1 cup small diced green papaya, 1 teaspoon crumbled dried oregano or 2 tablespoons chopped fresh cilantro leaves, 1 minced hot chile pepper (optional), ½ teaspoon (or to taste) Lizano sauce or Worcestershire sauce, and kosher salt and freshly ground black pepper to taste.

Picadillo de Arracache (a.k.a. Arracacha) (Costa Rican Root Vegetable Hash): Follow the recipe for Picadillo de Papaya but omit the papaya and substitute with small-diced arracache (available frozen online). After adding all the ingredients and sautéing, lower the heat, cover, and simmer until all the vegetables are tender.

Picadillo de Chorizo y Papa (Costa Rican Chorizo and Potato Hash): In a medium skillet over medium high heat, sauté 1 cup cooked chorizo and 1 cup diced onion until the onion is translucent, about 3 minutes. Add 2 cups small-diced and peeled Yukon Gold potatoes, 2 teaspoons Lizano sauce or Worcestershire sauce (or to taste), 1 teaspoon Tabasco sauce, and kosher salt and freshly ground black pepper to taste. Stir well and simmer, covered, until potatoes are cooked al dente, about 5 minutes.

Picadillo de Carne y Nopales (Mexican Cactus and Beef Hash): In a medium skillet over medium high heat, warm 2 tablespoons canola oil. Add the following ingredients in the order listed, sautéing each for 1 minute before adding the next ingredient: 1 ½ cups julienned red onion, 2 teaspoons minced garlic, 1 cup diced Roma tomatoes, 1 cup cooked ground or chopped beef, 1 cup fresh cooked small-diced cactus paddles, ½ cup cooked small-diced and peeled Yukon Gold potatoes, ¼ cup diced pickled or fresh jalapeños (optional), and kosher salt and freshly ground black pepper to taste. Adjust the heat to low, cover, and simmer to blend flavors for about 8 minutes.

Nopales con Tomate y Huevo (Mexican Egg and Tomato Hash): In a medium skillet over medium high heat, warm 2 tablespoons canola oil. Add the following ingredients in the order listed, sautéing each for 1 minute before adding the next ingredient: ¾ cup chopped onion, ½ cup diced Roma tomatoes, 1 cup fresh cooked small-diced cactus paddles, ¼ cup diced pickled or fresh jalapeños, and kosher salt and freshly ground black pepper to taste. Add 2 beaten eggs and cook until smooth, about 3 minutes.

PIBIPOLLO

Grilled Chicken in Sour Orange Sauce

SERVES 4 to 6

4 teaspoons minced garlic
½ teaspoon ground cumin
1 teaspoon crumbled
  dried oregano
Dash ground allspice
1 tablespoon ground achiote
1 teaspoon condimented
  achiote paste
½ cup fresh sour orange juice
  (jugo de naranja agria) or
  equal parts fresh orange and
  lemon juice (see note)
2 teaspoons red or white
  wine vinegar
2 tablespoons canola oil
2 ½ teaspoons kosher salt
Freshly ground black pepper
6 boneless, skinless chicken
  thighs, visible fat removed
1 whole fresh or frozen banana
  leaf, washed and wiped with
  a paper towel on both sides

1 recipe **Curtido de Cebolla
Roja** (Mexican Quick-Pickled
Red Onions, page 293)
1 lime cut into 8 wedges

I love the Mayan flavors of the Yucatán Peninsula because they so closely resemble some of those of my home country. Beyond being an iconic dish, cochinita pibil is one of my favorite dishes. It's traditionally made with pork, wrapped in banana leaves, and buried underground to cook under hot coals (pib), an ancient technique. This is my simplified home version with marinated chicken thighs, grilled and served on banana leaves. The flavors are just as delicious. The sauce is a careful orchestration of key ingredients, such as achiote and sour orange, combined with other spices. Serve with rice and black beans for a fantastic flavor experience, or shred the chicken and make tacos or sandwiches topped with pickled red onions and cilantro.

1. In a blender, combine the garlic, cumin, oregano, allspice, ground achiote, achiote paste, sour orange juice, vinegar, oil, salt, and black pepper to taste. Blend to make a completely smooth sauce.

2. Put the chicken in a bowl and combine it with the sauce. Cover and marinate for 6 to 8 hours in the refrigerator. For even marinating, move the chicken pieces around in the marinade at least once, preferably about halfway through the marinating time.

3. Preheat a grill or griddle over medium high heat. Season the grill or add a light coating of oil to the griddle and grill the chicken to medium brown, about 3 minutes per side. Reserve the marinade and cook it in a small skillet over medium high heat for 3 to 5 minutes. Transfer the chicken to a lidded ceramic or ovenproof dish lined with two layers of banana leaves. Pour the sauce on top, enclose the chicken well in the leaves, and cover the dish with the lid. Put the dish on the far side of the grill (or in the oven at 350°F) to cook the chicken through, about 15 to 20 minutes.

4. Serve in the cooking vessel with the pickled onions on the side.

AMALIA'S NOTES

- Condimented achiote (annatto) paste is available at major grocery stores, Latin stores, and online under the El Yucateco brand.

- Throughout this book, I use naranja agria (sour orange) to refer to Seville orange. Most people in Meso- and Latin America use this name. I also use the simplest way to mimic Seville orange's flavor, equal parts fresh orange and lemon juice, which produces the closest flavor I remember from my time growing up in Guatemala. Outside of Yucatán, sometimes people use a combination of juices such as lemon, lime, and grapefruit to mimic the Seville orange's flavor.

PULIQUE DE PATO CON TAMALITOS DE MILPA
Duck and Vegetable Stew with Mini Tamales Steamed in Corn Leaves

SERVES 4 to 6

Pulique, puliq', or pulik is a Mayan dish from the Guatemalan highlands, where it is often served for ceremonial and special gatherings. During my travels in Sololá and surrounding villages at the foot of the three volcanoes at Lake Atitlán, I had the privilege to make pulique and tamales with several families. Each one was unique yet shared some ingredients, but all of them contained masa as a key ingredient for flavor and as a thickener. The thickener turns the soup into a stew and gives it a distinctive touch. White or vegetable rice and small masa tamales wrapped in fresh corn leaves are traditional pairings. The tamales take the place of tortillas and build the experience further. This ancestral food began as a simpler meal containing only native ingredients (and quite possibly exotic animals), including turkey and duck, but after Spanish contact, the stew became hybrid with the addition of chicken, pork, beef, and many condiments. This is one of the easiest to make of all the Mayan stews. Here's my version of the Panajachel duck pulique using locally sourced duck in support of local farmers.

1 recipe **Tamalitos de Milpa**
(Mini Tamales Steamed in Corn Leaves, page 280)

1 fresh Muscovy or White Pekin duck, whole
1 small yellow onion, peeled and t-scored (see note on page 280)
1 ½ cups whole cilantro leaves and stems (roughly 1 bunch)
4 cups chicken stock, store-bought or homemade (see page 198)

1 ½ cups small-diced Roma tomatoes
½ cup husked, small-diced tomatillos
1 cup small-diced yellow onion
2 teaspoons minced garlic
1 teaspoon ground guajillo chile
¼ teaspoon ground achiote
¾ teaspoon crumbled dried oregano
¼ teaspoon dried thyme
Dash ground cloves
1 dried bay leaf
Kosher salt
Freshly ground black pepper

½ cup instant corn masa flour combined with ¾ cup cold stock or water

½ cup quartered güisquil or chayote squash, cooked al dente
4 whole medium carrots (stems partly on), cooked al dente
½ cup unpeeled, halved Yukon Gold potatoes, cooked al dente
1 cup thickly shredded cabbage (optional)

ADORNO (GARNISH)

Chopped cilantro

1. Make the tamalitos (recipe on page 280).

2. In a medium soup pot over medium low heat, cook the duck with the onion and cilantro in the stock until the duck is tender, about 25 to 30 minutes. Remove and reserve the onion and cilantro. Set aside the pot with the duck and stock.

3. In a blender or food processor, puree the tomatoes, tomatillos, diced onion, garlic, and reserved onion and cilantro.

4. Add the puree, guajillo, achiote, oregano, thyme, cloves, bay leaf, and salt and black pepper to taste to the pot of duck and stock. Bring to a quick boil over high heat, adjust the heat to medium low, and simmer, covered, for 5 to 7 minutes. Add the masa flour mixture gradually, using a whisk to prevent lumps, and stir well.

Continue stirring until the mixture thickens, about 2 to 3 minutes. Taste and add seasonings, if needed.

5. Nestle the cooked vegetables in the sauce around the duck and serve the stew garnished with chopped cilantro surrounded by the tamalitos.

Continued on page 280

TAMALITOS DE MILPA
(Mini Tamales Steamed in Corn Leaves)

MAKES 7 to 9 mini tamales

1 In the bowl of a stand mixer with the paddle attachment, combine the instant corn masa flour and the salt. While beating at speed 2, gradually add the stock to make very moist dough. Add the shortening and increase the speed to speed 4 and beat for 1 minute. Stop the mixer and scrape the sides and bottom of the bowl with a soft spatula. Add the cheese and fluff the dough at speed 6 for 2 minutes. (Alternatively, mix the ingredients by hand in a bowl with a wooden spoon and beat vigorously at the end to fluff the dough.)

2 Form the tamalitos by first dividing the dough into seven to nine equal portions. Lay the corn leaves vertically with the widest side toward you. Put a portion of dough near the end of the widest part of each leaf, matte side up, leaving a 1-inch gap. With your fingers, gently shape the dough into a 3-inch cigar. Fold the 1-inch leaf gap on top of the dough and press gently to secure in place. Fold the longer side of the leaf over the dough to enclose the dough inside and form 3x1 ½-inch short cylinders. Then, starting at the bottom, wrap the remaining leaf around the tamalito up as many times as it will go around to completely enclose the dough inside. Repeat until all the dough and leaves are used. Set aside.

3 In a medium pot with 3 cups water and a steamer basket, stack the tamalitos horizontally and evenly (end side down) throughout the basket. Make sure the water does not touch them. Bring the water to a quick boil over high heat, adjust the heat to medium low, and steam the tamalitos until cooked, about 20 to 25 minutes. They are cooked when the leaves have turned darker green and the dough is slightly shiny, not opaque. Let them sit in the pot for 10 minutes, or until ready to serve, with the heat off to firm up a bit before serving.

4 Serve the tamalitos on the side with the duck.

MASA (DOUGH)

1 cup instant corn masa flour
½ teaspoon kosher salt
1 cup chicken stock, store-bought or homemade (see page 198)
2 ½ tablespoons vegetable shortening
3 tablespoons crumbled Cotija cheese
7 to 9 fresh corn leaves (see note)

AMALIA'S NOTES

• To t-score an onion, make a ½-inch-deep cross-shaped cut at the narrowest end of the onion. The onion remains whole.

• Muscovy and White Pekin ducks are different in taste and fat content, with the latter being the fattiest. Muscovy is leaner and thus a drier meat. Both are delicious. Trim excess skin and visible fat prior to cooking. Skim the fat that floats to the surface of the pot during cooking.

• Look for corn leaves through your local farmer or Community-Supported Agriculture hubs (CSAs). The size of the leaves used will dictate the size and quantity of the tamales. If unable to source in winter, substitute with corn husks or banana leaves.

• This recipe can be made in parts. Make the tamalitos the day before, let them cool down, and refrigerate them until ready to use. Steam the cold tamalitos for 6 to 8 minutes before serving.

• Peel tomatillos under running water if you find the husks hard to remove.

GALLINA RELLENA
Roast Hen with Vegetable and Fruit Stuffing

SERVES 4 to 6

Gallina rellena, stuffed hen, is a delightful holiday plate from Nicaragua that is as easy to make as it is delicious. It is the dinner table centerpiece that wows guests. The panela, pineapple, jugo de naranja agria (sour orange juice), wine, and spices play a scrumptious role in the resulting broth. What I love about this dish is that the stuffing is high in vegetables. There are varying versions of the dish throughout Nicaragua. This is my version from Managua. For an amazing experience, pair it with Gallo Pinto Nica (Nicaraguan Red Bean and Cilantro Fried Rice, see note on page 283), Guacamol Nica (Nicaraguan Guacamole, page 187) and Chile Criollo (Nicaraguan Spicy Tomato and Cucumber Salsa, page 316). Find more ideas for sides in Chapters 5 and 6, pages 135 and 163, respectively.

1 (4-pound) butterflied or whole hen or chicken
1 teaspoon onion powder
1 teaspoon garlic powder
½ teaspoon ground cumin
½ teaspoon ground nutmeg
2 teaspoons ground achiote
1 ½ teaspoons kosher salt
Freshly ground black pepper
1 ½ cups fresh sour orange juice (jugo de naranja agria) or equal parts fresh orange and lemon juice

RELLENO (STUFFING)

3 tablespoons canola oil
4 tablespoons butter
1 ½ cups finely diced onion
1 tablespoon minced garlic
¼ cup panela (piloncillo) or dark brown sugar (see note on page 283)
½ cup raisins
3 small dried bay leaves
½ cup red wine (Malbec, Rioja, or Carménère)

1 ¼ cup julienned chiltomas or equal parts green and red bell peppers
1 ½ cups diced or julienned carrots
1 ½ cups diced Yukon Gold potatoes
1 ½ cups diced chayote squash
1 cup diced fresh pineapple
½ cup olives stuffed with pimentos
1 cup canned crushed tomatoes
1 ½ teaspoons kosher salt
Freshly ground black pepper
1 cup toasted bread cubes or mashed potatoes (optional)
1 cup chicken stock
1 (16-ounce) package fresh or frozen banana leaves, rinsed and wiped on both sides with a damp cloth

SPECIAL EQUIPMENT

Kitchen syringe
1 turkey-size oven bag

1. Rinse the hen inside and out. Pat dry with paper towels.

2. Combine the onion powder, garlic powder, cumin, nutmeg, achiote, 1 ½ teaspoons salt, and black pepper to taste in a bowl. Add 1 teaspoon of the mixed spices to the sour orange juice and stir well. Set aside. Rub the hen all over with the remaining spice mix, including inside the cavity. Using the kitchen syringe, inject the hen breast and legs with ½ cup of the spiced orange juice, distributing it evenly, and marinate the hen in the refrigerator overnight. Reserve the rest of the juice in the refrigerator for the stuffing.

3. When you're ready to prepare the hen, add the canola oil to a deep skillet over medium high heat and sear the hen on all sides until medium brown. Use tongs to help you hold the hen in place. Transfer the seared hen to another dish and keep it warm. Melt the butter in the remaining oil in the skillet. Add the onion and sauté until translucent, about 3 minutes. Add the minced garlic and sauté 1 minute. Add the panela, raisins, and bay leaves, stir well, and sauté 1 minute. Add the wine, deglaze the pan, and reduce the wine by half. Add the chiltomas, carrots, potatoes, squash, pineapple, olives, tomatoes, 1 ½ teaspoons salt, black pepper to taste, and bread cubes (if using), and the rest of the juice. Cook over high heat, uncovered, for 5 minutes. If using a butterflied hen, you will not be able to stuff it, so you will need to surround the hen with the stuffing as in step 5. Or, if using a whole hen, stuff the cavity of the hen loosely with as much stuffing as you can fit. Reserve the rest.

4. Fill a deep pot with 8 cups water, cover, and set it over low heat. Line a steamer basket with the oven bag and two layers of banana leaves, making sure the entire basket is entirely covered and the banana leaves also hang over the sides.

Continued on page 283

5. Place the hen in the basket and surround it with the remaining stuffing. Add the chicken stock, distributing it evenly on the stuffing around the hen. Enclose the ingredients in the banana leaves, pulling the leaves from the sides on top of the surface of the hen and stuffing to cover. Use additional leaves to ensure full coverage. Close the bag loosely, but do not tie it. You want to allow steam to escape, or the bag could burst open at the bottom.

6. Place the steamer basket in the pot with water. Increase the heat to medium high, put the lid on top of the bag, and steam the hen until the thermometer registers 165°F, about 1 ¼ to 1 ½ hours. Keep a close eye on it as steam builds up in the bag. If you need to release excess steam, simply lift the lid for a few seconds. Hold the hen on low heat, covered, until ready to serve.

7. Lift the lid, open the bag slightly and carefully, and beware of the steam. Grab the bag, wearing oven mitts to prevent burns. Gently and carefully pull the bag out of the steamer basket and put it in a deep oval or round serving dish. Cut the bag on two or three sides, carefully slide it out from under the hen, and discard. Attractively rearrange the banana leaves, hen, and stuffing in the dish. Serve.

AMALIA'S NOTES

- Kitchen syringes are available at major grocery stores and online. Alternatively, marinate the chicken in the spices and juice if you don't have a kitchen syringe and use the marinating juices when preparing the stuffing.

- Panela is very hard and must be broken for measuring or melting. To break it, put it in a double layer of resealable bags, wrap it twice in a kitchen towel, and pound it with the smooth side of a metal meat mallet until the panela is almost powdery.

- If you use bread cubes and desire the mixture to be more firm, soak the cubes in some stock before adding it to the stuffing. Or use an equal amount of mashed potatoes to thicken the sauce. The latter is naturally gluten free.

- I use an 8-quart pasta pot with a deep steamer basket to make this recipe. The oven bag is needed to catch all the juices from all the ingredients; otherwise, they would be diluted and lost in the steaming water.

- Frozen banana leaves must be washed well, as they have residual ash from their baking on open fires. This is needed to make them pliable for packaging and cooking. Handle the leaves carefully to prevent tears.

- The picture shows a butterflied hen (also referred to as a spatchcock hen), which has the backbone removed so it sits flat. This can be done easily with poultry scissors. Simply cut along one side of the backbone until cut all the way through. Then rotate the hen and repeat the cut along the opposite side of the backbone. Alternatively, buy a ready-to-use butterflied chicken at select grocery stores or online.

- Find the recipe for Gallo Pinto Nica (Nicaraguan Red Bean and Cilantro Fried Rice) in recipe variations under Arroz con Frijoles Rojos y Coco (Belizean Red Bean and Coconut Rice) on page 247.

TAMALES OAXAQUEÑOS
Oaxacan Mole Negro and Roast Pork Tamales

MAKES 8 rectangular tamales

I have fun memories of cooking with many generations of Zapotec women in outdoor kitchens in Oaxaca, seeding and roasting chiles, peeling garlic, toasting seeds, and selecting spices, all while exchanging precious interactions with each one. As we went through the process of making the masa and sauce, I realized how close the preparation of Oaxacan tamales is to Guatemalan tamales. They closely resemble tamales colorados and tamales negros in sauce preparation technique, although the number of ingredients and seasonings are different in both. It's the nuances of flavor that often make tamales unique. Many share a core ingredient, corn, but the recados and sauces separate them by country. If you appreciate a good tamale, Tamales Oaxaqueños are a special treat, and the secret is in the sauce. For study and contrast, here I also offer the Guatemalan version of Tamales Oaxaqueños, similar in preparation and some ingredients (see recipe variation on page 286).

2 cups Mole Negro (Chile and Chocolate Sauce, page 298)

2 ½ cups shredded roast pork

1 ½ cups chicken stock

MASA (DOUGH)

2 cups instant corn masa flour

1 ½ teaspoons kosher salt

3 ½ cups chicken stock, store-bought or homemade (see page 198)

¾ cup (about 6 ounces) vegetable shortening or lard

8 (14x11-inch) pieces banana leaves, wiped on both sides with a damp cloth

SPECIAL EQUIPMENT

8 (12x10 ¾-inch) aluminum foil sheets

1. Combine the Mole Negro with the pork and 1 ½ cups stock in a large saucepan and heat through over medium low heat to blend flavors, stirring often, about 5 minutes. Set aside.

2. In the bowl of a stand mixer with the paddle attachment, combine the corn flour and salt with the 3 ½ cups stock to make soft, moist dough. Add the shortening and fluff the dough for 3 minutes at medium speed. (Alternatively, put the ingredients in a deep bowl in the order listed and beat vigorously with a wooden spoon until well incorporated.) Divide the dough into 8 equal portions.

3. For each tamale, place 1 dough portion at the center of 1 piece of banana leaf, matte side up. Make an elongated well with a spoon and top with ⅓ cup mole pork and spread it out evenly on top of the tamale, pushing it gently into the masa. Repeat the process with the remaining banana leaves and dough portions. Distribute any remaining sauce evenly among all 8 tamales.

Wrap each tamale and seal it: Fold one leaf edge over the tamale and bring the other edge on top of it, gently wrapping the leaf around the tamale. With open edge side up, press the leaves flat from the outside in to hold the ingredients in the center and fold both sides inward toward the tamale to seal it. Wrap each tamale in aluminum foil.

4. Fill a deep pot with 10 cups water. Place all the tamales horizontally in a steamer basket and put the basket in the pot. Bring the water to a boil over high heat, cover the pot, and reduce the heat to medium low. Steam the tamales until they're cooked, about 1 ½ hours. When the tamales are done, the dough should hold the shape of the package and should be shiny and slightly translucent, not opaque. Let the tamales sit in the pot, covered, with the heat off for at least 1 hour before serving them. This resting time will bring the temperature down, and the tamales will firm up a bit.

Continued on page 286

RECIPE VARIATION

Guatemalan Tamales Negros (Sweet Christmas Rice Tamales with Mole Sauce):
Follow step 2 on page 284 to make the dough, combining 1 cup rice flour, 1 cup instant corn masa flour, 4 cups chicken stock (plus ⅛ teaspoon kosher salt and 3 tablespoons sugar dissolved), and ¾ cup vegetable shortening or lard. Instead of dividing the dough, transfer to a nonstick skillet and cook, stirring constantly, until the spoon leaves tracks and the dough starts lifting from the sides, about 15 minutes. Let it cool slightly. For fillings, assemble 16 (3x2-inch) pieces turkey or chicken thighs or pork loin seasoned with salt and black pepper, 8 prunes, 24 raisins, 16 blanched almonds, and 16 jarred roasted bell pepper strips. Follow step 3 to assemble the tamales and distribute the dough, the fillings, and 1 recipe Recado para Tamales Negros (Roasted Tomato, Guajillo, Mulato, Ancho, Pumpkin Seed, and Chocolate Sauce, see note). Steam the tamales as instructed in step 4.

AMALIA'S NOTES

- I use an 8-quart pasta pot with a deep steamer basket to make this recipe.

- Banana leaves are available frozen at Latin stores and some major grocery stores.

- Aluminum foil sheets (pop-up foil) are available at major grocery stores and online.

- Tamales refrigerate and freeze well. Reheat refrigerated tamales by steaming them for 15 to 20 minutes. To reheat from frozen, steam them for 20 to 30 minutes.

- Find the recipe for Recado para Tamales Negros (Roasted Tomato, Guajillo, Mulato, Ancho, Pumpkin Seed, and Chocolate Sauce) in recipe variation under Recado (Roasted Tomato, Guajillo, Mulato, Ancho, and Pumpkin Seed Sauce) on page 307.

10

Salsas, Recados y Aliños
Salsas, Sauces, and Dressings

LATIN ZEST

Sauces and salsas are often what give Latin cuisine its zest. They can make or break a dish. From Mexico to Costa Rica and beyond, there are countless preparations that complement a single dish or serve as a base for a variety of uses.

Dishes that scream for sauces are those that are mild and grilled. Tacos of many types require a sauce and another topping such as cabbage, onions, parsley, or cheese. Spicy sauces add a unique touch and dress these dishes beautifully.

Many easy-to-prepare sauces combine raw ingredients with vinegar, lime, and salt. Others may require cooking, grilling, or roasting some of the ingredients and combining them with other raw ingredients. Some are made with dried as well as fresh peppers.

One of my favorite flavorings is lime and naranja agria (sour orange), which are basic ingredients in the Mesoamerican kitchen. They're added to salsas, sauces, tamales, and ceviche and are used for marinating meats. I like flavoring pan-roasted or grilled fish with just these two ingredients.

Vinegar, especially white vinegar, is very common in the Central American kitchen to flavor sauces, salsas, and salads. Often it is used alone in combination with onions, carrots, cabbage slaw, or other vegetables.

Most of the recipes in this chapter take just minutes to make and are simple and full of robust flavor from hot peppers to herbs to citrus juices to spices.

Chile, aliño, chereban, pulik, chirmol (or chilmol or chimol), vinagreta, and mayonesa are all synonyms for sauce or salsa in the country or region where they originate. Some have indigenous names and derivatives, while others are traditional and modern terms.

Use these salsas for any of the recipes in this book, or for topping your favorite pupusa or tostada as your favorite dish. The sauces and salsas can be modified by adding fewer or more ingredients as well as other condiments and flavorings.

Salsas and sauces not only dress and complement dishes naturally at the Mesoamerican table, but they also add that needed traditional touch to a particular dish. Chirmol, for example, is an essential accompaniment to grilled meats in Guatemala and other parts of the area. It is an indispensable topping that adds authenticity to the dish. Other salsas and sauces that are part of specific dishes can be found throughout this book. In this chapter, I invite you to add Mesoamerican zest to any dish you like.

Sauce versus Salsa

In the Spanish-speaking Latin kitchen, the term *salsa* refers to raw or cooked preparations.

Many of the raw sauces in this chapter are not called sauces or even salsas. In Mesoamerica, they have indigenous or traditional names.

Recados or recaudos are more elaborate sauces. They take a bit longer to make than salsas. The hearty sauces of indigenous stews and tamales are more complex recados.

Chirmol or chimol is a quick and simple sauce that has multiple uses in Mesoamerican cooking.

Sofrito or refrito, another sauce, at its most basic level, can include just onions and garlic as well as bell peppers and sometimes tomatoes. From here, everyone makes it their own.

ENCURTIDO DE CEBOLLA
Spicy Pickled Onions and Carrots

MAKES 1 pint-size mason jar

3 ½ tablespoons red or white
  wine vinegar
¾ cup water
⅛ teaspoon dried thyme
⅛ teaspoon crumbled dried oregano
1 dried bay leaf
1 teaspoon kosher salt

1 yellow or red onion, julienned
1 large carrot, peeled and thinly sliced
1 cabro, jalapeño, serrano, or habanero
  chile, unseeded and thinly sliced

Encurtidos or curtidos (pickled vegetables) are a staple on the Mesoamerican table because they add a quick kick to any dish and are delicious and super easy to make. The pickles keep in the refrigerator for weeks, and as time goes by, the flavor is more intense. Not only are the onions and peppers scrumptious in this recipe, but the resulting juice is outstanding. I always have a jar of this preparation in my refrigerator and make it often, as it goes quickly. I vary the proportions of chiles to onions depending on what I have on hand. While visiting Roatán, Honduras, I had different versions of this encurtido as a topping with Baleadas (Green Onion Flour Tortillas with Beans, Scrambled Eggs, Avocado, Spicy Onions, and Cheese, page 65). To make this into a side dish, decrease the amount of spicy peppers, increase the amount of carrots, and add other vegetables, such as cooked cauliflower and broccoli florets.

1. Combine the vinegar, water, thyme, oregano, bay leaf, and salt in a pint-size mason jar. Close the jar and shake well. Add the onion, carrot, and chile to the jar in several layers, starting with a layer of onions, a layer of carrots, a layer of chile slices. Repeat the layers in the same order until all ingredients are used. Close the jar and shake vigorously. Let the ingredients pickle for 2 hours or overnight (the longer the vegetables sit in the vinaigrette, the better the flavor will be.) Serve immediately or reserve.

RECIPE VARIATIONS

Cebollas Encurtidas (Nicaraguan Pickled Onions): Use ½ cup white vinegar, ½ cup water, 1 teaspoon black peppercorns, 2 dried bay leaves, 1 teaspoon (or to taste) kosher salt, 2 teaspoons sugar, 4 julienned white or red onions, and 1 julienned red bell pepper. Follow the instructions above for Encurtido de Cebolla. Use a quart-size mason jar.

Cebollas Encurtidas Simples (Quick Nicaraguan Pickled Onions): Follow the recipe for Cebollas Encurtidas, omitting the red bell pepper.

Curtido de Cebolla (Salvadoran Spicy Pickled Onions): Use ½ cup white vinegar, kosher salt to taste, 4 julienned white onions, and 1 thinly sliced serrano or jalapeño chile. Follow the instructions for Encurtido de Cebolla. This recipe uses no water, but you may add it to taste. Use a quart-size mason jar.

Mi Encurtido de Cebolla (Amalia's Spicy Pickled Onions): Use ½ cup white vinegar, ½ cup water, 3 whole cloves, 2 dried bay leaves, ½ teaspoon crumbled dried oregano, 1 thinly sliced garlic clove, ½ teaspoon (or to taste) kosher salt, freshly ground black pepper to taste, 2 julienned red onions, 2 julienned white onions, 2 thinly sliced habaneros, 1 thinly sliced serrano, and 1 thinly sliced Fresno chile (seeds and veins included). Follow the instructions above and left for Encurtido de Cebolla. Use right away or refrigerate for later use. Optional: Use only 1 chile to make it less spicy. Use a quart-size mason jar.

Curtido de Cebolla Roja (Mexican Quick-Pickled Red Onions): Use ¼ cup white vinegar, 1 cup water, kosher salt and freshly ground black pepper to taste, 2 julienned red onions, and 1 thinly sliced habanero chile (seeds and veins included). Follow the instructions for Encurtido de Cebolla. Optional: Soak the onions in very hot water for 2 minutes prior to combining them with the rest of the ingredients to lessen their bite. Use a pint-size mason jar.

AMALIA'S NOTES

- You can add 1 or 2 teaspoons of olive oil to any of the recipes here. Typically, encurtidos only contain vinegar and water or only vinegar, but in some instances people add a teaspoon or two of olive oil for texture and looks.

- Make the recipe your own with other ingredients of choice, such as thinly sliced beets and cucumbers. Adjust the seasonings according to taste.

ADOBO
Fresh Achiote and Guajillo Paste

MAKES about ½ cup

This classic Mayan marinade, traditionally combined with pork, is a grill favorite in Guatemala that is sold in markets and grocery stores. The key to a great sauce is to use fresh ingredients, including the achiote paste, which is sold without any additives and can sometimes also be found wrapped in banana leaves in markets. It's quite possible that the base sauce started with only local ingredients—tomatillos, achiote, and wild garlic—and became a hybrid after Spanish contact. Adobo, or adobado, comes from the verb *adobar*, meaning to marinate, and can also be used with chicken or turkey. For delicious results, the meats should be marinated for one or two days and then either cooked on a lightly oiled griddle or well-seasoned grill. This delightful sauce is the cousin of the adobo (condimented achiote paste or recado) used in the Yucatecan dish cochinita pibil.

½ cup husked diced tomatillos
2 teaspoons minced garlic
1 teaspoon crumbled dried oregano
½ teaspoon dried thyme
½ teaspoon ground cumin
½ teaspoon ground canela (Ceylon cinnamon)
⅛ teaspoon ground cloves
2 tablespoons fresh achiote paste without condiment
½ teaspoon white wine vinegar or fresh sour orange juice (jugo de naranja agria) or equal parts fresh orange and lemon juice
1 tablespoon canola oil (optional)
1 teaspoon kosher salt
Freshly ground black pepper

1. Combine the tomatillos, garlic, oregano, thyme, cumin, cinnamon, cloves, achiote, vinegar, oil (if using), salt, and black pepper to taste in a blender and puree until fine and smooth. Use immediately to marinate chicken thighs and legs, pork tenderloin, or country-style pork ribs. Scale the recipe as needed.

AMALIA'S NOTES

• See Pibipollo (Grilled Chicken in Sour Orange Sauce, page 277) for a quick Yucatecan version of this sauce.

• Fresh achiote without condiment is available online.

RECIPE VARIATION

Adobo (Guajillo, Achiote, and Tomatillo Sauce): In a saucepan over medium low heat, cook ½ cup diced tomatillos, 1 cup diced Roma tomatoes, and 1 guajillo (or guaque) and 1 ancho (or pasa) chile, seeded and torn into small pieces, in ¼ cup water until soft, about 8 minutes. Let cool and add to a blender with ⅓ cup diced yellow onion, 1 tablespoon minced garlic, ¼ teaspoon crumbled dried oregano, 1 dried bay leaf, ¼ teaspoon ground cumin, ⅛ teaspoon ground cloves, ⅛ teaspoon ground canela (Ceylon cinnamon), ¼ teaspoon ground achiote, 1 tablespoon plus 1 teaspoon white wine vinegar, 1 tablespoon canola oil, 1 teaspoon kosher salt, and freshly ground black pepper to taste. Puree to a smooth consistency. The sauce should be thick and pasty so it will stick to the meat.

CHEREBAN IWAXTE
Spicy Pan-Toasted Pumpkin Seed Sauce

MAKES ¼ cup

5 tablespoons ground pan-toasted shelled pumpkin seeds

1 teaspoon Cobán chile powder or pan-toasted spicy dried chile powder

3 tablespoons water, chicken, or vegetable stock, store-bought or homemade (see page 198)

1 teaspoon fresh sour orange juice (jugo de naranja agria), equal parts fresh orange and lime juice, or just fresh lime juice

½ teaspoon kosher salt

Pumpkin seeds are a basic ingredient in Mesoamerican indigenous cooking, common in the cuisines of Mexico, Guatemala, and El Salvador, and used in combination with other seeds, dried chiles, and spices. Used in sauces, soups, and stews, and to dress fruits, vegetables, and more, this important ingredient adds complexity to any dish. The seeds can be used with the shell on or shelled, and the flavor changes when pan toasted. In Guatemala, they are called pepitoria (pepitas in Mexico) when shelled; otherwise they are pepita de ayote (squash seeds). A similar sauce is El Salvador's Salsa de Alguaishte (see recipe variation below). Iwaxte, or iguashte (pronounced *iguashtay*), is a name that comes from the word *alhuashte*, from the Nahuatl ayu (juice) and juashti (seeds). This simple sauce is big in flavor and can help build up dishes. Cherebanes are versatile and traditional sauces from the Maya people of Guatemala. They are basic, fresh, healthy, nutritious, and delicious. Cherebanes can dress beef, pork, poultry, sausages, vegetables, and more. They can be made in a grinding stone and modified to pair with any food or dish or can be a delightful snacking sauce. This sauce is also great for mild meatless tamales such as Boxboles (Corn Masa Dumplings in Chayote Leaves with Spicy Roasted Pumpkin Seed Sauce, page 109) and Tamalitos de Milpa (Mini Tamales Steamed in Corn Leaves, page 280), and together, they make the perfect vegetarian snack when tamales are made with vegetable stock and vegetable fat.

1 Combine the ground seeds, chile powder, stock, sour orange juice, and salt in a blender or food processor and puree to a smooth consistency. Serve.

RECIPE VARIATIONS

Iguaxte (Guatemalan Pan-Toasted Pumpkin Seed Sauce): Dry pan toast ½ cup shelled pumpkin seeds, 1 large Roma tomato, 2 medium tomatillos, 1 small yellow onion cut into ½-inch slices, and 2 small garlic cloves. Chop finely and combine with 1 teaspoon Cobán chile powder and ¾ teaspoon (or to taste) kosher salt.

Salsa de Alguaishte (Salvadoran Pan-Toasted Pumpkin Seed and Tomato Sauce): Dry pan toast 1 cup shelled or unshelled pumpkin seeds, 1 large Roma tomato (optional), 1 small yellow onion cut into ½-inch-thick slices, 2 garlic cloves, and 1 seeded and deveined guaque chile (or guajillo). Blend with kosher salt and freshly ground black pepper to taste, and

1 cup water until smooth. The sauce should have a grainy, puree-like consistency and will be green or pale yellow (if not using tomatoes), depending on the seeds used. If it's too thick, add more water. Optional: Add 2 to 3 teaspoons canola oil to a preheated medium skillet over medium high heat and pan fry the sauce for 2 minutes. Or cook all ingredients in the water first instead of dry pan toasting them, then blend and pan fry them.

AMALIA'S NOTES

- Cobán chile powder is available at Latin stores and online.

- This sauce tends to thicken as it sits. Add more stock or water as needed to thin it out.

- For a flavor twist, add ½ small onion and 1 vine-ripened tomato, both fire roasted, to the blender with the ingredients to the Cherebán Iwaxte recipe above.

- The ingredient proportion of any of these sauces can be adjusted to taste.

MOLE NEGRO

Chile and Chocolate Sauce

MAKES 8 cups

The king of moles, one of the seven Oaxacan moles, mole negro is a special treat from the Central Valleys as a stew or in tamales. As one of the most complex moles in Mexico, the sauce is a careful orchestration of fresh and dried ingredients and spices. A key technique consists of burning three ingredients, corn tortillas and the chile seeds and veins (which then must be specially treated to avoid bitterness), to add the distinctive black color and flavor nuances to the sauce in addition to the avocado leaves. As a stew, it is often made with turkey poached in onion and garlic first and then combined with the sauce. In tamales, the sauce is mixed with cooked shredded pork or chicken and then added to prepared corn masa. Mole, from the Nahuatl mōlli, and tamales are ancient preparations of Mesoamerica originally containing only native ingredients that became hybrids after Spanish contact. I had the pleasure of creating this masterpiece with a group of indigenous women in Teotitlán del Valle, Oaxaca. This is my simplified version.

5 chilhuacle negro chiles
2 chilhuacle rojo chiles
3 mulato chiles
2 pasilla chiles
6 taco-size corn tortillas

4 tablespoons lard or canola oil, divided
1 cup quartered Roma tomatoes
½ cup husked and quartered miltomate or tomatillos
1 medium yellow onion, cut into ½-inch-thick slices
2 large cloves garlic
1 small ripe but firm plantain, peeled and cut into 1½-inch slices
1½ tablespoons peanuts, dry pan toasted
1½ tablespoons sliced or whole almonds, dry pan toasted
1½ tablespoons walnuts or pecans, dry pan toasted
1½ tablespoons shelled pumpkin seeds, dry pan toasted
1½ tablespoons sesame seeds, dry pan toasted
5 tablespoons raisins
½ cup crumbled Mexican pan dulce (sweet bread)

SAZÓN (SEASONINGS)

½ teaspoon ground canela (Ceylon cinnamon)
½ teaspoon ground nutmeg
½ teaspoon dried thyme
1 teaspoon crumbled dried oregano
1 teaspoon dried marjoram
½ teaspoon ground allspice berries
¼ teaspoon ground cumin
¼ teaspoon ground anise
⅛ teaspoon ground cloves
2 teaspoons sugar
2 teaspoons kosher salt
Freshly ground black pepper
3 cups chicken stock, store-bought or homemade (see page 198)
1½ to 2 discs dark Mexican chocolate, broken into bits (see note on page 300)
3 fresh or dried avocado leaves, dry pan toasted

Continued on page 300

1. Devein and seed the chiles and reserve the veins and seeds. Dry pan toast them separately in a skillet over medium heat for about 3 minutes. Keep a close eye on them, as they can burn easily. Soak the toasted chiles in 3 cups very hot water until ready to use. Dry pan toast the reserved veins and seeds and toast them until burnt and smoking. Soak the burnt seeds and veins in 1 cup hot water for 10 minutes. Drain the water from the seeds and soak them again in a fresh 1 cup hot water for 10 minutes. Drain the water and set aside the seeds and veins. Burn the tortillas in a toaster oven or under a broiler until totally charred and smoking. Break them into pieces and soak them in 1 cup hot water for 10 minutes. Drain the water and soak the tortillas again in a fresh 1 cup hot water for another 10 minutes. Drain the water and set the tortillas aside.

2. Add 2 tablespoons lard to a large skillet over medium high heat and pan fry the tomatoes, tomatillos, onion, garlic, and plantain until medium soft, stirring from time to time, about 5 minutes. Gradually add the peanuts, almonds, walnuts, pumpkin seeds, sesame seeds, and raisins. Stir well for 2 minutes. Add the bread and stir for 1 minute.

3. In a blender, add the soaked chiles and ½ cup of the chile soaking water, the soaked seeds and veins, and the soaked tortillas. Puree to a smooth consistency. Pour into a bowl and reserve. Then puree to a smooth consistency the pan-fried ingredients, cinnamon, nutmeg, thyme, oregano, marjoram, allspice, cumin, anise, cloves, sugar, salt, black pepper to taste, and chicken stock. Reserve.

4. Heat the remaining 2 tablespoons lard in a medium saucepan over medium low heat. Add the 2 reserved purees and stir well to combine. Cook for 2 minutes, stirring constantly. Add the chocolate, starting with 1 ½ discs, and let it melt gradually while still stirring constantly. Add the avocado leaf, reduce the heat to low, and cook, stirring from time to time, to blend flavors, about 8 to 10 minutes. The sauce should be a little thicker than spaghetti sauce and should look black, smooth, and glossy. It should be mildly sweet. Taste and add the rest of the chocolate, if desired. If it's too thick, add a little stock. If it's too thin, cook it a little longer.

AMALIA'S NOTES

• You can also substitute 5 mulato, 2 pasilla, 3 ancho, and 2 guajillo chiles.

• This sauce is easy to make. It just takes preparation and proper planning and can be made in stages. One day ahead, select and measure all the ingredients, toast the nuts and seeds, and reserve them. The next day, prepare the rest of the ingredients and complete the sauce.

• The sauce can be reduced to a thick paste by cooking it for an extended period of time. Then it can be frozen in smaller portions and reconstituted with chicken stock to be used in a stew or tamales (see recipe for Tamales Oaxaqueños, Oaxacan Mole Negro and Roast Pork Tamales, on page 284). To make turkey or chicken stew, use thigh meat and cook it in chicken stock with 1 small onion and 2 garlic cloves. Then the mole paste can be gradually integrated into the stock, adding about ¾ cup mole (or more to taste) for each cup of liquid.

• The sauce is traditionally mildly sweet, and there are many variations of it. Make it sweeter by gradually adding more chocolate or sugar, or make it more savory by adding more salt. Make it blacker by increasing the number of burnt tortillas or by increasing the number of black chiles (chilhuacle negro or mulato).

• Dark Mexican chocolate discs weigh 3.15 ounces and are high in sugar. To break the chocolate disc into bits, wrap it in plastic, then wrap a towel around it and break it with a meat mallet.

CHIRMOLES
Mayan Sauces

MAKES 1 cup

1 cup diced vine-ripened
  tomatoes
1 guaque or guajillo chile,
  seeded and torn into
  small pieces
½ cup finely diced yellow onion
½ teaspoon minced garlic
¼ cup water
¾ teaspoon kosher salt
1 teaspoon canola oil
¼ cup finely chopped cilantro,
  equal parts cilantro and
  parsley, or epazote

Chirmoles are basic chunky salsas of Mayan origin throughout Guatemala present at just about every meal. Chirimol, chirmol, chilmol, and chimol are also names used in Mesoamerica to refer to this sauce, which has varying cooking techniques and seasonings by country. They can be basic or elaborate and made by combining cooked, raw, and dried ingredients. Chirmoles can be simmered and fried, grilled, pan fried, half raw, and half cooked. Depending on the purpose and your taste, you can modify them to fit any style by adding spices and fresh herbs. These sauces can be used to top sunny-side-up or hard-boiled eggs, fritters, chiles rellenos, rolled tacos, or open-faced tortillas filled with grilled meats, or as a base for rice, beans, stews, or soups. Traditionally chirmoles are chunky, but they can be pureed too. The first sauce is Chirmol con Chile Guaque (Tomato-Guaque Chile Sauce), and on page 303 I present a variety of chirmol sauces, including a Salvadoran version of chirmol.

1. Combine the tomatoes, guaque chile, onion, and garlic with the water and salt in a saucepan. Bring to a boil over high heat, stir well to combine, and adjust the heat to medium low. Simmer, covered, until very soft, about 8 minutes. Puree with an immersion blender or regular blender.

2. Add the oil to a preheated skillet and pan fry the sauce for 2 minutes. Add the cilantro and stir well. Serve.

AMALIA'S NOTES

- All these sauces can be altered according to taste using less or more salt, lime juice, garlic, onion, and so on.

- Another variation of the Chirmol Frito recipe on page 303 is to add 1 minced garlic clove and 1 teaspoon dried or fresh chile pepper.

- Another variation of the Chirmol Salvadoreño recipe on page 303 is to make the sauce with all raw ingredients. You can add chopped radishes or use sour orange juice instead of lime juice. Sour orange juice can be substituted with a combination of equal parts of fresh orange and lemon juice.

Continued on page 303

RECIPE VARIATIONS

Chirmol Asado (Pan-Roasted Tomatillo-Zambo Chile Sauce): Follow the recipe on page 301, substituting 4 whole tomatillos for the tomatoes and 1 teaspoon ground Zambo chile for the guaque chile. Pan roast the tomatillos in a dry skillet over medium high heat until they are charred and soft, about 8 minutes. Chop them finely and combine them with the rest of the ingredients. Do not pan fry the sauce. Serve.

Chirmol Chapín (Charred Tomato and Mint Salsa): Dry pan roast 3 whole Roma tomatoes until they're charred all over and soft, about 12 to 15 minutes. Chop them coarsely, but do not peel them. Combine the tomatoes with 2 tablespoons finely diced onion, 1 tablespoon finely diced chopped mint, 1 tablespoon finely chopped cilantro (optional), 2 teaspoons freshly squeezed lime juice, ½ teaspoon minced fresh chiltepe (piquín) or hot chile pepper of choice, and ½ teaspoon kosher salt. Stir well. Serve.

Chirmol Frito (Basic Pan-Fried Tomato and Onion Sauce): Pour 2 teaspoons canola oil into a preheated skillet over medium heat. Add 2 ½ tablespoons finely diced Roma tomatoes, 1 tablespoon finely diced yellow onion, 3 tablespoons water, and ¼ teaspoon kosher salt. Cook over medium heat until saucy and thick, about 3 minutes. Serve.

Chirmol de Zapatero (Pan-Roasted Tomato, Tomatillo, and Garlic sauce): Dry pan roast or grill 4 tomatillos and 1 vine-ripened tomato until charred and soft, about 8 minutes. Chop them finely and combine with ¾ teaspoon minced garlic and ½ teaspoon kosher salt. Serve.

Chirmol de Miltomate (Pan-Roasted Spicy Tomatillo Salsa): Dry pan roast or grill 8 small tomatillos and 1 serrano chile until charred and soft, about 8 minutes. Chop them finely and combine with 1 ½ tablespoons finely diced onion, ½ tablespoon finely chopped parsley, ½ tablespoon finely chopped cilantro, 1 teaspoon freshly squeezed lime juice, and ½ teaspoon kosher salt. Serve.

Chirmol Salvadoreño (Tomato and Chile Salsa with Lime): In a bowl, combine 2 dry pan-roasted, peeled, and finely chopped vine-ripened tomatoes, ½ cup finely diced onion, ¼ cup finely chopped cilantro leaves and stems, 1 tablespoon minced fresh hot chile of choice (such as chiltepe, serrano, or jalapeño), 1 tablespoon freshly squeezed lime juice, ¾ to 1 teaspoon kosher salt, and freshly ground black pepper (optional). Serve.

SALSA DE CHILTEPE
Fresh Piquín Chile Sauce

MAKES about 1 cup

It doesn't get simpler than this, a sauce as Guatemalan as it comes. Chiltepe is Guatemala's national chile pepper, and it's used in multiple preparations, from basic sauces to ceviches. There are many variations with few or many ingredients, including vinegar or lime juice or both. This is a sauce you can use in place of a bottled sauce to add a quick, bold, delicious punch to just about anything you want to make spicy. It's a favorite in my home, and when I make it, it's gone within a day or two.

¼ cup chopped fresh chiltepe or bird's eye chiles

½ cup husked diced tomatillos

1 teaspoon minced garlic

¾ cup water

½ cup finely diced yellow onions

¼ cup finely chopped cilantro leaves

1 teaspoon white wine vinegar or freshly squeezed lime juice

¾ teaspoon kosher salt

1. Combine the chiles, tomatillos, and garlic with the water in a saucepan, bring to a quick boil over high heat, cover, and cook until soft, about 5 to 8 minutes. Blend with an immersion or regular blender until saucy yet still chunky. Allow it to cool slightly.

2. In a bowl, combine the puree with the onions, cilantro, vinegar, and salt. Serve.

RECIPE VARIATIONS

Salsa de Chiltepe con Miltomate y Samat (Chiltepe Chile, Tomatillo, and Culantro Sauce): Blend ¼ cup roughly chopped fresh chiltepe chiles, ½ cup husked diced tomatillos, 1 bunch chopped culantro, ¼ cup water, ½ cup diced onion, 1 tablespoon white wine vinegar, and 1 teaspoon (or to taste) kosher salt in a blender until saucy yet still chunky. Serve.

Salsa de Chiltepe y Ajos Asados (Pan-Roasted Chiltepe Chile and Garlic Sauce): Pan roast ¼ cup roughly chopped fresh chiltepe chiles and 4 garlic cloves in a skillet over medium high heat until charred, about 3 to 5 minutes. Finely chop and combine with ½ cup finely diced onions, 2 teaspoons white wine vinegar, and ½ teaspoon (or to taste) kosher salt. Serve.

AMALIA'S NOTES

• This sauce can also be made without cooking the chiles, tomatillos, and garlic. Simply puree them in the blender and then combine them with the rest of the ingredients.

• Add cilantro, parsley, or mint (or all or a combination of two of these) to the sauce or any variations to elevate them to a new level.

• Culantro (the serrated leaf herb) in Guatemala is called samat. If unable to source samat, use cilantro instead.

RECADO

Roasted Tomato, Guajillo, Mulato, Ancho, and Pumpkin Seed Sauce

MAKES about 2 cups

1 cup quartered Roma tomatoes (about 2 large tomatoes)

½ cup husked, quartered tomatillos (about 2 to 3 small tomatillos)

½ cup chopped, seeded red bell pepper

1 small yellow onion, cut into ½-inch-thick slices

2 large cloves garlic, peeled

1 guaque or guajillo chile, seeded

½ Zambo or mulato chile, seeded

½ pasa or ancho chile, seeded

1 tablespoon shelled pumpkin seeds

1 tablespoon sesame seeds

2 tablespoons canola oil

1 ½–2 teaspoons ground achiote, mixed with a little water

½ teaspoon ground canela (Ceylon cinnamon)

Kosher salt

Freshly ground black pepper

AMALIA'S NOTES

• Achiote is available as a fresh paste, dried seeds, and ground at most Latin stores, some grocery chains, and online.

• This recado can also be used for Tamales Colorados (Guatemalan Red Chicken or Pork Tamales in Banana Leaves). Find the recipe in variations under Tamales de Arroz y Pavo (Guatemalan Red Chile Sauce and Turkey Rice Tamales) on page 265.

Guatemalans use slightly varying ingredients and techniques to make this sauce. Some cooks prefer to simmer all the fresh ingredients in a little water instead of pan roasting them first. Pan roasting adds another layer of flavor. When my mom made tamales for Christmas, I used to watch her as she carefully pan roasted the sauce ingredients and strived to reach the right sazón (seasoning). This is my version of the sauce, which you can create easily at home. My sauce is a bit spicy and very flavorful. For a milder sauce, use only half a guaque or guajillo chile. You can use this sauce for Tamales de Arroz y Pavo (Guatemalan Red Chile Sauce and Turkey Rice Tamales, page 265); for a Saturday favorite, Tamales Colorados (Guatemalan Red Chicken or Pork Tamales in Banana Leaves, see note below); for topping grilled meats, chicken, or pork; or as a base for a red pepián (stew). Traditionally this sauce, with some modifications, is also used as a base for Guatemalan Tamales Negros (Sweet Christmas Rice Tamales with Mole Sauce, page 286). This sauce freezes well in resealable plastic bags, so store any leftover sauce for later use.

1. Heat a skillet for 2 minutes over medium heat, then add the tomatoes, tomatillos, bell pepper, onion, and garlic. Pan roast them until they're charred all over and mushy, about 8 minutes.

2. Separately dry pan toast the chiles in a skillet over medium heat for 3 to 5 minutes. Keep a close eye on them, as they burn easily. Soak the roasted chiles in 1 cup very hot water for 10 minutes.

3. Separately dry pan toast the seeds in a skillet over medium heat for 3 to 5 minutes. Keep a close eye on them, as they burn easily. Grind the seeds with a coffee mill or a small food processor.

4. Combine all the pan-roasted vegetables with the soaked chiles and half of the soaking water and puree in a blender. The sauce should look smooth and velvety.

5. Heat the oil in a medium saucepan over medium high heat and add the puree, achiote liquid, ground seeds, cinnamon, and salt and black pepper to taste. Adjust the heat to medium low and simmer for 5 minutes. Taste and add additional seasonings, if needed. The sauce should be bright orange and should have the consistency of spaghetti sauce. If it's too thick, add a little chicken stock or water. If it's too thin, cook it a little longer.

RECIPE VARIATION

Recado para Tamales Negros (Roasted Tomato, Guajillo, Mulato, Ancho, Pumpkin Seed, and Chocolate Sauce): Follow the recipe given, but add 3 to 4 pitted prunes or 1 ½ tablespoons raisins, soaked in very hot water, to the blender with the vegetables and chiles. Omit the achiote and use only ½ teaspoon kosher salt. Sweeten the sauce with ¾ to 1 cup Guatemalan chocolate and 1 ½ teaspoons sugar, or to taste, adding them with the puree to the saucepan. The ending sauce should be dark brown, similar to the color of chocolate. To darken the sauce further, add either more chocolate or 3 to 4 tablespoons browned instant corn masa flour. Brown the flour on a dry pan over medium low heat until it's medium brown. Add the flour to the sauce gradually, making sure it doesn't clump in the sauce, or combine the flour with a little cold water first. Traditionally this sauce is thickened with ground blackened plantain peel. If the sauce becomes too thick, add a little water.

SALSA DE MILTOMATE Y AGUACATE
Tomatillo, Avocado, Serrano, and Cilantro Sauce

MAKES 2 cups

This Mexican tomatillo sauce is one of my favorites to top grilled chicken, steak, pork, or tacos. Salsa de Miltomate y Aguacate will dress any salad beautifully. Add it to cold cubed potatoes with chopped hardboiled eggs for a delicious potato salad twist, use it as a dip for chips, or combine it with your preferred snack. This sauce is the bomb in Memelitas (Herbed Achiote Corn Masa Cups Filled with Chopped Flank Steak and Vegetables, page 87). It is mildly spicy, and you can change the flavor profile of the sauce by cooking or grilling part of the ingredients as indicated under recipe variations below. See Chirmol de Miltomate (Pan-Roasted Spicy Tomatillo Salsa), a Guatemalan version of this sauce, on page 303.

1 cup husked petite-diced tomatillos

1 teaspoon minced garlic

⅓ cup finely chopped yellow onion

¼ cup roughly chopped cilantro leaves and stems

1 ripe avocado, skin and pit discarded

1 tablespoon freshly squeezed lime juice

¼ cup water

¾ teaspoon kosher salt

1 tablespoon minced serrano or jalapeño chile, including veins and seeds

1. Combine the tomatillos, garlic, onion, cilantro, avocado, lime juice, water, salt, and serrano in a blender and pulse to make a puree or chunky sauce.

2. Use immediately or refrigerate for later use. The sauce keeps in the refrigerator for 2 days.

AMALIA'S NOTES

- This sauce is mildly spicy. Increase the amount of minced chile to make it spicier, if desired.

- Add more water if you want the sauce to be runnier, or use less if you want the sauce to be thicker.

RECIPE VARIATIONS

Salsa de Miltomate Cocida (Cooked Tomatillo Sauce): Follow the recipe given, except cook the tomatillos and the chiles in the water until soft, about 5 minutes. Let them cool and proceed with the recipe. Omit the avocado. Adjust the seasonings to taste.

Salsa de Miltomate y Tomate (Tomatillo and Tomato Spicy Sauce): Follow the recipe for Salsa de Miltomate y Aguacate, except use equal parts tomatillos and tomatoes and cook the tomatillos and tomatoes and chiles in the water until soft, about 5 minutes. Let them cool and proceed with the recipe. Omit the avocado. Adjust the seasonings to taste.

Salsa de Miltomate Asado (Grilled Tomatillo Sauce): Follow the recipe for Salsa de Miltomate y Aguacate, except dry pan roast or grill the tomatillos whole (use about 5 medium tomatillos) and the pepper whole (use about ½ a serrano chile) before proceeding with the recipe. Omit the avocado. Adjust the seasonings to taste.

ALIÑO DE NARANJA AGRIA
Sour Orange Vinaigrette

MAKES about 1 ½ cups

¼ cup chopped shallots or
   sliced green onions

1 tablespoon kosher salt

1 tablespoon sugar

Freshly ground black pepper

1 tablespoon Dijon mustard

½ cup fresh sour orange juice
   (jugo de naranja agria),
   or equal parts fresh orange
   and lemon juice

1 cup extra-virgin olive oil

I like quick and easy sauces that pack a punch. I come from a culture where lime is king, so my taste buds crave tart foods. Besides being easy and delicious, this dressing is a cold sauce that can dress leafy greens or a simple salad with lettuce, avocado, red onion, and tomatoes. It is on the strong side by design, so a little goes a long way. It is a healthy way to add flavor without adding a lot of calories. Basic Central American salad dressings are usually light and often consist of just lime, sour orange, vinegar, or any other acidic ingredient, depending on the country or region, plus basic seasonings. The best part is that the vinaigrette keeps in the refrigerator for one week. This is my go-to dressing for busy weekdays.

1. Combine the shallots, salt, sugar, black pepper to taste, mustard, and sour orange juice in a blender and blend for 1 minute. With the motor running on low, slowly incorporate the oil in a thin stream to make a homogeneous sauce. The vinaigrette will thicken and can be stored in the refrigerator in a jar with a tight lid for up to 1 week.

AMALIA'S NOTE

- This basic dressing can also be a marinade for seafood, chicken, beef, or pork. Add other ingredients such as dried and fresh herbs to build different flavor profiles according to taste. If using on fruit, leave the onion, mustard, and oil out and replace with one tablespoon toasted pumpkin seed powder and 1 teaspoon dried chile powder. Use half the salt as well, or adjust the seasonings according to taste.

SALSA DE MOLCAJETE
Spicy Manzano Tomato and Guaje Sauce

MAKES 1 cup

While in Oaxaca and Mexico City, I had the opportunity to make a variety of salsas with local cooks. As in the rest of Mesoamerica, sauces and the techniques used to make them vary within towns, cities, and regions. A molcajete, a concave stone made from volcanic rock with an arm (tejolote), has been used by the Aztec and Maya for millenia, since pre-Hispanic times and is a tool and technique to crush ingredients by grinding. The sauces are typically chunky, a key characteristic, similar to Guatemalan chirmoles (see page 301). Some are simple, and others more elaborate. All are fresh and delicious and enhance any food topped with them. Some of my favorite sauces are those that can be made in a matter or minutes and provide an experience for family or friends. This one is a winner, as it combines a variety of common and lesser-known ingredients, many native to Mesoamerica, including yellow manzano tomatoes (with a sweet and tart apple taste), guaje, pipicha, and allspice berries. Guaje originates in Oaxaca and is a tree legume that grows in long, skinny pods. It's similar in color and appearance to shelled pumpkin seeds, although guaje is more tender with a unique flavor. Pipicha, also from Puebla and Oaxaca and parts of Central America, is a delicate herb used in traditional cooking for sauces and soups. The sauce has flavor nuances that are best appreciated when eaten with chips or used to top roast pork or chicken tacos.

4 medium manzano tomatoes
1 small yellow onion, cut into ¼-inch slices
2 small cloves garlic
4 allspice berries
½ teaspoon kosher salt
¼ cup shelled guaje legumes (from a handful of pods)
1 dried morita chile, seeded, soaked in hot water for 10 minutes, and drained
1 tablespoon roughly chopped pipicha (pepicha), epazote, or cilantro (or a combination of all)

1. Pan roast the tomatoes, onion, and garlic in a dry skillet over medium high heat until charred and mushy, about 8 minutes. Cut the tomatoes in half but do not peel them. Set aside.

2. Crush the allspice berries and salt to a fine powder in the molcajete by first pounding them gently and then moving the arm in a circular motion, starting at the center and moving around to the side, to crush and distribute the ingredients evenly. Add the guaje and repeat.

3. Continue adding ingredients one at a time: the garlic, onion, soaked chile, tomatoes cut in halves, and pipicha. Mix well between each addition. The sauce should be saucy yet chunky.

4. Serve in the molcajete.

AMALIA'S NOTES

- The sauce can be made with tomatillos or Roma tomatoes.

- Manzano tomatoes and guaje pods are available at Mexican markets.

- Pipicha (pepicha) is available online as an herb and in seeds to grow at home.

CHILE FRITO

Spicy Pan-Fried Cobán Chile Sauce

MAKES ½ cup

1 teaspoon canola oil

¼ cup minced yellow onion

1 teaspoon minced garlic

½ cup petite-diced
   vine-ripened tomatoes

⅓ cup water

1 tablespoon crushed Cobán
   chile (or substitute guajillo,
   piquín, puya, or árbol)

2 tablespoons chopped
   cilantro leaves

½ teaspoon kosher salt

Las Verapaces, which is located in the Mayan highlands and contains Alta and Baja Verapaz in north-central Guatemala, is a multiethnic and multilingual indigenous area with some of the best culinary traditions in the country. Cobán chile, a small hot pepper used fresh and dried, is native to Cobán, the capital of Alta Verapaz. When dried, it is smoked and then sold in markets whole, crushed, or ground to a powder. Cobán and chiltepe (piquín) are the two most popular chiles in Guatemala and are consumed daily in many preparations, alone as a topping, in simple sauces, or added to fresh fruits or stews. Although fiery, the chile is truly delicious and has many flavor nuances that are best appreciated when eaten with fresh fruit. Interestingly, the burn doesn't last too long after eating it. Street carts use it to add kick and awesome flavor to the popular bags of fruit found in city corners, parks, plazas, and crowded places. Chile Frito is the perfect way to add a quick punch to black beans, rice dishes, stews, or ceviche. A little goes a long way.

1 Add the oil to a preheated small skillet over medium high heat and pan fry the onion and garlic until translucent, about 2 minutes. Add the tomatoes and water and cook until saucy yet chunky, about 2 minutes.

2 Add the crushed chile, cilantro, and salt, and cook 2 minutes. Serve immediately.

RECIPE VARIATION

Chile Cobanero (Dried Chile Base):
Combine 1 cup crushed Cobán chile, ¼ cup ground pan-toasted and peeled fresh cocoa beans, and ½ teaspoon kosher salt. Store in an airtight jar until ready to use. See the Kixnank' (Artisan Chocolate with Vanilla Bean and Cinnamon) recipe on page 39 for instructions on how to pan toast and peel cocoa beans.

AMALIA'S NOTES

• Buy Cobán chile at Latin markets or online.

• To extend the life of Chile Frito, add 1 tablespoon white vinegar to the mixture. Then store in a small mason jar. The sauce keeps in the refrigerator for up to 1 week with added vinegar.

SALSA CRIOLLA FRÍA

Quick Homestyle Sauce

MAKES 2 cups

Criollo is the term used for a person of Spanish descent born in Latin America, and this sauce is so named because it combines Spanish and Latin ingredients. *Fría* means cold, as this is meant to be eaten cold. This recipe is from my personal collection, and it's perfect for grilled meats, empanadas, or cooked rice or roasted potatoes. It could also be a nice dip for baked corn chips. There are many criollo sauces in Mesoamerica, and they are all delicious and easy to make. For a twist in flavor and appearance, add fresh herbs of choice and blend to create a velvety red sauce.

1 cup petite-diced vine-ripened tomatoes
1 cup petite-diced red bell pepper
¾ cup finely chopped yellow onion
2 teaspoons minced garlic
½ cup water
½ cup extra-virgin olive oil
1 tablespoon red wine vinegar
1 teaspoon kosher salt
1 teaspoon crumbled dried oregano
Freshly ground black pepper

1. Combine the tomatoes, bell pepper, onion, garlic, water, oil, vinegar, salt, oregano, and black pepper to taste in a medium saucepan. Stir to combine, bring to a quick boil over high heat, reduce the heat to medium low, and simmer, covered, for 5 minutes.

2. Uncover the pan, simmer another 5 minutes, and let cool. Serve.

RECIPE VARIATIONS

Salsa de Tomate Picante (Guatemalan Spicy Tomato Sauce): Follow the recipe above, except replace half the tomatoes with tomatillos, omit the oregano, and add 1 teaspoon minced fresh jalapeño, ½ teaspoon dried thyme, and 1 dried bay leaf. Instead of simmering the ingredients, pan fry them in the olive oil. Serve warm or cold.

Salsa de Tomate Ciruela (Guatemalan Quick Tomato Sauce): Follow the recipe for Salsa Criolla Fría, except add ¼ cup finely diced celery and ½ teaspoon sugar. Simmer the sauce without the olive oil for 5 minutes, puree with a blender, and pan fry in the oil. Serve warm or cold.

Salsa de Tomate con Orégano (Guatemalan Oregano Tomato Sauce): Cut a shallow X in the bottom of 2 medium vine-ripened tomatoes and blanch them in boiling water for about 1 ½ minutes. Plunge immediately in cold water, then peel. Chop the tomatoes and puree them with ¾ teaspoon minced garlic with a blender. Pan fry the puree in ¼ cup olive oil, and add ½ teaspoon crumbled dried oregano and ½ teaspoon kosher salt. Serve warm or cold.

Salsita de Chile Guaque (Guatemalan Guajillo Tomato Sauce): Add 1 cup roughly chopped grilled Roma tomatoes, 2 guaque chiles (or guajillo), seeded and soaked in hot water, ¼ cup finely chopped onion, 1 teaspoon minced garlic, ¼ teaspoon dried thyme, 1 teaspoon white wine vinegar, and ½ teaspoon kosher salt to a blender or food processor and puree to the consistency of spaghetti sauce. Taste for seasoning and add more salt if needed. Serve warm or cold.

Salsa Salvadoreña (Salvadoran Basic Quick Tomato Sauce): To a small saucepan, add 1 cup roughly chopped vine-ripened tomatoes, 2 tablespoons chopped onion, 2 small cloves garlic, 1 to 2 teaspoons minced jalapeño or serrano, ⅛ teaspoon dried thyme, ½ teaspoon crumbled dried oregano, 1 small dried bay leaf, ¼ cup water, 1 teaspoon white wine vinegar, and ¼ teaspoon kosher salt or to taste. Bring to a quick boil over high heat, reduce the heat to low, cover, and simmer for 5 to 8 minutes. Remove and discard the bay leaf. Puree with an immersion blender or regular blender and heat through or continue to cook it to thicken as desired. Use the sauce immediately or store it in a mason jar in the refrigerator for up to 1 week.

Chile Criollo (Nicaraguan Spicy Tomato and Cucumber Salsa): Combine ½ cup finely diced vine-ripened tomatoes, 2 tablespoons finely diced yellow onion, ½ cup finely diced cucumber, 1 teaspoon minced jalapeño, 1 tablespoon freshly squeezed lime juice, and ½ teaspoon kosher salt in a bowl and mix well. Serve cold.

AMALIA'S NOTES

- Unless the sauce contains vinegar, use the sauce within a day or two. Sauces containing vinegar can last in the refrigerator up to 1 week.

- For a flavor twist, use pasa (ancho) chiles or a combination of both in the Salsita de Chile Guaque recipe.

11

La Panadería y Postres
Cookies, Bread, Cakes, and Desserts

PAN DULCE

A symbol of comfort, pan dulce is a perfect pairing with a good cup of coffee or hot artisan chocolate during a cozy conversation with family or friends. It also is a fast breakfast food or happy ending to a nice meal.

Pan dulce is the traditional term for sweet bread, which can be a wide variety of breads consumed daily in many parts of Mesoamerica. In Guatemala, pan dulce is also known as pan de manteca, and it can also refer to the rolls shaped like conchas, or scallop shells, coated with a paste made of sugar and butter or shortening, that are prominent at many Latin markets. *Manteca* can mean either lard or shortening, which can be used interchangeably.

Baking is an old trade and used to be rustic, much like the initial corn-based tortillas in Mesoamerica. Early breads (flat cakes) were unleavened in the Middle East (and are still made in some cultures today). Toasted, crushed wheat mixed with water was likely cooked on hot stones or other rustic means, and fermentation (yeast) probably happened by accident. The first bread bakers were the Greeks, who used ovens heated by wood fires. Then the Romans proliferated bread production and used honey and oil to create sweet breads (pastries).

With the fall of the Roman Empire, bread nearly vanished, though it resurfaced in France during the latter part of the Middle Ages. Baking gained prominence, and a guild of bakers created a wave of bakers that elevated the baking and pastry profession to a high level. During conquest of the Americas, sugar, chocolate, and vanilla were imported and played a key role in pastry making.

Breads and pastries then were for the upper classes, but after the French Revolution, bakers were no longer required to cook for royalty and started to find ways to survive and bring the breads to regular people. The Spanish and later immigrant French bakers introduced bread and baking as it is known today to Meso- and Latin America around the nineteenth century, and everyone contributed their own twist.

When I was little, my grandmother used to make artisan bread without the use of any fancy equipment. She used a bowl and a wooden spatula to combine ingredients by hand and baked her bread in an igloo-like wood-heated earthen oven, an ancient practice still alive today in rural Guatemala. It took her three times the effort and time than when I use her recipes in my modern kitchen.

Wheat versus Corn

Although wheat reigns supreme worldwide and is second only to rice, in Mesoamerica, it is second to corn.

Wheat has been around since 10,000 BC and corn around 7000 BC, and both developed independently in two key agricultural world regions.

Wheat came to Meso- and Latin America through Spain, and although it did not dethrone corn, it came to coexist and remain present in the diet of Latin Americans.

Wheat has a high gluten content, making it ideal for bread and cakes, and in Meso- and Latin America, the techniques used for breadmaking have French influences.

Although there are similarities in the breads of the region, there are distinctive recipes that make them unique by country. Many breads, cakes, and pastries have been adapted to local tastes as well as to local ingredients.

Wheat and corn at times coexist within the same recipe, making the item a hybrid mix of two world staples and cultures.

This chapter contains some of my favorite breads, pastries, and sweets. I chose carefully to reflect their hybrid nature and cultural blending with the use of a variety of ingredients, some of which are native to the Mesoamerican region, making them different from the rest of Latin America. Wheat, corn, cornstarch, and yuca play recurring roles in Mesoamerican cooking, as they can be used for savory and sweet foods. Fruits and their juices as well as canela (Ceylon cinnamon), vanilla, sugar, honey, milk, cream, cheese, butter, gelatin, and rum are prevalent ingredients in bread, cakes, and desserts.

Rum, a byproduct of distilled sugarcane juice (not native), is an important ingredient in drinks as well as a flavoring in sauces for specialty cakes, such as Borracho (Spiced Rum Cake, page 337). I favor high-quality rums from Mesoamerica to enhance fruit desserts such as

Bananitos Flameados con Ron (Caramelized Bananas with Butter and Cinnamon Flamed with Rum, page 338).

The blending of ingredients and flavors that resulted from the Exchange and beyond came to create a new category of breads and sweets in Mesoamerica. It forever altered and expanded the repertoire in this area, as the native cuisine included sweets that came mostly from nature, agave and fruit. It also introduced richer and higher-calorie foods.

Sugarcane and its byproducts (sugar and panela or piloncillo) introduced a whole new group of sweets, which I go into more in depth in Chapter 12 (see page 351). Now I invite you to discover or rediscover new or familiar breads, cakes, and sweets with a Mesoamerican twist.

CHAMPURRADAS

Guatemalan Cookies

MAKES 28 cookies

4 cups (22 ounces) aerated all-purpose flour, plus more flour for dusting (see note on page 324)

1 tablespoon baking powder

1 cup (7 ounces) sugar

¼ teaspoon kosher salt

4 large eggs

1 teaspoon esencia de crema (cream essence) or vanilla extract

½ cup (4 ounces) butter, at room temperature and cut into ¼-inch slices

½ cup (4 ounces) vegetable shortening

2 tablespoons sesame seeds

SPECIAL EQUIPMENT

3-inch cookie cutter

One of my favorite sweet treats from Guatemala City, champurradas are crispy cookies topped with sesame seeds. I like to dunk them in cold milk, hot coffee, or Guatemalan artisan hot chocolate. They are easy to make and delicious. Traditionally, they are about five inches in diameter, but you can make them in any size or shape you wish. I like to use fun cookie cutters of different sizes to fit the purpose. They make a fun dessert with a cup of coffee after a nice elegant dinner with friends or can pair with your favorite hot drink during a cozy gathering with family. Kids love them and can't get enough. I also make them with a combination of wheat and corn flour (see recipe variation below) with equally delicious results. Champurradas are a very special treat in my home.

1. Line a baking sheet with parchment paper. Preheat the oven to 350°F.

2. In the bowl of a stand mixer with the dough hook or paddle attachment, combine the flour, baking powder, sugar, and salt. Stir at the lowest speed to mix these ingredients and break up any clumps.

3. Break the eggs into a small bowl and add the esencia de crema, but do not mix them. While the mixer is running at slow speed, add the eggs one by one, and add the butter and shortening in between each egg. Continue mixing just to bring all ingredients together. The mixture will become doughy and collect at the center of the bowl. Do not overmix.

4. Transfer the dough to a floured surface and divide it into two parts. Return one part to the mixing bowl and place it in the refrigerator, covered with plastic, until ready to use. Flatten the other half with a rolling pin to about ¼ inch thick. Use round cookie cutters to cut circles 3 inches in diameter (they will extend more when you flatten them on the baking sheet). Using a thin spatula, transfer each cookie to the baking sheet. Repeat the procedure with the rest of the dough.

5. Flatten the cookies even more with your fingers to about ⅛ inch thick and 4 inches in diameter. The cookies will rise back to ¼ inch thick during baking. Score four or five lines in the center of each cookie with a pastry cutter or paring knife, or make diamond shapes by crisscrossing the cuts. Sprinkle the sesame seeds equally over all the cookies. Push the seeds gently into the dough with your fingers.

6. Bake for 10 minutes, rotate the baking sheet 180 degrees for even baking, and bake for another 10 minutes. Rotate the baking sheet 180 degrees once more and bake until the cookies appear medium brown and crispy, about 5 additional minutes.

7. Serve immediately or let them cool completely and store in airtight containers or resealable plastic bags.

RECIPE VARIATION

Champurradas (Guatemalan Cookies with Corn Flour): Follow the recipe above, except use 3 cups aerated all-purpose flour and 1 cup instant corn masa flour.

Continued on page 324

AMALIA'S NOTES

- Aerate the flour prior to measuring it by simply stirring it around with a wire whisk within the container to fluff it. Then scoop the flour into the measuring cup and use a knife to level the flour across the top of the measuring cup.

- Work fast, as too much contact with the hands softens the dough quickly. Transfer it to the refrigerator if the dough becomes too soft, or it will be hard to transfer the cookies to the baking sheet.

- The cookies can be made earlier in the day, set on baking sheets lined with parchment paper, covered with plastic, and stored in the refrigerator to be baked later in the day.

- These cookies can be made and shaped by hand. Using a sturdy spatula, combine all the ingredients in a bowl in the order listed. Using a cookie scoop for uniformity, form a ball and flatten it with your hands slightly. Place the cookie on the baking sheet before flattening it further to the desired thickness and size.

- Although sesame seeds are the traditional garnish, you can use poppy seeds or other seeds of choice for variety.

PAN FRANCÉS
Guatemalan French Bread

MAKES 32 pieces

1 cup plus ⅓ cup lukewarm
    water, divided
1 teaspoon sugar
2 (0.25-ounce) packets
    active dry yeast

4 cups (22 ounces) aerated
    all-purpose flour, plus more
    for dusting (see note on
    page 326)
1 teaspoon kosher salt
2 ½ tablespoons vegetable
    shortening, plus more
    for coating the bowl

Most Guatemalans prefer corn tortillas at mealtimes, but pan Francés (French bread) is also popular, especially in Guatemala City. Pan Francés came to Guatemala with immigrant French bakers in the nineteenth century. What is unique about this bread is its shape. It does not look like your typical baguette or loaf but rather like two dinner rolls baked together, which can be easily detached if one only wants a little bread. It is crispy on the outside and soft inside, quite similar to French bread. People often run to the nearby store to buy freshly baked bread for breakfast or dinner. In some neighborhoods, el pan (sweet and savory bread) arrives daily by bicycle in large and wide baskets. The vendor rings the bike's bell to announce he has arrived. Guatemalans eat pan Francés with tamales and other foods. Other popular savory breads include pirujos, elongated buns with pointed ends that are a bit larger and wider (hot dog bun size). Pan Francés and pirujos are great as sides but also for sandwiches called panes. Panes are quick sandwiches made with black bean puree, cheese, or both, and chiles rellenos, chicken, turkey, roast pork, and more.

1 Line a baking sheet with parchment paper and dust it lightly with flour.

2 In a large clear measuring cup, combine 1 cup water and sugar and whisk to dissolve well. Add the yeast and whisk again. Allow the yeast to bloom, covered, until very foamy and doubled in volume, about 15 to 20 minutes.

3 In a stand mixer with the dough hook attachment, stir the flour and salt on the lowest speed for 20 seconds. With a soft spatula, make a well in the center of the flour and add the yeast mixture and shortening. Stir to combine them on the lowest speed, about 1 minute. When the dough is starting to come together but still looks stringy and dry, increase the speed to number 2 and add the remaining water in a very thin stream down the side of the mixing bowl while the machine is still running. The dough is ready when it looks smooth and elastic and doesn't stick to the bottom or sides of the mixing bowl, about 8 to 10 minutes.

4 Gather the dough in a ball with your hands, then lightly coat the mixing bowl with a very thin layer of shortening just to keep the dough from sticking to the bowl. Return the dough to the mixing bowl, tightly cover the bowl with plastic, and let rise in a warm place until it has doubled in volume, about 30 to 40 minutes. Remove the plastic and transfer the dough to a clean, lightly floured working surface.

5 With a stainless steel scraper, divide the dough in half. Divide each half in half again and repeat until you have sixteen roll-size portions. (Alternatively, using a baker's scale, weigh each portion to your desired size.)

Continued on page 326

6. Working with one portion at a time, holding the palm of your hand fairly flat, roll the dough in a tight circle on the work surface. Do not use too much flour for dusting, as the dough must stick to the work surface a little for this technique to work. As the dough takes on a round shape, gradually cup your hand. The finished ball of dough should have a smooth surface, except for a slight pucker on the bottom. This should take about 30 seconds per ball. Repeat until all the dough has been used.

7. Line up four balls in a row so that they are touching each other. With a thin rolling pin or the side of your hand, make a deep trench horizontally across the middle of the ball row, without breaking the dough completely in half. The balls will now look like half balls joined by the flattened middle dough and connected to each other. With your palms placed at each end of the row, gently squeeze the row together toward the center. Repeat with the remaining dough balls to make three more rows, for a total of four rows.

8. Transfer the rows to the baking sheet, leaving 2 inches of space in between each row for the rolls to expand during proofing and baking. Cover with plastic and proof until the rows have doubled in volume and the dough springs back slowly when touched, about 30 to 40 minutes. If the dough is still firm and elastic, it needs more proofing. If the dent remains in the dough, the dough is overproofed, but you can still bake the bread.

9. While the dough is proofing, preheat the oven to 425°F.

10. Place a small rimmed baking sheet or round cake pan almost full of water on the oven floor. (The water's intense heat is needed to add the moisture the bread needs to form a nice crust while remaining soft inside.) Bake on the top rack for 10 minutes, then very carefully, and wearing oven mitts to prevent burns, remove the water pan from the oven and rotate the bread baking sheet 180 degrees. Continue baking until the bread is golden brown and sounds hollow when thumped, about 5 additional minutes.

AMALIA'S NOTES

- For the recipe to turn out, it's important to measure the ingredients with the appropriate measuring tools for dry and liquid ingredients and to machine-knead, rest, and proof the dough as indicated. Enough moisture in the oven is also essential for a nice crunchy crust.

- Aerate the flour prior to measuring it by simply stirring it around with a wire whisk within the container to fluff it. Then scoop the flour into the measuring cup and use a knife to level the flour across the top of the measuring cup.

- If you need to add any water to the dough, do it in increments of half teaspoons.

- Imperfectly shaped pan Francés will make it look artisan and homemade. You can also top the bread with a light dusting of flour using a sifter or strainer.

- I prefer to use active dry yeast for this recipe, as I have found it works the best. There are other yeasts out there, but not all of them will produce the same results.

- Hard-crusted breads ideally should be consumed the day they are made, as they can become stale quickly. To extend freshness, you can freeze them once cool, and when you're ready to eat them, reheat the bread in the oven or small toaster oven.

- Serve Pan Francés as a side, or make Guatemalan sandwiches with it. Sandwich fillings can be as simple as frijoles volteados (bean puree) with cheese and crema, chiles rellenos (stuffed peppers), or stewed chicken or turkey.

TORTA DE QUESO Y YUCA

Yuca Cheesecake

SERVES 14 to 16

Nonstick baking spray
  with flour

1 pound frozen shredded
  yuca, thawed
1 cup whole milk
1 ½ cups (6.7 ounces)
  shredded Nicaraguan dry
  grating cheese or Cotija
½ cup unsalted crema or
  Mexican table cream
2 large eggs
¾ cup (5.25 ounces) sugar
1 teaspoon baking powder
½ teaspoon kosher salt
¼ cup (2 ounces) butter,
  melted

Berries, mint leaves,
  and flowers

This Nicaraguan yuca cheesecake is the bomb. It's super easy to make and delicious. Yuca is an important ingredient in Central and Latin American cooking, and it's consumed in varying forms, mostly in savory preparations. As a dessert, yuca pairs well with cheese and cream or requesón (Latin ricotta) and makes a delightful slightly firm and moist gluten-free dessert. Serve it as is, or top it with fresh fruit.

1 Preheat the oven to 350°F. Coat a 9-inch round cake pan with baking spray.

2 Combine the yuca, milk, cheese, crema, eggs, sugar, baking powder, salt, and butter in a stand mixer with the paddle attachment. Mix on speed 2 for 2 to 3 minutes.

3 Pour the mixture into the cake pan and bake until a knife inserted in the center of the cheesecake comes out clean, about 40 to 45 minutes. Allow the cheesecake to cool down.

4 Garnish with berries, mint leaves, and flowers right before serving.

AMALIA'S NOTE
• Frozen shredded yuca is available at Latin markets.

EMPANADAS DE MADURO

Sweet Plantain and Melting Cheese Turnovers

MAKES 4 empanadas

Ripe plantains are versatile and can be fried, baked, grilled, steamed, and poached. They're also great in atole (the hot beverage) or beef and vegetable soups. Mash them and prepare Guatemalan Rellenitos (Plantain Dumplings with Chocolate-Bean Puree, see recipe variation below), or stuff them with cream and cheese. This Nicaraguan treat will please any crowd as a snack or dessert, or in a smaller size as an appetizer. Dress them with a bit of sugar or drizzle them with dark chocolate sauce and top with berries and you have a gourmet dessert. Fill them with beef or pork picadillo (see Enchiladas Nicas, Pork Picadillo–Stuffed Corn Tortillas Topped with Cabbage-Tomato Slaw and Spicy Vegetable Pickles, page 82), cooked chorizo, or black bean puree and create a totally different and delightful empanada.

1 ripe yet firm unpeeled plantain
2 tablespoons all-purpose flour, plus more for dusting

¾ cup (4.5 ounces) shredded Oaxaca cheese or crumbled queso fresco (or a combination), divided
½ cup canola oil

1. Wash the plantain and cut it into 2-inch slices, ends included. Place them in a saucepan and add enough water to cover the slices completely. Bring to a boil over high heat, adjust the heat to low, cover, and cook until soft, about 10 minutes from boiling. Drain the plantains, peel them, and put them in a stand mixer with the paddle attachment. Mix on the lowest setting to make a puree. Add the flour gradually, stop the mixer, scrape the sides at least once, and mix until doughy, about 1 minute. (Alternatively, use a potato masher to mash the plantains and flour in a bowl.)

2. Form four equal-size balls with the help of a cookie scoop or spoon. Use the extra flour as you are forming the balls to keep the mashed plantains from sticking to your hands. Dust the balls with flour and set them aside.

3. Use two pieces of sturdy plastic from a resealable bag to flatten each ball. Dust a thin layer of flour on the bottom plastic piece, place one ball on top, and place the second piece of plastic on top. Flatten the balls between the plastic pieces with the back of a small skillet to ¼ inch thick and 5 ½ inches in diameter. Dust more flour as needed on the top of the dough ball before putting on the second piece of plastic to keep the dough from sticking to the plastic. Peel the top layer of plastic off. Put 3 tablespoons cheese in the center, distribute it evenly with your fingers, leaving about a ¼-inch edge, and enclose the pocket by folding it in half with the help of the bottom plastic layer. Gently seal the edges with your fingers. It's important to seal the edges well to keep the filling from oozing out during frying. Repeat the procedure with the remaining three dough balls.

4. Preheat a griddle or wide nonstick skillet over medium low heat, add half the oil, and fry two empanadas at a time until medium brown, about 2 to 3 minutes per side. Transfer them to a plate lined with paper towels to absorb excess oil and keep them warm covered with a cloth.

5. Serve immediately.

RECIPE VARIATIONS

Guatemalan Rellenitos (Plantain Dumplings with Chocolate-Bean Puree): Follow the recipe given, except omit the cheese and use a chocolate-bean puree as the filling. Combine 1 cup pureed black beans, ½ teaspoon vanilla extract, 2 ounces Guatemalan chocolate, 2 tablespoons sugar, and ⅛ teaspoon kosher salt. Fill the flattened dough balls with this puree and shape them to resemble small fat cylinders or little American footballs. Dust them with a little flour and pan fry them in the canola oil until light brown all around. Roll the rellenitos in cinnamon-sugar and serve.

Costa Rican Empanadas de Plátano (Plantain Turnovers): Follow the recipe for Empanadas de Maduro, except add 2 teaspoons sugar to the plantain dough when mixing. Fill with cheese or bean puree. Fry in equal parts butter and oil.

AMALIA'S NOTE

• Add chopped jalapeños, chopped fresh herbs, and onions to the cheese filling for a savory twist.

MAGDALENA
Orange Coffee Cake

SERVES 10 to 12

Nonstick baking spray
  with flour

½ cup (4 ounces) butter,
  at room temperature
2 cups (14 ounces) sugar
2 teaspoons minced
  orange rind

4 large eggs
3 cups (16.5 ounces) aerated
  all-purpose flour (see note)
2 teaspoons baking powder
½ teaspoon kosher salt
1 cup freshly squeezed
  orange juice
½ cup whole milk

2 oranges, sliced ¼ inch thick,
  then cut into quarters
22 mint leaves

Central Americans and Mexicans are very social people who often meet for a refacción or merienda (snack time) and cozy chat over a cup of coffee and a piece of magdalena or other pan dulce (sweet bread) in small shops or cafeterias. Sometimes girlfriends will gather at someone's home to catch up, gossip, or celebrate friendship. Refacciones (a Guatemalan term) are smaller bites between meals typically accompanied by café, Café con Leche (Coffee with Milk, page 35), or hot chocolate. There's a version of this cake in the Mesoamerican region and beyond, with everyone giving it their own twist. This is my version of this scrumptious coffee cake. In Guatemala, a magdalena is traditionally made in a tube pan, and this is how you can tell it apart from other sweet breads.

1. Preheat the oven to 350°F. Coat a 10x4-inch-deep tube pan with baking spray.

2. In a stand mixer with the paddle attachment, cream the butter, sugar, and orange rind for 3 minutes at speed 4. Stop and scrape the bottom and sides of the bowl with a soft spatula halfway through the mixing time.

3. Decrease the speed to 2, and while continuing to beat, add the eggs one at a time and mix for 2 minutes total. Incorporate the flour, salt, and baking powder into the creamy mixture a little at a time, alternating with the orange juice and milk. Make sure the dry ingredients are well blended into the dough. Stop and scrape the bottom of the bowl and sides with a soft spatula after everything is added and beat for 1 more minute.

4. Pour the batter into the tube pan and bake until a knife inserted near the center of the ring comes out clean, about 45 to 50 minutes.

5. Allow the cake to cool down, then decorate with overlapping pieces of orange quarters and mint leaves in between.

RECIPE VARIATION

Magdalena Borracha (Drunken Coffee Cake): Make the rum syrup from the Borracho (Spiced Rum Cake, page 337) recipe and follow the steps for applying it to the cake.

AMALIA'S NOTE

- Aerate the flour prior to measuring it by simply stirring it around with a wire whisk within the container to fluff it. Then scoop the flour into the measuring cup and use a knife to level the flour across the top of the measuring cup.

PAN DE MAÍZ Y QUESO OREADO
Corn Masa and Fresh Farmer Cheese Bread

SERVES 10 to 18

Corn reigns supreme in Mesoamerica, and it's no surprise that people have created everything you can think of from it. Pan de maíz, with varying ingredients, is popular throughout this region. In my grandmother's small town, women sold freshly baked pan de maíz and other artisan foods door to door. Sometimes I was out playing with my friends at the nearby basketball court, and when I noticed the vendors selling my favorite treats, I'd ask them to give me a piece and then go to my grandmother's to collect the money for it. This Guatemalan version contains fresh farmer cheese and anise extract, but in Nicaragua it is made with requesón (ricotta cheese) and panela (piloncillo). This can be a delightful casual dessert or a very special pastel de cumpleaños (birthday cake), and it's gluten free.

Nonstick baking spray

3 cups (15.5 ounces) instant corn masa flour
3 cups water
2 ¼ cups (15.75 ounces) sugar
2 teaspoons baking powder
2 cups (½ pound) shredded queso oreado (fresh farmer cheese)
8 large eggs
1 cup (½ pound) butter, melted, divided
1 teaspoon anise extract
1 tablespoon sesame seeds

Edible flowers

① Preheat the oven to 350°F. Coat a 9-inch round springform pan or a 9x13-inch cake pan with baking spray.

② In the bowl of a stand mixer with the paddle attachment, combine the corn flour and water to make a soft dough. Add the sugar, baking powder, and cheese, and mix at speed 2 for 1 minute. With the mixer running, alternate adding two eggs at a time and ¼ cup butter, making sure the batter has absorbed each ingredient before adding the next. Proceed until all the butter and eggs have been incorporated into the batter. This will take 2 to 3 minutes. Add the anise extract and mix at speed 2 for 30 seconds. Fluff the dough at speed 4 for 2 minutes.

③ Pour the batter into the pan and bake until a knife inserted in the center comes out clean, about 1 hour and 10 minutes. Allow the bread to cool. To unmold, if not using a springform pan, place a cutting board on top of the cake pan and invert it. Remove the pan. Place a cake plate upside down on top of the bread and invert it again onto the plate. Allow the cake to cool down.

④ Decorate with edible flowers, slice, and serve.

AMALIA'S NOTE

• Alternatively, you can use 7x11x2-inch-long or 8x8-inch square baking pans. Baking time will vary, so keep a close eye on it. Start checking for doneness after 15 to 20 minutes, and add time in 5-minute increments, as needed. Fill each baking pan half to two-thirds full so the batter doesn't pour over the sides.

BORRACHO

Spiced Rum Cake

SERVES 10 to 12

Nonstick baking spray
with flour

6 large eggs
¾ cup (5.25 ounces) sugar
1 teaspoon vanilla extract

1 ½ cups (8.25 ounces) aerated
all-purpose flour (see note)
1 teaspoon baking powder
¼ teaspoon kosher salt

MIEL DE RON (RUM SYRUP)

1 cup water
¾ cup (5.25 ounces) sugar
1 (5-inch) stick canela
(Ceylon cinnamon)
Half the rind of an orange or
the entire rind of a lime
3 whole cloves
4 allspice berries
½ cup good-quality rum,
such as Guatemalan Zacapa
Centenario or Nicaraguan
Flor de Caña

ADORNO (GARNISH)

Berries, mint, and Chantilly
cream (optional)

I grew up eating this delicious cake. The last time I had it was when one of my nephews graduated from college in Guatemala City. This is a truly delightful dessert. Like Magdalena (Orange Coffee Cake, page 333), there are versions of this cake under differing names, such as sopa borracha or borrachito, in El Salvador, Costa Rica, Nicaragua, and elsewhere in Latin America. Traditionally, this borracho cake (meaning drunkard) is garnished very modestly, but modern versions add other toppings. This is my version, the way I remember it from my time growing up in Guatemala.

1. Preheat the oven to 350°F. Coat a 15x10-inch glass baking dish or equal-size sheet cake pan with baking spray.

2. In the bowl of a stand mixer with the whisk attachment, whisk the eggs and sugar at speed 4 until they have tripled in volume and are at the ribbon stage (thick and fluffy), about 15 minutes. Add the vanilla and whisk 30 seconds.

3. Remove the bowl from the mixer. In a separate bowl, combine the flour, baking powder, and salt, and mix well with a fork. In folding strokes using a soft spatula, incorporate the flour mixture into the eggs, using a small strainer or sifter, shake about one-third of the flour mixture on top of the egg mixture and fold it into the egg mixture using a soft spatula. Make sure the flour is well incorporated before adding the next third of the flour mixture. Repeat the process with the final third of flour. Do not overbeat.

4. Pour the batter in the prepared pan and bake until the center of a knife inserted in the center of the cake comes out clean, about 25 to 30 minutes. Let cool.

5. Meanwhile, make the rum syrup by combining the water, sugar, cinnamon, orange rind, cloves, and allspice in a medium saucepan. Let the mixture simmer over medium low heat, covered, until very aromatic, about 15 minutes. Allow the syrup to cool slightly. Add the rum and stir well.

6. Invert the cake on a platter and use a pastry brush to dab the cake with the syrup. Work from left to right and around the sides, making sure the cake has fully absorbed the syrup before adding more. Repeat until half of the syrup (or more to taste) has been used. Save the remaining syrup to serve with the cake.

7. Chill the cake until ready to serve. Garnish with your choice of toppings.

AMALIA'S NOTES

- Aerate the flour prior to measuring it by simply stirring it around with a wire whisk within the container to fluff it. Then scoop the flour into the measuring cup and use a knife to level the flour across the top of the measuring cup.

- Chantilly cream is easy to make. Whip 1 cup cold heavy cream by hand or with a mixer until soft peaks form, add 1 tablespoon powdered sugar and ½ teaspoon vanilla extract, and whip again until stiff peaks form. Do not overwhip, or the cream can separate.

BANANITOS FLAMEADOS CON RON

Caramelized Bananas with Butter and Cinnamon Flamed with Rum

SERVES 4

I favor simple yet delicious desserts, especially if they are made with fruit. For this dessert, use ripe yellow bananas when they are at their peak; they will still work if they have a few brown dots. When combined with cinnamon, sugar, and butter, the bananas acquire a light brown tone, and the texture becomes creamier. The flavor is elevated to a gourmet level by flaming them with rum. Build this dessert further with chocolate shavings, berries, and crema. Or serve it à la mode with a scoop of vanilla ice cream on the side.

2 tablespoons butter

4 ripe yet firm bananas, peeled

3 tablespoons sugar

3 tablespoons high-quality rum, such as Guatemalan Zacapa Centenario or Nicaraguan Flor de Caña

¼ teaspoon ground canela (Ceylon cinnamon)

ADORNO (GARNISH)

Berries and mint

1. Melt the butter in a nonstick medium skillet over low heat. Place the bananas on top, increase the heat to medium, and brown for 4 minutes. Using a wide, heat-resistant spatula, turn the bananas over, being careful not to break them.

2. Sprinkle the sugar along the length of each banana, dividing it evenly among the four bananas. Brown for 2 minutes.

3. Pour the rum into a small dish or measuring cup. If using a gas stovetop, increase the heat to high and remove the skillet from the flame to pour the rum in a zig-zag pattern on top of the bananas. Return the skillet to the flame and tilt the skillet toward the flame to ignite the rum. While the rum is flaming, keep the skillet as far away from your face as possible.

4. When the rum has stopped flaming, sprinkle with cinnamon. Slide the bananas onto a plate, garnish with berries and mint, and serve immediately.

AMALIA'S NOTES

• For safety, follow the flaming directions carefully. Never pour rum directly from the bottle into the pan with high flames, as the bottle could explode. Flaming with rum or other high-alcohol-content liquor can be dangerous if not done properly and safely. Do not allow children to be close while flaming.

• If flaming on a stove other than gas, use a match or butane lighter.

• Ripe plantains, whole or in slices, can also be an option for this preparation. Pan fry them, increasing the amount of butter to 4 tablespoons, until medium brown, 4 minutes per side for whole plantains, or 1 ½ to 2 minutes per side for slices.

PASTEL DE CUMPLEAÑOS
Birthday Cake with Strawberry Compote and Vanilla Meringue

SERVES 10 to 12

Nonstick baking spray
with flour

1 cup (½ pound) margarine,
at room temperature
1 ⅔ cups (12 ounces) sugar
5 large eggs, separated
1 teaspoon vanilla extract
4 cups (22 ounces) aerated all-
purpose flour (see note
on page 342)
3 teaspoons baking powder
½ teaspoon kosher salt
1 cup whole milk

MERMELADA DE FRESA (STRAWBERRY COMPOTE)

1 pound fresh strawberries
6 tablespoons sugar
1 tablespoon lime juice
2 tablespoons cornstarch
dissolved in ¼ cup water

TURRÓN DE VAINILLA (VANILLA MERINGUE)

1 cup (7 ounces) sugar
½ teaspoon vanilla extract
¼ cup water
4 large egg whites
½ teaspoon cream of tartar

ADORNO (GARNISH)

Mixed berries, edible flowers,
or mint

I had few birthday party celebrations as a child, and the ones I remember are when I was asked what I wanted. I almost always requested helados de la Austria (ice cream from a no-longer-existent wonderful European-style pastry shop in downtown Guatemala City) or pastel de fresas con crema, strawberry and cream cake, layered with real whipped cream and fresh strawberries at the center and the top of the cake. I wanted to recreate that sweet memory, this time using my grandmother's pastel (cake) recipe, and give it my own twist. In Latin America, following Christian tradition, el Día del Santo (or Saint's Day) is the day one is born that corresponds with a saint on the calendar, making this day even more special. Virgen de los Dolores and Santa Catalina de Génova are my birthday saints. Some time ago, children used to be named after their birthday saint. Today this is not always the case, but it is good to make the connection to where this tradition started.

1 Preheat the oven to 350°F. Coat two 9-inch round cake pans with baking spray.

2 In a stand mixer with the paddle attachment, cream the margarine and 1 ⅔ cups sugar at speed 4 until very creamy and fluffy, about 5 minutes. Reduce the speed to 2 and add the 5 egg yolks one at a time, making sure each one is well incorporated into the creamy mixture before adding the next one. Add 1 teaspoon vanilla and beat 1 minute. Scrape the sides and bottom of the bowl with a soft spatula and beat 1 more minute.

3 Combine the flour, baking powder, and salt in a large bowl. Incorporate them into the creamy mixture ½ cup at a time, alternating with the milk, making sure the dry and liquid ingredients are well blended into the batter before adding more flour or milk. Stop and scrape the sides and bottom of the bowl with a soft spatula at least twice during the process. Beat at speed 2 until the batter looks smooth and uniform, about 2 minutes.

4 Separately, whisk the 5 egg whites until soft peaks form. Remove the bowl from the mixer. Using a soft spatula, combine the fluffy egg whites with the batter using folding strokes. Blend until thoroughly incorporated and the batter looks smooth.

5 Divide the batter equally between the cake pans and bake until a knife inserted in the center comes out clean, about 30 to 35 minutes. Let cool slightly and unmold. Set aside.

6 To make the strawberry compote, rinse the berries, save six to eight whole strawberries for garnish, and hull and slice the rest to end up with about 2 ½ cups. Combine the strawberries, sugar, lime juice, and cornstarch-water mixture in a large saucepan and cook over medium low heat, stirring constantly until the mixture thickens, about 5 minutes. Stop stirring and let the compote simmer, uncovered, for 2 minutes. Turn the heat off and let cool completely.

Continued on page 342

7. To make the meringue, start with very clean and dry equipment, free of grease or debris, or the meringue will not work. Combine the 1 cup sugar, ½ teaspoon vanilla, and water in a small saucepan. Do not stir; just swirl the pan around to mix the ingredients, and cook over medium low heat until clear and syrupy, about 5 minutes. Using a stand mixer with the whisk attachment, combine the 4 egg whites with the cream of tartar and whip at speed 4 until soft peaks form. While whipping, incorporate the hot syrup by pouring it slowly down the side of the bowl into the egg whites in a steady, thin stream. Continue whipping until the mixture is cool, has increased in volume, and forms stiff peaks, about 7 minutes.

8. Put the first cake layer on a serving platter and top it with the compote. Put the compote first in the center and carefully distribute it evenly with a knife or offset spatula. Be careful not to go too close to the edges, preferably leaving about a 1-inch border. Carefully place the other cake on top and line it up evenly. If any compote juice has oozed out the sides, dry it with a paper towel. Place a big dollop of meringue in the center of the cake, and with a metal offset spatula, push down gently and spread the meringue over the top of the cake and toward the edges, making sure the spatula stays on top of the meringue at all times without touching the surface of the cake. Use more meringue to coat the sides of the cake.

9. Garnish with the reserved whole strawberries, cut in half, and any other garnishes of preference. Refrigerate the cake until ready to serve.

AMALIA'S NOTES

- Aerate the flour prior to measuring it by simply stirring it around with a wire whisk within the container to fluff it. Then scoop the flour into the measuring cup and use a knife to level the flour across the top of the measuring cup.

- Use Chantilly cream (recipe on page 337) as a topping instead of meringue. For best results, eat the cake within a day or two.

- If using flowers when decorating, add them right before serving the cake, as they will wilt if refrigerated uncovered.

PAI DE HIGO
Fig and Pastry Cream Pie

MAKES 1 pie

COSTRA DE GALLETA (COOKIE CRUST)

2 cups Maria cookie crumbs (from about 32 cookies)

½ cup (4 ounces) unsalted butter, melted

CREMA PASTELERA (PASTRY CREAM)

3 cups whole milk

1 (5-inch) stick canela (Ceylon cinnamon)

4 egg yolks

¾ cup (5.25 ounces) sugar

½ teaspoon kosher salt

½ cup (2.5 ounces) cornstarch

¼ cup (2 ounces) unsalted butter, at room temperature and cut into 1-inch cubes

7 ounces mission figs, cut into bits (reserve 4 and cut them lengthwise into quarters for garnish)

12 ounces (about 2 cups) whipped cream cheese spread, at room temperature

Edible flowers (optional)

While not traditionally Guatemalan, this pie is popular in cafeterias, bakeries, and coffee shops in Guatemala City. This is my version. What makes it truly delicious is flavoring the milk with canela (Ceylon cinnamon) and using Maria cookies (a Spanish import) in the crust. Crystalized figs are traditional snacks in Guatemala along with dulces típicos (artisan sweets), which encompass a wide array of artisan fudge candies, fruit conserves and preserves, and candied fruits (see Chapter 12, page 351). Sometimes after school, I would stop by a restaurant nearby to enjoy a piece of this decadent pie with my schoolmates. It's common to see the word *pie* spelled *pai* or *pay*, as it sounds in Spanish, but sometimes it is spelled in English too.

1. To make the cookie crust, combine the cookie crumbs and melted butter in a bowl and stir well to blend. Transfer the mixture to a 9-inch pie pan and distribute it evenly over the bottom and sides, pressing firmly with your fingers to form the crust. Transfer the pan to the refrigerator and chill until needed.

2. To make the custard, combine the milk with the cinnamon stick in a medium saucepan and scald it over your stovetop's lowest heat setting until very aromatic, about 20 minutes. Stir from time to time to keep the milk from sticking to the bottom of the pan or scorching. When it's ready, remove the cinnamon stick and discard. Keep the milk hot.

3. In a medium mixing bowl, combine the egg yolks and sugar and whisk until creamy, about 2 minutes. Add the salt and whisk for 10 seconds. Add the cornstarch in three batches, whisking to integrate it with the mixture until it becomes a thick paste that's hard to whisk.

4. To temper the paste, add 1 tablespoon hot milk to the paste and whisk for 30 seconds. Add another tablespoon and whisk for 30 seconds. Then 2 tablespoons, whisk for another 30 seconds, and repeat. Then add ½ cup milk and whisk well for 30 seconds, until the mixture is very runny. Pour this mixture into the remaining hot milk in the saucepan and continue cooking over low, whisking

continuously, until the mixture thickens into a custard, about 3 to 5 minutes. Turn the heat off. Add the fig bits and cubed butter and stir continuously with a soft spatula to combine with the custard, about 30 seconds. Use the pastry cream as soon as it is ready, as it is easier to work with while hot.

5. To assemble the pie, pull the pie pan out of the refrigerator and pour the custard in the center. With a wide, soft spatula, carefully spread the custard over the cookie crust. Do not allow the spatula to touch the bottom or sides of the crust. Chill the pie until set, about 2 to 3 hours.

6. After the pie is set, put some of the cream cheese in the center of the pie. With an offset spatula, gently and slowly spread the cream cheese over the custard, pulling from the center outward and around to cover the whole pie. Add the remaining cream cheese and spread until the entire pie is almost covered, leaving a half-inch gap between the cream cheese and the crust, exposing some of the pastry cream. The cream cheese should be a thin layer on the surface of the pastry cream. Decorate with the reserved quartered figs and flowers, if using. Chill the pie, covered with plastic, until ready to serve.

Continued on page 344

AMALIA'S NOTES

• An easy way to make cookie crumbs is in a food processor. Simply add the cookies to the bowl and pulse to the desired texture.

• A cookie crust does not cut the same as a traditional pie crust. Keep in mind that when you cut the pie, you will need to scrape out some of the crust remaining in the pie pan after each slice is cut. This makes it similar to a crumble dessert and is by design.

• You can also make this pie with a store-bought prebaked pie crust, available frozen at most grocery stores. Try both versions to see which one you prefer.

• Packaged figs have a high sugar content, and when mixed with the pastry cream and chilled, they will bleed into the custard. It's important that they are mixed into the pastry cream while it's still hot to keep their sugar content from causing cracks in the pastry cream.

• You can also top the pie with the fig bits instead of adding them to the pastry cream. If using this method, garnish the pie after the cream cheese layer has been added. A 7-ounce bag yields about 1 cup fig bits plus the 4 whole figs used for garnish. Use all or fewer figs as you prefer.

• If you prefer a thinner layer of cream cheese, use only 8 ounces instead of the full 12.

CARLOTA ARCO IRIS
Chilled Gelatin Confetti Delight

SERVES 12 to 14

Nonstick baking spray

4–6 (3-ounce) boxes
multicolored flavored
gelatin of choice (strawberry,
pineapple, lime, kiwi,
apricot, mango, black
cherry, grape, etc.)

4–6 cups hot water, divided,
1 cup per package of
flavored gelatin

3 (0.25-ounce) envelopes
flavorless gelatin (see note)

½ cup cold water

1 cup hot whole milk

½ teaspoon freshly
ground nutmeg

2 teaspoons vanilla extract

¾ cup honey

1 (12-ounce) can ice-cold
evaporated milk

1 cup unsalted crema or
Mexican table cream

As kids, my siblings and I were treated to many special foods, including desserts. This simple and delicious dessert was a delight every time my mom made it. She used a rectangular Pyrex dish and cut it into squares to serve it, but the cake can be made in any decorative mold. Carlota Arco Iris is today served at some restaurants in Guatemala City. For me, it's a nostalgic sweet that reminds me of my childhood and fond times with my family. This is my rendition of my mom's creation.

1. Coat a 10-cup Bundt cake pan or rectangular clear mold(s) with baking spray.

2. Make the flavored gelatins in separate molds using only 1 cup hot water per package. Let the gelatins set in the refrigerator until very firm, about 2 ½ to 3 hours. Unmold by dipping each container in warm water for 10 seconds and running a soft spatula around the edges of the container. Cut each color into ½-inch cubes. Keep colors separate and return the gelatins to the refrigerator until ready to use.

3. In the bowl of a stand mixer, combine the unflavored gelatin and ½ cup cold water and allow it to bloom for 5 minutes. With the whisk attachment, whisk at speed 2 for 30 seconds. In a steady stream, add the milk, then add the nutmeg, vanilla, and honey. Whisk at speed 4 until the milk is lukewarm, about 3 to 5 minutes. Add the evaporated milk and crema and whisk to combine, about 1 ½ minutes.

4. Working quickly, layer and alternate all the ingredients in the mold: Begin by adding one layer of gelatin cubes of mixed colors, then add a layer of the milk mixture to cover the first layer. Add another layer of the gelatin cubes, another thin layer of the milk mixture, and so on until all the ingredients are used, finishing with the gelatin cubes. If any of the cubes stick out at the end, push them gently into the milk mixture with a soft spatula.

5. Refrigerate, covered with plastic, until the gelatin is completely firm, several hours or overnight. To unmold the gelatin on a serving platter, place the platter on top of the gelatin mold and invert it. If the gelatin doesn't release easily, either dip the bottom of the mold in warm water for 10 seconds at a time, shake it gently from left to right, rotate the pan, and repeat, or allow it to sit inverted on a plate for 5 minutes. Slice the gelatin with a knife dipped in warm water and serve.

AMALIA'S NOTES

- You can customize gelatin flavors by mixing tropical fruit juices like passion fruit, papaya, marañón (cashew fruit), or other juices with unflavored gelatin according to the package directions.

- Keep the knife dipped in the warm water right next to the gelatin so you can dip it as needed, wiping it and dipping it after each slice.

- Unflavored gelatin comes in 1-ounce boxes containing 4 envelopes.

FRESAS CON CREMA
Strawberries and Bananas with Almond Honey Cream

SERVES 4 to 6

El Lago de Los Cisnes in Los Aposentos, a few miles south of Chimaltenango, Guatemala, is a forested park with natural springs and two lakes where cisnes (swans) have made their home. This is a resort my siblings and I used to visit on weekends with my dad when we were little, and one of the special foods I fondly remember and looked forward to was the locally grown fresh strawberries with a dollop of Guatemalan crema that street vendors sold, a true delight. They put them in small paper cups and provided a small plastic spoon. Strawberries and cream are popular in Latin America and in other parts of the world. What I like about this is the simplicity, deliciousness, and precious memories from my time with my father. I have added bananas, almond extract, and honey, which elevate the dessert to another level. This can be a scrumptious lighter ending after a heavy meal with friends or family.

½ cup unsalted crema or Mexican table cream
1 teaspoon almond extract
1 tablespoon honey

1 pound strawberries, washed, hulled, and sliced ¼ inch thick
2 bananas, peeled and sliced ¼ inch thick

ADORNO (GARNISH)

Mint leaves and sprigs, sliced starfruit, whole strawberries, or flowers

1. Combine the crema, almond extract, and honey in a medium bowl and stir with a whisk to dissolve the honey.

2. Just before serving, add the strawberries and bananas to the crema and mix gently with a soft spatula until the fruit is evenly coated. Garnish and serve.

RECIPE VARIATIONS

Fresas con Crema de Ron (Strawberries with Latin Cream, Vanilla Bean, and Honey-Rum Sauce): Follow the recipe given, except omit the almond extract and substitute with ¼ teaspoon fresh vanilla bean pulp and 3 to 4 teaspoons high-quality rum, such as Guatemalan Zacapa Centenario or Nicaraguan Flor de Caña.

Fresas con Crema Chantilly (Strawberries with Chantilly Cream): Follow the recipe given, except substitute the crema, almond, and honey with Chantilly cream (see page 337).

AMALIA'S NOTE

• For best results, consume this dessert the day you make it. Once the strawberries have been exposed to water after washing, they start to lose their firm texture, so it's important to use the freshest strawberries for this dessert. After washing, allow the strawberries to dry on a paper towel prior to combining with the crema.

12

Dulcería Artesanal
Artisan Sweets

DULCES TÍPICOS

White Gold

Sugar, once called white gold, was a scarce luxury item only the European affluent could afford. It did not look the way we know it today; it was rustic and had to be chiseled or pounded for consumption.

Sugar cultivation was traced back ten thousand years to New Guinea and again in the fourth century BC to Persia, ancient Arabia, and India but did not reach the Western world until the eighth century, when the Moors occupied the Iberian Peninsula.

Introduced to the New World by Columbus in 1493 from the Canary Islands, sugarcane was a back-breaking, labor-intensive, and highly perishable crop once cut. Europeans were not willing to work for it, although demand and greed was high.

White gold fueled the wealth of European nations to finance their colonies, all at the expense of unwilling enslaved people who endured harsh working conditions. The precious commodity came to us at a not-so-sweet price.

Dulces típicos are artisan sweets different from desserts. They are usually small or bite-size because they are very sweet. Available at specialty stores, they are a special treat people look forward to enjoying as a snack at the store, in the street, and at fairs or celebrations.

Sugar production in the Americas created a chain reaction of new product development, from rum to sweets, in Mexico and the rest of Mesoamerica and beyond. Guatemalan dulces típicos originated in colonial times around 1524, creating a whole new category of confections. Arab-influenced Spanish sweets came to fuse with Guatemalan traditions and native ingredients.

In Guatemala, as in the rest of Mesoamerica, artisan sweets making is centralized by region, and each region has specialties, with Antigua Guatemala being the center, followed by Mixco, Quetzaltenango, Cobán, Esquipulas, Amatitlán, and San Martín Jilotepeque. This chapter contains a sampling of artisan sweets from throughout these regions.

Panela (piloncillo), a byproduct of sugarcane juice, along with honey, came to occupy a new place in sweets-making kitchens in the region and blended deliciously with other imported byproducts and products such as milk, butter, eggs, cinnamon, and sesame seeds. Similar and unique regional treats throughout Mesoamerica concurrently came into being, with each country giving them their own touch and name.

In contrast, pre-Hispanic food had virtually no sweets of this category in its system. Flowers or nectars of native trees were probably used if anything needed to be sweetened. Likely, if chocolate or other food was ever sweetened by the indigenous people, it was the exception rather than the rule, as nearly all post-Hispanic traditional desserts are a blend of cultures. As you go through the recipes in this chapter, notice the wide variety and contrasting textures of each recipe. All may have similar ingredients, but they have been used in very unique ways, fusing local ingredients and recreating ancient techniques.

From Canillitas, Colochos de Guayaba, Mazapán, and Turrón to Pepitoria and Bolitas de Tamarindo, you are bound to rediscover a new sweet spot in your taste buds through this sampling of treats.

CANILLITAS

Caramelized Milk and Cinnamon Fudge

MAKES 8 canillitas

2 cups whole milk
1 (1 ¼-inch) piece canela
  (Ceylon cinnamon)
¾ cup (5.25 ounces) sugar

These melt-in-your-mouth brown canillitas are my favorite Guatemalan artisan sweet of all time. They're from Antigua, although they are available throughout Guatemala City. One or two go a long way as they are very sweet but scrumptious. This is dulce de leche, which is popular in varying forms and names in Meso- and Latin America. In Guatemala, they are called canillitas de leche, or little milk legs, because their shape resembles little legs. The shape and recipe are traditionally Guatemalan, and canillitas are the centerpiece of artisan sweets in the country. Canillitas can also be made with powdered milk, but this version is the traditional one.

1 Prepare a sheet of parchment paper on the counter. Combine the milk and cinnamon in a heavy saucepan and cook over low heat until very aromatic, about 7 minutes. Discard the cinnamon and any pieces from it. Add the sugar and stir well with a whisk to dissolve. Increase the heat to medium and bring to a slow boil without stirring. As the mixture approaches a boil, it will foam up. Quickly remove it from the heat before it boils over and stir.

2 Reduce the heat to low, set the pan back on the heat, and cook slowly, stirring frequently with a wooden spoon while the mixture gradually caramelizes. The fudge is ready when it is thick but can still be scooped and poured with a spoon. Keep a close eye on it, as the fudge can burn easily toward the end. This entire process can take about 80 to 90 minutes. Remove from the heat.

3 With a soup spoon, scoop small quantities of the fudge onto parchment paper and give them a non-uniform elongated shape, about 3 ½ inches long by 1 inch wide. Pour the mixture from the spoon as if you were making a horizontal line, then toward the end, bring back the spoon over the line and pour the rest of the fudge to round off the edge.

4 Let cool completely. The canillitas should be firm on the outside and fudge-like inside. Store in airtight containers or cellophane bags. For freshness, canillitas should be eaten within a few days, or they start drying up.

AMALIA'S NOTES

• Alternatively, let the fudge cool in an 8x8-inch square baking pan lined with parchment paper. Use a slim, sharp knife or a stainless-steel scraper to cut long or square shapes, wiping it between every cut if the fudge sticks to it.

• Caramelized sugar can cause serious burns. Make sure children are not near the stove or involved in this activity.

COLOCHOS DE GUAYABA
Sweet and Tart Guava Curls

MAKES 14 colochos

Colochos, meaning curls, are some of the most delicious guava treats you may encounter. This is a traditional Guatemalan sweet, and what makes them unique is that the guava paste is black and they are shaped like curls and dusted with white sugar. Unlike other artisan sweets, this one is gooey and very sweet, so one is perfect per person. Serve them as a sweet appetizer with champagne, a snack, or an after-dinner treat with black coffee. They are easy to make and require only a few ingredients. If you are lucky to have access to fresh guavas, the paste can be made from scratch; otherwise, using readily available guava paste is convenient and delicious, and can save some time.

1 (14-ounce) package guava paste
¼ teaspoon black liquid food coloring
½ cup (3.5 ounces) sugar

SPECIAL EQUIPMENT

1 small baking sheet, covered with a thin layer of butter
1 stainless-steel spatula for cake decorating, covered with a thin layer of butter
1 stainless-steel scraper, covered with a thin layer of butter
1 small baking sheet, lined with parchment paper

1. Unwrap and cut the guava paste block into smaller chunks and put it in the bowl of a stand mixer with the paddle attachment. Add the food coloring and mix on the lowest speed, occasionally stopping to scrape the sides and bottom of the bowl to make sure the paste is thoroughly black. This will take about 2 minutes.

2. Transfer the paste to the baking sheet covered with butter. Slowly spread the paste and flatten it to a ½-inch-thick layer using the butter-covered spatula. Clean the spatula with paper towels and coat again with butter as needed to prevent the paste from sticking to it. With the help of the butter-covered scraper, shape the paste into an 8x5-inch rectangle, gently pushing the paste toward the center from all sides and flattening the rectangle at the end to make it even.

3. With the scraper, mark ½x8-inch strips. Put the baking sheet in the freezer for 20 to 30 minutes. This will make it easier to cut and roll.

4. Pull the baking sheet out of the freezer and work quickly. Cut the strips with the buttered scraper where previously marked, using the scraper positioned lengthwise under each strip to lift and separate it from the remaining paste. Roll each strip into a 1-inch spiral (curl). Place the curls on the side of the same buttered baking sheet until all the guava paste has been used.

5. Put the sugar in a small bowl. Gently roll one curl at a time in the sugar, making sure each one is well coated on all sides, including the center. Transfer to the baking sheet lined with parchment paper. Repeat until all the curls have been covered with sugar.

6. Serve immediately or store them flat, covered with plastic. Eat within a few days for freshness.

AMALIA'S NOTE

- Guava paste is available at Latin markets and online.

ALBOROTOS
Panela Popcorn Balls

MAKES 8 alborotos

1 (3.29-ounce) bag microwave gourmet popping popcorn

4 neon gel (squeeze tubes) food colors of choice

1 (8-ounce) cone panela or piloncillo, broken into bits (see note)

2 tablespoons water

SPECIAL EQUIPMENT

Disposable gloves

An alboroto, literally meaning ruckus or commotion, is a mishmash of ingredients put together and formed into a ball. When I was a child living in my grandmother's town in Quezaltepeque, Chiquimula, I always looked forward to the annual municipality fair, which brought together artisans of all kinds from the region. They brought dulces de colación (white sugar figurines) and conserva de coco (candied coconut loaf) from Esquipulas; alborotos from Jutiapa; and much more. The colorful balls stood out from the rest of the sweets at each vendor's stall. I'd buy one and spend a good amount of time eating it like a chipmunk. This can be a fun activity for a special get-together with friends. Traditionally, alborotos have been made with plain sorghum (maicillo), a very nutritious tiny kernel from the corn and sugarcane family used in Mesoamerica at times in place of corn to make a variety of foods. This is my version using gourmet popcorn. The butter, panela (piloncillo), and crunchy popcorn are a match made in sweet heaven.

1. Pop the popcorn in the microwave as indicated on the package. Carefully open the package to avoid steam burns. Empty the bag into a large mixing bowl and let the popcorn cool. Divide the popcorn equally into four parts and put them into four medium bowls. Choose the first gel color to use. Drizzle the gel (about a teaspoon) in a zig-zag fashion over the popcorn in one bowl. Wearing disposable gloves, quickly stir with your hands to make the color stick. Drizzle the gel again and repeat. The popcorn does not have to be completely covered and can have white spots remaining. Repeat this procedure with the remaining bowls of popcorn and gel colors.

2. Combine the panela and water in a small heavy saucepan, stir lightly with a soft spatula, and melt over low heat. Cook until syrupy, about 2 to 3 minutes. Keep it hot over low heat, or the syrup will start hardening.

3. Drizzle about 2 teaspoons of hot syrup with the spatula over one bowl of popcorn. Using a wooden spoon, quickly and gently combine the hot syrup with the popcorn. Drizzle again to create sticky popcorn. Return the syrup to the stove to keep it hot. The syrup mixed with the popcorn will have cooled now but will remain sticky for a short amount of time, so it's important to work quickly. Grab a handful of popcorn in each hand and press gently yet firmly to form two equal-size balls. Repeat with the rest of the popcorn bowls.

4. Serve immediately or store the popcorn balls in an airtight container or large resealable plastic bags. Eat within a day or two, or the popcorn will become stale and soft.

AMALIA'S NOTES

- Alternatively, create rainbow designs by drizzling gel colors in two or four sequences per bowl.

- Panela is very hard and must be broken for measuring or melting. To break it, put it in a double layer of resealable bags, wrap it twice in a kitchen towel, and pound it with the smooth side of a metal meat mallet until the panela is almost powdery.

- Working with hot syrup can cause severe burns. Make sure children are not near the stove or involved in this activity. Also make sure the syrup is cool before you touch the popcorn with your hands.

- If the syrup becomes too thick, add water in increments of 1 teaspoon at a time to thin it out. If the syrup has too much water, it will not stick to the popcorn, so it's important to keep it thick yet thin enough to drizzle.

- If the popcorn has too much gel, the syrup will not work, so it's important not to over-coat it with the gel food colors.

- Caramelized sugar can be an alternative to using panela.

TARTARITAS
Almond Pudding Tartlets

MAKES 12 to 14 tartaritas

One of my favorite treats as a child was these tartlets from Antigua Guatemala, which were filled with this almond pudding or cream custard, almond paste, or homemade fruit preserves. I like all of them; they are equally delicious and a good way to add variety. A way to add flavor variety is by using extracts and essences (see note). Tartaritas are another light, sweet way to end a meal. The tartlets can be a petit four along with Turrón (Lime Meringue, page 367) or other sweets in this chapter, accompanied by a cup of Guatemalan coffee.

1 Combine the flour, sugar, and salt, then place the mixture on a clean work surface and make a well in the center. Add the butter and bind these ingredients together with a fork or pastry cutter. As the mixture becomes dry and mealy, gradually incorporate the egg yolk and orange juice. Pick up the mixture with your hands, squeeze it together, then knead it for 1 minute or so to make it look uniform. The dough should look smooth. Wrap the dough in plastic and let it rest for 30 minutes.

2 Line a small baking sheet with parchment paper.

3 Transfer the dough to a lightly floured surface, and with a floured rolling pin, roll the dough to ⅛ inch thick. Cut circles with the cutter. With the help of a pastry scraper, lift the circles. Firmly pinch the edges of each circle up to form tartlets resembling bottle caps. Transfer them to the baking sheet lined with parchment paper. Poke the flat bottom of the tartlets many times with the tip of a paring knife, toothpick, or fork to prevent them from inflating. Put the baking sheet with the tartlet shells in the refrigerator until ready to fill.

4 Preheat the oven to 325°F.

5 To make the pudding, combine the milk, water, egg yolk, sugar, cornstarch, and almond extract in a small saucepan and cook over medium low heat until aromatic and thick, stirring continuously, about 4 to 5 minutes.

Transfer the pudding to a medium bowl, spread it as flat as you can, and allow it to cool in the refrigerator for 10 minutes.

6 Take the baking sheet out of the refrigerator. Fill the tartlets with about 2 teaspoons of the pudding, pushing it gently into the tartlet shell to fill all the empty spaces.

7 Bake until the dough looks cooked and opaque but still pale, not necessarily golden, about 25 to 35 minutes, rotating the baking sheet 180 degrees at half baking time. Let cool completely. Garnish with cinnamon.

AMALIA'S NOTES

- Aerate the flour prior to measuring it by simply stirring it around with a wire whisk within the container to fluff it. Then scoop the flour into the measuring cup and use a knife to level the flour across the top of the measuring cup.

- If the dough feels dry, add juice in 1-teaspoon increments. If it feels wet, add a little flour and knead lightly. If it's too soft, put in the refrigerator to chill for 10 to 15 minutes.

- Tartaritas can be flavored in a number of ways. The recipe given (but without almond) is the traditional way. You can use other extracts of choice to flavor the dough or custard, such as vanilla, coconut, lemon, or chocolate. Various flavors and essences are available at major grocery stores and pastry shops.

TARTARITAS (TARTLETS)

1 cup (5.5 ounces) aerated all-purpose flour, plus more for dusting (see note)

1 teaspoon sugar

¼ teaspoon kosher salt

2 tablespoons chilled unsalted butter, cut into ¼-inch cubes

1 large egg yolk

3 tablespoons plus 1 teaspoon freshly squeezed orange juice

MANJAR (ALMOND PUDDING)

½ cup skim milk

¾ cup water

1 large egg yolk

⅓ cup plus 1 tablespoon (2.7 ounces) sugar

¼ cup (1.1 ounces) cornstarch

1 teaspoon almond extract

ADORNO (GARNISH)

Ground canela (Ceylon cinnamon)

SPECIAL EQUIPMENT

3-inch circle cutter

COCADAS

Coconut and Rum Crisps

MAKES 12 cocadas

¼ cup canned coconut water

½ cup (3.5 ounces) sugar

2 ½ cups (about 10.6 ounces) sweetened flaked coconut

2 egg yolks

2 tablespoons high-quality rum, such as Guatemalan Zacapa Centenario or Nicaraguan Flor de Caña

SPECIAL EQUIPMENT

#40 cookie scoop

Cocadas are a crispy and sweet yet light treat with a hint of rum, sometimes presented as a conserva (loaf) or as a small treat in Livingston and the eastern departments of Guatemala. Although they don't appear easy to make, they are. Cocadas, made of coconut, could be a nice dessert after a dinner party. Coconut is a usual ingredient in the cuisine of Guatemala and Mesoamerican tropical and coastal regions, and rum is a common ingredient in beverages, cake sauces, and candy making.

1. Preheat the oven to 350°F.

2. Combine the coconut water and sugar in a medium saucepan and cook over medium high heat until syrupy, about 3 to 5 minutes.

3. Add the coconut, and with a soft spatula, fold the coconut into the syrup until the mixture looks wet. Cook for 1 minute. Let cool completely in the saucepan.

4. Line a baking sheet with parchment paper. In a small bowl, combine the egg yolks with the rum using a whisk. Add it to the coconut mixture and fold together until combined. Use the cookie scoop to scoop as much of the mixture as you are able, pack it firmly against the bowl, and place each half-round 1 inch apart on the baking sheet lined with parchment paper. When releasing the coconut mixture from the scoop onto the baking sheet, make sure it stays packed. Repeat until all the coconut mixture has been used.

5. Bake until crispy and medium brown, about 20 minutes. For even baking, rotate the baking sheet 180 degrees halfway through the baking time. Serve immediately.

AMALIA'S NOTE

- Store any leftovers lying flat in an airtight container for up to 1 week.

BOLITAS DE TAMARINDO
Sweet and Tart Tamarind Balls

MAKES 30 balls

If you like tamarind, you'll love these easy-to-make, sweet-tart treats. They are a traditional sweet in Guatemala, Mexico, and the rest of Mesoamerica with varying ingredients. For a twist in flavor, roll the balls in a little dried spicy pepper and salt before rolling them in sugar. Rolling them in red sugar crystals gives them a whole new look.

1 (15.5-ounce) package natural sugar-free 100% tamarind
1 cup (7 ounces) sugar
1 (2.25-ounce) bottle red sugar crystals

SPECIAL EQUIPMENT

Disposable gloves
#100 cookie scoop

1. Wearing disposable gloves, combine the tamarind pulp and sugar in a medium bowl. Work the tamarind seeds and inner tougher membrane out by squeezing the paste between your fingers. This is a necessary step, as some of the seeds are ingrained in the pulp. This will take about 1 hour.

2. Divide the pulp into equal-size portions using the #100 cookie scoop and form balls, rounding them by hand. Work quickly, as the pulp will stick to your palms as it warms and softens.

3. Put a small amount of red sugar on a plate and roll the balls over it, pressing gently to cover them thoroughly. Serve immediately or store them in a single layer in an airtight container. Do not pack them on top of each other. They also can be wrapped individually in small cellophane mini bags.

AMALIA'S NOTE

- Tamarind is available in vacuum-packed blocks at Latin and Asian stores. Make sure the mixture does not contain sugar or other additives. This is easier than working with fresh tamarind pods, and the results are equally delicious.

TURRÓN

Lime Meringue

SERVES 6 to 8

4 large egg whites
1 cup (7 ounces) sugar
1 tablespoon fresh lime juice
Mini ice cream cones
    (optional)

ADORNO (GARNISH)

Ground cinnamon or nutmeg
    (or both)
Multicolored sprinkles,
    dragées, candy beads,
    edible glitter and gold
Edible flowers

Meringue is made in a variety of ways depending on purpose. This is a simple yet unique Guatemalan treat. As a street food, turrón (stiff meringue) is traditionally served in mini ice cream cones or in dried corn husk squares topped with ground cinnamon or multicolored sprinkles. The sweet can be elevated to a finer level by serving it in small cups, dressed in any style. It is deliciously light and perfect as an after-dinner dessert. Fresh lime juice is a Guatemalan flavor enhancer favorite for savory and sweet foods, and in this dessert, it blends in nicely and cuts back a bit on the sweetness. Every spoonful is a velvety treat. Turrón can be a fun and inexpensive treat for a kid's birthday party too.

1. Fill a medium saucepan with water about halfway. Bring it to a boil over medium high heat. Reduce the heat to low until ready to use.

2. Start with very clean and dry equipment, free of grease or debris, or the meringue will not work. Combine the egg whites and sugar in the stainless-steel bowl of a stand mixer. Put the bowl over the saucepan of hot water. Stirring frequently, cook until the sugar is well integrated with the egg whites and the mixture has become translucent, about 4 to 5 minutes.

3. Transfer the bowl to the stand mixer fitted with the whisk attachment. While whisking at speed 4, steadily add the lime juice in a thin stream. Whisk until the mixture is cool and very thick and stiff peaks form, about 10 minutes.

4. Put the meringue into a piping bag and pipe it into mini ice cream cones or small cups. Or put all of it into a serving bowl and allow everyone to serve themselves. Refrigerate until needed.

5. Garnish with ground cinnamon, nutmeg, or sprinkles of choice, and flowers.

AMALIA'S NOTES

- As an alternative, add food coloring of choice to the meringue in the last 2 minutes of whisking.

- This meringue can be used to top other desserts or to cover small or large cakes.

HIGOS CRISTALIZADOS
Crystallized Figs

MAKES 8 figs

These are a favorite of Guatemalans usually purchased in an Antigua dulcería, a traditional artisan sweets store. Figs are great as a snack, in desserts such as Pai de Higo (Fig and Pastry Cream Pie, page 343), or on top of vanilla ice cream. Because they are very sweet, these treats are usually made in small portions. Depending on their size, figs are grouped into two or three per order and are known as a maleta de higos (a fig suitcase). Crystallizing is an old technique also used by other cultures as a fruit preservative. Cal or calcium hydroxide (a.k.a. slaked lime or pickling lime) has been used in Mesoamerica for millennia for processing corn into nixtamal to remove the skin or pericarp, make it digestible, and increase its nutrition. It also helps fruit retain its shape during extended cooking. Crystallizing makes fruit delicious and translucent, slightly dry on the outside and soft and moist on the inside, a desired trait.

1 tablespoon cal (slaked lime or calcium hydroxide)
8 green, firm figs, t-scored 1 inch deep at the stem (see note)

2 ¼ cups (15.75 ounces) sugar, divided
1 (1 ½-inch) piece canela (Ceylon cinnamon)

1. Make sure your equipment is fully clean, free of grease or debris, before beginning. In a large bowl, dissolve the cal in 4 cups water. Stir well with a whisk. Add the figs to the prepared water and soak 8 hours or overnight. Drain the water and rinse the figs thoroughly, then soak them for 15 minutes in enough cold water to cover them. Drain the water and set the figs aside.

2. Line a baking sheet with parchment paper. In a medium heavy saucepan, combine 1 ¾ cups sugar with 2 cups water and add the cinnamon stick. Bring to a quick boil over high heat, reduce the heat to low, and simmer, covered, until aromatic, about 10 minutes. Discard the cinnamon stick and any pieces from it. Add the figs and simmer gently, uncovered, without stirring, for 30 minutes. With tongs, carefully transfer them to the baking sheet lined with parchment paper.

3. Add ½ cup sugar to the remaining syrup and increase the heat to high to bring to a quick boil. Reduce the heat to low and cook, uncovered, for 5 minutes. Return the figs to the syrup and simmer over medium low heat, uncovered, for 5 minutes. With the tongs, turn the figs once to make sure all sides are covered with the heavier syrup. Transfer the figs back to the baking sheet and let them air dry for at least 1 hour. When they're ready to eat, they will look translucent, have a light glaze, and should not be mushy. Serve immediately or store in one layer in a small square container lined and tented with parchment paper. Eat the figs within 1 week.

AMALIA'S NOTES

• Cal is available at Latin stores or online and is the best option for this recipe. Baking soda is also used for crystallizing fruit in the United States; however, the two cannot be swapped in this recipe.

• For this recipe, green and firm figs are preferred as opposed to ripe and soft figs so they stay whole during cooking, even after soaking in cal.

• To t-score a fig, make a 1-inch-deep cross-shaped cut at the narrowest end of the fig closest to the stem. The fig remains whole.

• Traditionally, figs are peeled in Guatemala, but I choose not to peel them for added nutrition. The peel also helps keep the fig firmer during cooking.

• Other foods that can be crystallized are tubers (camote), squash (chilacayote), and certain fruits, such as oranges, orange slices, orange peel, lemons, and ripe papaya.

• Melting sugar can cause serious burns. Make sure children are not in the kitchen when you are preparing this treat.

MAZAPÁN
Pumpkin Seed Marzipan

SERVES 4 to 6

½ cup (3.4 ounces) rice
¾ cup (3.6 ounces) shelled
  pumpkin seeds
1 cup (7 ounces) sugar
1 cup whole milk
1 teaspoon almond extract
2 tablespoons raisins or toasted
  sliced almonds

½ cup (2.4 ounces) toasted
  pumpkins seeds

Mazapán brings memories of weekends in Amatitlán, a municipality within the Guatemala Department about forty minutes from Guatemala City with a beautiful volcanic lake of the same name. The beachside is surrounded by eateries and street vendors offering grilled corn with lime, tortillas filled with grilled meat and sausage, and a variety of artisan sweets. Traditional Guatemalan mazapán is made with pumpkin seeds combined with rice. Other varieties include mazapán made with almonds or yuca, and some are garnished with raisins and flavored with cinnamon. The texture can vary depending on the main ingredient and can be pasty or a bit gooey. Mazapán comes in blocks or in individual portions in traditional round small containers made with soft wood. To eat it on the go, people open the container, break the lid in half, and use one half as the utensil to eat the mazapán. It's a fun and casual way of enjoying it in the company of friends or family. I roll this mazapán in chopped toasted pumpkin seeds to give it a gourmet effect.

1. In a small bowl, soak the rice for 30 minutes in 1 ½ cups cold water. Drain the rice thoroughly in a colander.

2. In a blender, combine the rice, raw pumpkin seeds, sugar, milk, and almond extract and blend to make a smooth puree.

3. Transfer the puree to a medium skillet, add the raisins (if using almonds, save those for garnish at the end), and cook over medium low heat, stirring constantly with a soft spatula. Alternate with a whisk to break up any lumps, if needed. Cook until it becomes a thick paste that's hard to stir and comes off the sides of the skillet, about 15 to 20 minutes.

4. Transfer the paste to a 5 ¾x3x2-inch mini loaf pan (or similar small container) lined with plastic and let it cool completely.

5. Pulse the ½ cup toasted pumpkin seeds in a food processor to a coarse texture. Transfer to a cutting board or plate.

6. Remove the mazapán from the pan, carefully peel off the plastic, and press each side into the seeds. Cut portions of desired size to serve immediately, wiping the knife with each cut, or store it wrapped in new plastic in the mini loaf pan until ready to eat. When left unwrapped, mazapán tends to become dry on the outside, but it remains soft on the inside. Eat within a few days for freshness.

SEMILLAS DE MARAÑÓN CARAMELIZADAS
Caramelized Roasted Cashew Clusters

MAKES 4 to 6 clusters

Roasted seeds are common ingredients in savory and sweet dishes in Guatemala. Toasted pumpkin and sesame seeds are often caramelized either in sugar or panela (piloncillo), as are cashews and peanuts. This easy-to-make snack with varying ingredients and presentation forms is popular throughout the Mesoamerican region. You can make small, medium, or large clusters.

2 cups (10.6 ounces) raw cashews

1 cup (7 ounces) sugar

1. Spread the cashews evenly on a baking sheet and roast in a preheated oven or toaster oven at 350°F. Move them around with a heat-resistant spatula to ensure even roasting until medium brown, about 2 to 4 minutes. Keep a close eye on them, as they can burn easily.

AMALIA'S NOTE

• Melting sugar can cause serious burns. Make sure children are not in the kitchen when you are preparing this treat.

2. Line a baking sheet with parchment paper. Add the sugar to a medium saucepan and melt over medium low heat without stirring until it starts caramelizing around the edges. Stir with a whisk to blend the sugar at the top with the melted sugar at the bottom. Keep stirring until the sugar is clear and amber in color. This whole process will take about 10 minutes.

3. Turn the heat down to low. Add one-third of the cashews and stir quickly with a wooden spoon to ensure they are well coated with the caramelized sugar, being careful not to break the cashews. Add another one-third of the cashews, stir, and repeat with the remaining cashews. It's important to work quickly, as the caramel will start to harden fast.

4. With a serving spoon, carefully scoop four to six clusters of the mixture and transfer each one to the baking sheet lined with parchment paper. The clusters are ready to eat within minutes. For freshness, eat within a day or two.

BOCADILLO DE PEPITORIA
Toasted Pumpkin Seed Brittle

SERVES 6 to 8

Nonstick baking spray

½ cup (2.4 ounces) shelled
pumpkin seeds
¾ cup (5.25 ounces) sugar
or panela (piloncillo)

A favorite at patronal saint celebrations and fairs, bocadillo de pepitoria is a classic artisan sweet from Amatitlán, Guatemala, that contains only two ingredients. Pumpkin seeds are a basic ingredient in some Mayan stews and moles, as well as in drinks and desserts. Caramelized sugar is the delicious binding ingredient to hold the toasted seeds together. This sweet treat can also be made with other toasted seeds or nuts, such as sesame seeds or peanuts.

1. Spread the pumpkin seeds evenly on a small baking sheet and toast them in a preheated oven or toaster oven at 350°F until medium brown, about 2 to 4 minutes. Remove from the oven and set aside.

2. Prepare two 12x15-inch pieces of parchment paper and spray each with a thin layer of nonstick baking spray. Lay one on the counter right next to the stove. Have the other one handy nearby.

3. Add the sugar to a stainless-steel medium skillet and melt over medium low heat without stirring until the sugar starts caramelizing around the edges. Stir with a whisk to blend the sugar at the top with the melted sugar at the bottom. Keep stirring until the sugar is clear and amber in color. This whole process will take about 10 minutes.

4. Turn the heat down to low. Add the pumpkin seeds in two batches, stirring quickly and carefully with a wooden spoon between batches to make sure the seeds are fully covered with the caramel. Transfer the mixture to the parchment paper by the stove, cover it with the other parchment paper piece, oiled side down, and quickly and gently flatten the seeds with a rolling pin to ¼ inch thick. It's important to work quickly, as the caramel will start to harden fast.

5. Remove the top piece of parchment paper, and while still warm, cut the brittle into squares or longer pieces of desired size. You can also break pieces by hand when the brittle has cooled slightly to be safe enough to handle. Let cool completely, about 8 to 10 minutes.

RECIPE VARIATION

Bocadillo de Ajonjolí o Manías (Sesame Seed or Peanut Brittle): Follow the same procedure as given but use toasted sesame seeds or toasted peanuts instead. Or use a combination of all three and use panela instead of sugar. Add 1 or 2 tablespoons water to the broken panela to get it to melt faster.

AMALIA'S NOTES

• Panela is very hard and must be broken for measuring. To break it, put it in a double layer of resealable plastic bags, wrap it twice in a kitchen towel, and pound it with the smooth side of a metal meat mallet until the panela is almost powdery. Then measure the desired amount.

• Melting sugar can cause serious burns. Make sure children are not near the stove or participating in this activity.

CAJETA DE LECHE
Soft Milk Bites

MAKES 50 bites

Milk and sugar are combined into various desserts in Meso- and Latin America. From dulce de leche to this special dessert, all of them are delicious. This Costa Rican treat is super easy to make. It can be a fun activity for kids, as it is safe, involves just a few ingredients, and forming the milk treats into bite-size portions can take a little time. They don't require cooking and are ready to eat immediately. Add other flavorings such as chocolate powder or vanilla or almond extract, or make different colors and shapes.

1 (14-ounce) can sweetened condensed milk
1 ½ tablespoons butter, at room temperature
2 ¾ cups (about 12.4 ounces) powdered whole milk, plus more for dusting

ADORNO (GARNISH)

Toasted shelled pumpkin seeds
Sliced almonds or other nuts
Candied or crystallized fruit

SPECIAL EQUIPMENT

#100 cookie scoop

1. Add the condensed milk and butter to a medium bowl and combine with a sturdy spatula or wooden spoon. Gradually add the powdered milk, making sure each addition is well incorporated into the condensed milk before adding more. Stir the milk mixture until a dough-like paste forms and soft peaks form. (Alternatively, combine all ingredients in a stand mixer using the paddle attachment.)

2. Line a baking sheet with waxed paper or parchment paper and dust it lightly with powdered milk. Set aside. Use the cookie scoop to form a bite-size ball of the mixture. Put the ball on your palm and, while the ball is in your hands, dust it with powdered milk to ease rolling. Place it on the prepared baking sheet. Repeat until all the paste has been used. The balls may flatten a bit as they sit.

3. Dust a paring knife with powdered milk and make a ⅛-inch-deep cross at the top of each ball. Dust the knife with more powdered milk between cuts as needed. Place your garnish of choice at the center of the cross. As the balls sit, they will become firmer. Store them in the baking sheet or equal size container, loosely covered with plastic wrap. Consume this treat within a day or two, for freshness.

AMALIA'S NOTES

- For firmer balls, add more powdered milk. For a looser cajeta, begin testing the paste for your desired consistency after adding the second cup of powdered milk.

- If this treat will be served outdoors, chill it for at least an hour (or longer) before serving. Warm weather will soften and flatten the balls and make them harder to pick up.

INGREDIENT SOURCES

Before shopping online, check your local grocery store.
Some major chains now carry a wider variety of Latin American products.

Amigo Foods: Your Latin Food Store on the Internet

Shop here for Incaparina, chow mein, Ducal canned beans, pacaya flowers, jarred chiltepes, Picamás hot sauce, and more.
www.amigofoods.com

Goya Foods

Shop here for a wide variety of dried and canned goods and frozen fruits and vegetables from throughout Latin America.
www.goya.com/en

La Tienda: The Best of Spain

Shop here for bomba or calasparra rice, saffron, olive oil, capers, olives, and more.
www.tienda.com

Melissa's: The Freshest Ideas in Produce

Shop here for banana leaves, chayote squash, dried chiles, Jamaica flowers (hibiscus), pumpkin seeds, panela (piloncillo), jarred pimentos, and more.
www.melissas.com

Latin Foods Market

Shop here for a wide variety of Latin American products.
www.latinfoodsmarket.com

The Latin Merchant

Shop here for dried chiles and spices.
www.thelatinmerchant.com

Sabor a País

Shop here for ingredients and foods from Mexico to Nicaragua and beyond.
saborapais.com

Penzey's Spices

Shop here for chile peppers (dried and powdered), achiote, canela (Ceylon cinnamon), extracts, vanilla beans, and more.
www.penzeys.com

Zocalo Foods: Online Latin Food Market

Shop here for Central American foods.
www.zocalofoods.com/pages/central-american-food-products

MEASUREMENT CONVERSIONS

US to Metric Conversions

Measure	Equivalent
⅕ teaspoon	1 milliliter
1 teaspoon	5 milliliters
1 tablespoon	15 milliliters
1 fluid ounce	30 milliliters
⅕ cup	50 milliliters
1 cup	240 milliliters
2 cups (1 pint)	470 milliliters
4 cups (1 quart)	0.95 liter
4 quarts (1 gallon)	3.8 liters
1 ounce	28 grams
1 pound	454 grams

Metric to US Conversions

Measure	Equivalent
1 milliliter	⅕ teaspoon
5 milliliters	1 teaspoon
15 milliliters	1 tablespoon
30 milliliters	1 fluid ounce
100 milliliters	3.4 fluid ounce
240 milliliters	1 cup
1 liter	34 fluid ounces
1 liter	4.2 cups
1 liter	2.1 pints
1 liter	1.06 quarts
1 liter	0.26 gallon
1 gram	0.035 ounce
100 grams	3.5 ounces
500 grams	1.10 pounds
1 kilogram	2.205 pounds
1 kilogram	35 ounces

US Dry Volume Measurements

Measure	Equivalent
1/16 teaspoon	dash
⅛ teaspoon	pinch
3 teaspoons	1 tablespoon
⅛ cup	2 tablespoons (1 standard coffee scoop)
¼ cup	4 tablespoons
⅓ cup	5 tablespoons plus 1 teaspoon
½ cup	8 tablespoons
¾ cup	12 tablespoons
1 cup	16 tablespoons
1 pound	16 ounces

US Liquid Volume Measurements

Measure	Equivalent
8 fluid ounces	1 cup
1 pint	2 cups (16 fluid ounces)
1 quart	2 pints (4 cups)
1 gallon	4 quarts (16 cups)

Oven Temperature Conversions

Fahrenheit	Celsius	Gas Mark
275°F	140°C	gas mark 1 (cool)
300°F	150°C	gas mark 2
325°F	165°C	gas mark 3 (very moderate)
350°F	180°C	gas mark 4 (moderate)
375°F	190°C	gas mark 5
400°F	200°C	gas mark 6 (moderately hot)
425°F	220°C	gas mark 7 (hot)
450°F	230°C	gas mark 9
475°F	240°C	gas mark 10 (very hot)

ACKNOWLEDGMENTS

A cookbook is undoubtedly a major undertaking by the author, and her work is only as good as her support system. What happens behind the scenes of a beautiful cover and glossy pages is a careful orchestration of many resources, from editors, proofreaders, indexers, book and graphic designers, sketchers, photographers, endorsers, publishers, and printers to distributors.

My second experience as an author has taught me good discipline and helped me anticipate and lessen unneeded anxiety. Taking note from past experience has made my book vision and purpose more fluid, despite the challenges I have endured in the process. As a professional chef, I feel at home writing, testing, and styling each recipe to fit my style.

I am grateful to my publisher, Wise Ink, for being flexible and for connecting me to the needed resources to make my book happen. I also want to thank my photographer, Todd Buchanan, for agreeing to work with me once again and for always making the photoshoot sessions productive, creative, fun, and relaxing.

A huge thank-you to all the great cooks from Mexico to Costa Rica who opened up their kitchens to me unconditionally. And to my husband, Kenn, and son, Jens, and to my extended family in Guatemala, Los Santa Cruz, for all their love and support of my work.

I also want to express gratitude to my dear Guatemalan friend and artist based in West Palm Beach, Florida, Andy E. Pereira, for creating this special painting for my book, showcasing delicious cashew fruit (shown below).

I am profoundly grateful to all my friends in the Mesoamerican region who shared their homes and wisdom with me. Thank you, thank you all for helping me realize my second dream.

WORK WITH AMALIA

Book Amalia for brand representation, product development, keynote speaking, cooking demonstrations, and other custom culinary experiences. For more information, visit AmaliaLLC.com or contact Amalia@AmaliaLLC.com.

Connect with Amalia on:
Instagram @amaliamorenodamgaard
Facebook @AmaliaLatinGourmet
LinkedIn Amalia Moreno-Damgaard

INDEX